Marwa El Daly
Al Waqf

Maecenata Schriften

Edited by
Dr. phil. Rupert Graf Strachwitz,
Dr. sc. Eckhard Priller and
Dr. phil. Siri Hummel

Volume 21

Marwa El Daly

Al Waqf

Philanthropy, Endowments and Sustainable Social Development in Egypt

DE GRUYTER
OLDENBOURG

ISBN 978-3-11-069696-7
e-ISBN (PDF) 978-3-11-069703-2
e-ISBN (EPUB) 978-3-11-069708-7
ISSN 1866-122X

Library of Congress Control Number: 2021953292

Bibliographic information published by the Deutsche Nationalbibliothek
The Deutsche Nationalbibliothek lists this publication in the Deutsche Nationalbibliografie; detailed bibliographic data are available on the Internet at http://dnb.dnb.de.

Printing and binding: CPI books GmbH, Leck

www.degruyter.com

Foreword

This book is a continuation of an academic and practical on-the-ground initiative started by Marwa El Daly, the author of this book, who holds her PHD from Humboldt University in Berlin. The book derives excerpts from her PHD Thesis that was a full fledgled study on philanthropy and the Third Sector in Egypt. El Daly obtained her BA and Master's degree from the American University in Cairo (AUC). Her MA was obtained in affiliation to the Political Science Department with a specialization in Professional Development with a Thesis entitled: Private Philanthropy in Egypt: Local Philanthropy as an Alternative Giving Mechanism for Sustainable Development in Egypt. This thesis was a pioneering exploratory research in the field of philanthropy and the social responsibility of the private sector towards development and it made evident that more comprehensive and representative research interventions are needed, especially that primary quantitative data on neither philanthropy nor corporate social responsibility (CSR) in Egypt existed. Upon fulfilling her MA thesis, El Daly received a Rockefeller scholarship to join the Center for the Study of Philanthropy and Civil Society in the City University of New York as an International research fellow. This fellowship resulted in a study on Islamic philanthropy in the United States, its mechanisms and the Diaspora community and how its resources are channeled to development work.

Upon returning back to Egypt, El Daly resumed her professional life in the Third Sector. As a senior staff and the creator and Program Manager of Philanthropy for Development Program in the Center for Development Services (CDS) which is an international development organization affiliated to the Near East Foundation (NEF). El Daly developed a proposal to undertake a comprehensive study on philanthropy in Egypt to be the primary reference on local philanthropy and means to direct giving and volunteering to development work. This proposal was met with interest by the CDS and a proposal for cooperation was submitted to the Ford Foundation, which in return funded this national study on philanthorpy in part of its larger interest and initiative in this field and as the base for what became the Philanthropy Center at the American University in Cairo (AUC) Meanwhile the Maecenata Institut for Third Sector Research in Germany welcomed Marwa El Daly as an international fellow and through this link the El Daly was admitted as a PHD candidate with Professor Peter Heine at the Humboldt Universitaet Berlin, who kindly accepted to be the supervisor for this work.

Thus, this book is one of Marwa El Daly's recommendations in her MA Thesis at AUC and an update of her PHD Thesis at Humboldt University of Berlin. This linkage between the academic world and the field work it entails with the experience of the researcher as a development practitioner who seeks to use the results of the study to translate it into development programs and on the ground interventions to enhance living conditions, is another distinctive measure characterizing this work.

https://doi.org/10.1515/9783110697032-202

In 2007 and while completing her Doctoral Thesis, Marwa El Daly founded the first Community Foundation in Egypt registered in 13 May 2007 as Waqfeyat al Maadi al Ahleya or Waqfeyat al Maadi Community Foundation (WMCF) to revive the concept and application of a *waqf* or endowed foundation with a modern secular function and structure. It is not only the first community foundation serving one geographical area, Maadi and its outskirts, to be established in Egypt, but it is the first *waqfiyya* institu-tion to be termed as such and registered as a foundation under the Ministry of Social Solidarity. Upon this achievement, which together with the national study on philan-thropy is considered the ground breaking field work for this work, El Daly was se-lected as a Social Entrepreneur from the Arab Region by Ashoka in July 2007 in recog-nition for her efforts in promoting institutionalized philanthropy and reviving the *waqf* endowment system to achieve change and development. The Waqfeyat al Maadi Community Foundation was considered by this international organization a ground-breaking model that paves the way for further innovative revolutionary changes in world development. Synargos Institut also recognized El Daly as an Arab Social Inno-vator and embraced El Daly as a fellow as well. In 2013, El Daly received the African Philanthropy Award by the African Global Network for this work on philanthropy. In 2014, El Daly put a clause in Egypt's new constitution (clause 90) that commits the government to revive and modernize the waqf model. Thus, this has been a continu-ous work linking theory with tractice, establishing models and lobbying for change.

Marwa El Daly is currently an Assistant Professor teaching management of NGOs, Philanthropy and Corporate Social Responsibly (CSR) at the American University in Cairo (AUC), the School of Global Affairs and Public Policy (GAPP) at the Public Policy and Administration Department (PPAD).

Abstract

The main challenge that this study attempts to confront is the lack of information and knowledge about philanthropic trends and practices in Egypt and in return the absence of a reference indigenous development foundation model that is local in essence, modern in structure, and revolutionary in its practical approach towards driving real change in the community it serves. Instead there are a number of Civil Society Organizations (CSOs), either secular or religious, which follow an organizational structure that is originally Western and suffers from the absence of a cultural heritage as well as any sustainable financial mechanism that guarantees their continuity and independence while the Arab and Islamic cultures have known financially sustainable and perpetual civic foundations, known as *waqf* (singular; *awqāf* plural) strongly outliving centuries and centuries.

The analytical problem from this perspective involves exploring this rich theoretical philanthropic framework and looking into possibilities of channeling local philanthropic resources towards development and change rather than exhausting it in a vicious circle of charity given as person-to-person aid or through charity programs that rely on distributing food and ad-hoc services by CSOs. This approach involves investing in and building on the results of the surveys and in-depth interviews employed in order to create a new model for the development world that employs all aspects of community and textual strengths as discovered in the communities and brought to light throughout the study process.

In addition to the ground breaking results that are driven out of the study like determining the faith-based nature of giving and volunteering and estimating the monetary strengths of the philanthropic resources and identifying the motives and preferences behind giving, the study's strengths lie in the practical application of knowledge to launch the first community foundation model in Egypt that the grass-roots interviewed helped in orienting the author of this study about its application. Upon fulfilling the field-work, the researcher founded the first Community Foundation to be introduced in Egypt and built its modern structure on the basis of waqf, the indigenous sustainable *ṣadaqa* (*ṣadaqa jāriyya*) model. The study revealed the tendency by philanthropists to invest in their less advantaged family members and their community and also that the legislations of *zakāt* favors spending in one's community until meeting all existing needs. Giving and volunteering among Christians and Muslims appeared to be very similar and indigenous *waqf* structure, although it has textual connotation in Islam, it has been applied by Jews, Christians and Muslims, not only in Egypt, but in the Arab region at large, including societies influenced by the Islamic culture like Spain or by a predominantly Muslim communities like Indonesia.

Hence, a model of a secular community waqf is established by the researcher to give credibility and to link theory with practice. This community *waqf* model has attracted a strong Board of Trustees that includes prominent figures in the neighbor-

https://doi.org/10.1515/9783110697032-203

hood of Maadi representing socially responsible business persons, development practitioners and academia. Since the creation of the Ministry of Endowment, this is the first *model* of a *waqfiyya* which is called Waqfeyat al Maadi Community Foundation (WMCF) to be established. Hand in hand with the currently running activities, work with different stakeholders and the government, embodied in the Ministry of Social Solidarity is taking place to do necessary reforms to allow for a more encouraging legal framework that encourages the development of similar models of modern civic *awqāf*. Bringing about investments, whether Islamic or secular, to help create capital and invest on existing resources to benefit the sustainability of growth of the foundation model and its work is being developed by this institutional model. It has a library of over 2000 resources on philanthropy to encourage further research and progress in this field.

Dedication

I dedicate this work to my mother, Prof. Dr. Fatma Abu Nawareg and my father, Eng. Ahmed Fakhr El Din El Daly, my everlasting source of light, and to my Husband, Eng. Manuel Mercier and our three beautiful children Marwan, Manon and Morgan, in addition to our two little ones in heaven Mario and Miriam.

I would like to start this book by sharing this story:

Once upon a time, there was a child ready to be born. The child asked God, "They tell me you are sending me to earth tomorrow, but how am I going to live there being so small and helpless?" God replied, "Among the many angels, I chose one for you. Your angel will be waiting for you and will take care of you." The child further inquired, "But tell me, here in heaven I don't have to do anything but sing and smile to be happy." God said, "Your angel will sing for you and will also smile for you every day. And you will feel your angel's love and be very happy." Again the child asked, "And how am I going to do when I want to talk to you?" God said, "Your angel will place your hands together and will teach you how to pray." "I've heard that on Earth there are bad men. Who will protect me?", God said, "Your angel will defend you even if it means risking its life. But I will always be sad because I will not see you anymore." God said, "Your angel will always talk to you about me and will teach you the way to come back to me, even though I will always be next to you." At that moment there was much peace in heaven, but voices from Earth could be heard and the child hurriedly asked, "God, if I am to leave now, please tell me my angel's name." "Her name is not important. You will simply call her Mom."

For my mom, the endless source of giving and my inspiration for life.

https://doi.org/10.1515/9783110697032-204

Acknowledgment

I start by thanking my mother, Prof. Dr Fatma Abu Nawareg, the wonderful Art Professor who taught me love by living it in every moment and to my father, Eng. Ahmed Fakhr El Din El Daly, whose belief, both of them, and confidence, brought me to carry the honor and burden of social development in my country. They are and will always be my role models and guides; the ethics and education they tought me by example will continue and spread as a good running sadaqa that shall spread in every step I take to extend beyond my life through the knowledge I give, offspring and students whom I inspire and the waqf I strive to revive.

Role models like my Eastern parents I have found in the West, as caring, encouraging and giving. Professor Dr Peter Heine, whose name was an unreachable fairy figure of a great Professor and Reference in Islamic studies, became possible to approach because of the most encouraging efforts of Graf Dr. Rupert Strachwitz who selected me as a fellow to the Maecenata Institute to Humboldt University. What I might fail to say and rather write is simple: Without this belief in my work which I have witnessed by Graf Dr. Strachwitz and the incredible patience and support I have received by Dr Peter Heine, this work would not have seen the light as it's initial study has allowed me to obtain my PHD from Humboldt University in Berlin. As much as I am a researcher, I am a devoted development practitioner, and oftentimes people like me get overwhelmed by field work on the expense of their academic accreditation. I am so grateful to both of them to have given me the possibility to consolidate my field work with such a strong academic work that by all means is a ground breaking primary reference to philanthropic studies in Egypt in specific and to the Arab region at large.

I am grateful to every person who took part in the field work; the names are plentiful and I mentioned them in detail in my first chapter. However, I would like to refer to the outstanding efforts of my colleague and friend Ms. Heba Heleil, who was the gear behind carrying out the procedures for the establishment of the Waqfeyat al Maadi Communtiy Foundation as the byproduct of a scientific approach to development work, by the people to the people in every aspect of it.

I would also like to show gratitude to Dr Ali Almoselhy, the Minister of Social Solidarity in Egypt at the time of my field work, who started giving space and freedom to new initiatives and models to see the light and building the capacity of the civic sector to enable it to be a key partner in the development process. His new vision and reform strategy made me believe in a possible change.

Finally, I express my sincere gratitude to Dr Omar Z. Youssef, the great surgeon, who is also Waqfeyat al Maadi Community Foundation's Board of Trustees' member and my dearest supporter and guide in life. His guidance was enlighting for me to proceed with this book.

https://doi.org/10.1515/9783110697032-205

Last but not least, I thank my husband, Eng. Manuel Mercier for his encouragement and support. I could only produce this book because of his support in travelling with me to attend conferences and sharing the responsibility of our beautiful children Marwan, Manon and Morgan. Elhamdulillah, as we say in our part of the World, I thank God for showing me the right way, for this inner strengths and peace and for being surrounded by such great people. May we all find the right path to bring about positive change in the lives of all humanbeings by accelerating science, philanthropy and social justice.

Contents

List of figures

https://doi.org/10.1515/9783110697032-207

List of tables

https://doi.org/10.1515/9783110697032-208

Abbreviations and Acronyms

AUC	The American University in Cairo
BoD	Board of Directors
Bpuh	Blessings and Peace be Upon Him
CAPMAS	Central Agency for Population Mobilization and Statistics
CDAs	Community Development Associations
CSOs	Civil Society Organizations
CSR	Corporate Social Responsibility
DANIDA	Danish International Development Agency
ICA	The Institute of Cultural Affairs
MoSA	Ministry of Social Affairs (later named as Ministry of Social Solidarity)
NGOs	Non-governmental Organizations
PPS	A Probability Proportionate to Size
SPSS	Statistical Package for the Social Sciences
UNDP	United Nations Development Program
UNICEF	United Nations Children's Fund

https://doi.org/10.1515/9783110697032-209

1 The Problem, the Scope, the Solution, Theoretical Framework and Research Methodology

1.1 The Problem

Despite a rich history of hundreds of centuries of Arab and Islamic civil institutions in the form of endowments referred to as *waqf* (singular) or *awqāf* (plural) signaling a strong civil society with credible institutionalized philanthropic tools for community development and social interdependence, the Arab region and the majority of the Muslim World today are challenged by severe development problems and they are lacking the effective role that could be played by civil society organizations.

In spite of the work of international aid agencies and development assistance programs in a country like Egypt, there are not much efforts invested in understanding and consolidating the local giving mechanisms to allow people eventually to rely on themselves in funding development, especially with the international aid being unsustainable and taking into account the rich history of organized philanthropic efforts in the region. Hence, it was of dire need to study the local giving mechanisms and resources, their potentials and the challenges they face in order allow them to play a role in development. Up to this point before this research is conducted, there was no reference or information with regard to the size of philanthropy or local assets that could be geared towards development in Egypt, nor of the philanthropic trends, motives or forms. In a faith-based country where religious teaching of giving is a driving force behind many behavioral patterns, historical mechanisms of local interdependence (*takāful*) constitute a major reference. These include the formation of *waqf* (endowments), Muslim *zakāt* or Christian tithes giving, *ṣadaqāt*, nudhūr, and volunteer efforts. However, the problem here is two-fold: what is their size and magnitude, and second, what is the possibility of channeling these resources of local giving towards development work and not towards charitable ad-hoc and unorganized giving?

Over the last 15 years poverty and inequality are on the rise in Egypt. In the UNDP HDR report of 2019, it is indicated that 28% of Egyptians live under poverty line (signaling an increase in poverty within the last 15 years) and inequality is measured to be on the rise in Egypt, where it is currently ranking 116 out of 176 countries[1]. According to the UNDP Egypt Human Development Report 2005, over 20% of the Egyptian population lived under poverty line and faced harsh economic conditions as well as health problems. Strong positive correlation between poverty and illiteracy makes the situation difficult for development. Egypt is amongst the 9th countries with the highest illiteracy rate in the world, where it reaches 40% among men and around 60% among women and rates highest among the rural communities. According to the

1 Human Development Report 2019

https://doi.org/10.1515/9783110697032-001

World Bank Report 2004, 45% of the world's poor are illiterate and that it is 24% more probable for an illiterate person to become poor. Thus, it is a pending challenge to break this poverty cycle. Illiteracy and poverty by all means put great pressure on the country's resources and hinder development efforts. In addition, unemployment is another national challenge. The World Bank's data on unemployment[2] for Egypt from 1991 to 2019 provides the following: The average value for Egypt during that period was 10.4 percent with a minimum of 7.95 percent in 1999 and a maximum of 13.15 percent in 2013. Thus, poverty, illiteracy and unemployment remain challenges that over the last 15 years still face Egypt and which strategic philanthropy needs to address from the core.

In a country, where faith-based giving manifests in all forms and occasions and where *zakāt* is a compulsory behavior, local philanthropy should rate high, yet is not necessarily serving the development vehicle and far by being strategic. The problem remains that local resources are not assessed, under estimated, and definitely not considered as a funding mechanism to development. When NGOs start looking outward for help (mostly from international sources), inward strengths shift to strengthen the ability to ask for help. Meanwhile and gradually, indigenous mechanisms to combat difficulties die out. Poverty, illiteracy, unemployment and other problems facing Egypt should have a considerable local contribution by committed stakeholders and organizations. Individuals, philanthropists, the Diaspora and concerned civic structures must unite to combat the national challenges and direct their contributions in an efficient and strategic way. The problem remains at this point in assessing these contributions, the willingness, awareness and strengths of the existing partners and environments and the challenges and real potential for local philanthropy as a vehicle for social change and social justice. In 2020, the biggest local NGOs in Egypt spend millions of Egyptian Pounds to promote their services on TV and their advertisement only revolve around two things: mostly asking for donations to buy food for the needy or buy medicine for hospitals.

1.2 The Scope

Islam is a Religion that is built upon 5 pillars called in Arabic *arkān al Islam*[3]. The third pillar among the five crucial cornerstones that make a Muslim, is giving *zakāt* (alms-tax) as an obligatory act of philanthropy. In this context, philanthropy is well defined in the Quranic verses as well as in Prophet Mohamed's Sayings (*aḥādīth* (plu-

2 https://www.theglobaleconomy.com/Egypt/unemployment_rate/

3 The first pillar (*rukn*) of Islam is declaring faith in the One God and His last Prophet Mohamed (May Peace be Upon Him-MPUH), the second pillar is doing the prayers, the third is giving the *zakāt* (alms-giving), the fourth is fasting during the holy month of Ramadan and the fifth pillar is pilgrimage to Mecca (for those who could afford it– physically and financially).

ral), *ḥadīth* (singular). Accordingly, generosity and social interdependence (*takāful*) have always been characteristic of the Muslims, whether the rich amongst them, or the poor who slaughter their only possessed poultry to provide food to a passing stranger. In addition, for many centuries, Muslim beliefs manifested in traditions that contributed enormously in shaping cultures of social interdependence – *takāful* that grew and flourished upon solid foundations of philanthropy and civil society institutions. These traditions diffused within cultures of diverse beliefs and different countries and nations bonding people and bridging diversities, not only through charitable giving but also through institutionalized philanthropic mechanisms that enjoyed legal and financial autonomy and sustainability, such as the Islamic *waqf* (endowment) establishments.

In the world of today, all Muslim countries, and the majority of the Muslim populations living within non-Muslim societies, are impoverished and are classified within the category of the developing world countries and third-world citizens. Most of these countries face problems of high illiteracy rate, rising unemployment rates, inflation, deficits and heavy debt burdens. Moving from the Muslim World at large and looking at the Arab World, which constitutes one-fifth of the Muslim Population and the majority of which consists of Muslims, one finds no exception to this rule. According to previous UNDP[4] estimates, 90 to 100 million Arabs (out of a total Arab population of around 250 million) live in poverty and do not possess means that allow them to obtain nutritionally adequate diet. The recent estimates by the global report of mulidimentional poverty by UNDP and OPHI (2018) indicates that around one-fifth of the Arab population (around 65 millions) live in extreme poverty. The Arab Multidimensional Report of 2017 suggested a total number of multidimensional poor at 116.1 million, which is 40% of the Arab population. It also indicated that volunerability to multidimensional poverty is as high as affecting one quarter of the population. This means that two thirds of the Arab population either poor or volnurable to multidimensional poverty (ESCWA et al, 2017)[5].

In addition, the Arab region at large is marked by political and economic instability rising due to growing social inequalities, capital concentration in the hands of a few at the expense of a widening strata of the poorest of the poor and other factors continuously contributing to this vicious circle of poverty and stagnation. Many of these countries lie within the endless chain of receiving aid and find themselves losing local mechanisms of social interdependence to acquire dependency-driven methods to fund programs sustaining on international donations threatened to stop at any time.

However, while studies reveal that the Arab world today has suffered a twenty-year growth slowdown, nonetheless, poverty levels in the Arab world are not as bad as in countries with similar levels of income. The reason given by the Arab World Com-

4 UNDP: Arab Human Development Report. July 2002
5 (ESCWA et al, 2017)

petitiveness Report 2002–2003 is that among the major explanations is the “cohesive system of private social responsibility” that distinguishes the Arab region, and within which families help their disadvantaged members through religious giving systems (24). However, and according to the same report, to reduce poverty over time can be best achieved through increasing the growth rate of the economy. This is all associated with inefficient investments, political instability, a weak business environment, low quality of human capital, primarily education and knowledge advances (25–31).

The Arab Competitiveness Report in 2018 stressed on a new factor for growth that was not measured before, namely innovation. It mentions that weakness in education as well as innovation have negative implications to the quality of life in the Arab countries. The Arab World ranks very low compared to other countries in the level of the quality of education especially in Math and Science. Simmilar is the low level of innovation that characterizes most Arab countries (xvi). Without creating an enabling environment for innovation that includes thinking out of the box, supporting research and development as well as building human capital, the Arab World will continue to lag behind. The Muslim and Arab Worlds find themselves now in a position that requires them to start thinking about reviving their long dormant strengths, introducing innovative models to solve problems, re-explore their potentials, re-discover their assets and look for ways to realize development strategies that would help accelerate growth with social justice in their societies.

1.3 The Solution

The Arab Competive Report of 2018 argues that there is a recent phenomenon of rising social entrepreneurship in the Arab World. Social entrepreneurship could be private for-profit, non-profit or hybrid organizations with a social mission. In essence social entrepreneurs tend to be driven by values. They take risks and use innovation to solve problems facing their communities (77). In addition and according to the UNDP Human Development Report 2005 recommend “by virtue of physical proximity to local communities and through a better understanding of local demands and needs, decentralized bodies and NGOs, as well as civil society leaders are best suited to develop and implement programs” (28). In line with this recommendation and in accordance with the mindset promoting social entrepreneurship and innovation, the study argues that local philanthropic organizations and social enterprises should undertake the developmental challenge of the country, by depending on local funding mechanisms and innovating the country’s rich faith-based philanthropic heritage and by closing partnerships with the private sector and the concerned government bodies as real partners collaborating for positive change. This collaborative approach should produce the developmental agenda of the country, its benchmarks, timeframe, resources, roles, monitoring and evaluation and the accountability system it entails. Current Civil Society Organizations are best suited, yet they are not as ready as they should be. They face challenges in the structure and scope of their work, in their internal governance, their funding mechanisms, and in most cases suffer from credibility issues vis-à-vis other entities and the public. To what this thesis is concerned, one of the main challenges is the lack of civic decentralized financially autonomous structures serving specific geographical areas, a model manifested in community foundations, or what I like to refer to as "community *waqf* foundations".

This study argues that innovating faith-based philanthropic mechanisms such as the waqf and alleviating the level of knowledge about other local giving tools and advocating for building an encouraging legal environment would pave the way for civic modern philanthropic structures of traditional basis to emerge. Applying this model to specific geographical areas to benefit from faith-based giving tendency to respond to people of geographical proximity and simultaneously allow for better monitoring and evaluation techniques is a path-breaking initiative that will contribute significantly in solving the problem of Community Based Organizations' (CBOs) financial dependency, governance issues and enable them to monitor, evaluate and accredit their programs in an efficient manner.

Thus, to begin with solving the problems presented above, it was necessary to conduct a national research on philanthropy in Egypt representing the population as the local individual philanthropic power and the CBOs as the institutionalized philanthropic sector. It was necessary to explore whether this local power existed, to asses and quantify it as well as explore all the potentials and challenges that could either lead of hamper change-driven philanthropy.

1.4 The Theoretical Framework

In order to understand philanthropy in the Muslim context, one must go back to forms of giving as it originates in Islam. This is not necessarily what is practiced by Muslims; many practices might be traced to the origin, but also many of the practices that existed or dominated a certain epoch might have been lost within the course of history and find either no, or limited, traces today.

According to Chapra[6], the Islamic word-view is based on three fundamentals: *tawḥīd* (oneness of God), *khilāfa* (vicegerency of human beings) and *ʿadāla* (justice). *Tawḥīd* implies the uniqueness of the Supreme Being, the creator of the Universe. Khilāfa indicates that the human being is the vicegerent of God on earth, implying that the resources granted to him/her are a trust (Quran, 57:7). Thus, everyone, regardless of his/her race, gender, origin is a *khilāfa* of God on earth making all people brother/sisters in humanity. This brotherhood had to be accompanied by justice, ʾ

6 M.Umer Chapra. *Islam and Economic Development*. Malaysia: The International Institute of Islamic Thought and Islamic Research Institute, 1981.

ʿadāla, or else it would have been void (6). In this respect Islam brings up a whole system of *takāful* or social interdependence that emphasizes on achieving social justice (Elwan[7], 25). Establishing and consolidating justice has accordingly been declared by the Quran as one of the most primary objectives that God's messengers on earth should seek to achieve (Quran, 57:25). The Quran places justice closest to piety in terms of its importance (5:8) in the Islamic belief (6). Thus, begging for instance is inconsistent with the dignity that should be imbedded within the *khilāfa* of God and it is accordingly the responsibility of each healthy person to strive for a dignified life through work. Since, in complex societies there are people who might not be skilled or able to work, the ʿadāla concept should compel those who can, to help those who can not. Help in this context does not lie in charity where a top-down paternalistic status prevails, but in enabling the impoverished to develop themselves as brother/sisters whose development translates into a stronger united society. Hence, providing training, education, job opportunities are the core ideas of *takāful* or social interdependence, as embedded in Islam and where the weakest have rights on the more powerful.

These rights would constitute the first capacity building ingredient that the weak get, as they become conscious that they are entitled to share in the money of the more fortunate *khilāfa*; his/her brother or sister in God's delegation as human beings. According to Qaradawy[8], Islam, the message that was brought to humanity over fourteen centuries ago, dealt with the problems of poverty and made the weakest amongst them conscious about their rights (7). In propagating for this "rights-based approach" to philanthropy, An- Na ʿim[9] argued that the basic thrust of this approach is derived from Islamic jurisprudence (*sharīʿa*) and lies in the social and moral right of the beneficiaries to receive assistance with due respect for their human dignity. "And those in whose wealth is a **recognized right**, for the beggar and the destitute" (Quran 2:29), this recognized right indicated refers to the entitlement of the weak to a set percentage of the wealth of those who could afford (9). Therefore, the various forms of giving in Islam are strictly listed in such detail reflecting for some its obligatory status and for others its significance as God or Allah's wealth, which His *khilāfa* on earth should spend a recognized part of for those in need and who are entitled to receive it through him/her.

These forms are classified into obligatory and voluntary acts of social responsibility. Thus, philanthropy in Islam is divided into two forms: 1. Obligatory Giving, which includes the giving of *zakāt* in general (*zakāt al māl* with all its different kinds),

7 Abdallah Naseh ʿElwan, *Al takafol al ijtima'i fil Islam*. Cairo, Dar Al Salam publishers, 6th edition, 2001.

8 Youssif Al-Qaradawy. Fiqh Al-Zakah: A Comparative Study to the Rules and Philosophy of Zakat in Light of the Quran and Sunnah. Cairo: Wahba Library (24th edition), 2003.

9 Abdullahi Ahmed An- Na ʿim and Asma Mohamed Abdel Halim. Rights Based Approach to Philanthropy for Social Justice in Islamic Societies.

zakāt al fitr, paying al *nudhūr*, paying al *kaffārāt, fulfilling the aḍāḥī*, as well as emergency aid to rescue the hungry and the needy[10]; the other form, which is considered voluntary philanthropy involves endowing family and charity *waqf* (*al waqf al ahlīwa al khayrī*) that is synonymous to what is known as the sustainable ṣadaqa (*ṣadaqa jāriyya*) in Islam; this voluntary form also entails writing the will before death allocating a sum to relatives and charity, showing hospitality to strangers and wayfarers, lending goods to others known as *'iʿāra*, preferring others to benefit known as *īthār* , and finally gifts known as *hiba* (plural: *hibāt*).

In the coming section of this chapter, I will present explanation to the theoretical implications underlying obligatory as well as voluntary philanthropy with special focus on *zakāt* and *waqf* as the primary philanthropic forms. In the chapters to come, there will be definitions explaining the legislations and types; thus the purpose of this section is to high light and investigate theoretically some of the philanthropic duties.

1.5 Obligatory Giving

1.5.1 Zakāt

Zakāt linguistically indicates different meanings. As Al-Marsafy[11] explains, *zakāt* derives from growth accompanied with bless, like a plant growing or a soul developing. Another meaning is associated with purity, like purifying one's soul. "Of their goods, take alms, that so thou mightest purify and sanctify them; and pray on their behalf. Verily thy prayers are a source of security for them: And Allah is One Who heareth and knoweth" (Quran, 9:103). In Quran, *zakat* was strongly connected to praying, whereby the two were the main sources for purifying one's soul. The two follow each other in the pillars of Islam and *zakāt* was mentioned twenty-six times in verses in the holy Quran in relation to prayers (*al ṣalāt*), signaling its significance[12]. Moreover, the application of *zakāt* was mentioned in immense detail in the Quran in the sense that it is considered the main source of social interdependence (*takāful*) in the Islamic faith and the executive arm for the realization of social justice. Quranic verses encouraging spending are 234 verses, a considerable number of messages reflecting the significance of giving versus capital stagnation[13]. *Zakāt* is considered the good money lent to God or what is termed as *qarḍ al ḥasan*. Even the proceedings of praying (how people should pray) were not elaborated in Quran and were left to the Prophet's *sunna* to elaborate, while

10 See: Abdallah Naseh ·Elwan, *Al takafol al ijtima'i fil Islam*. Cairo, Dar Al Salam publishers, 6th edition, 2001.

11 Said Al-Marsify. Al-Mas'uliya al-ijtima'iya fi al-Islam. Al-Mansoura: Dar Al Yaqin, 2004.

12 Nea·mat Mashhour. Al-Zakat Mawared wa Masaref. www.islamonline.net/arabic/economics/2000/12/article2.shtml.

13 Ahmed Isma·il Yehia. Al Zakat: 'ebada maleya wa idarah iqtisadeya. Cairo: Dar Al Ma'aref1986.

zakāt was profoundly explained in details in the Quran to reflect not only its importance, but also that it is not an individual act left to the freewill of the giver and accordingly should be calculated in utmost details as it belongs to God and the people He assigned it for. *Zakāt* accordingly is considered a means to worship God; it is a monetary *ʿibāda* (worship) and not a tax, as Al Sheikh[14] put it. Forms of *zakāt* and its outlets (those who deserve to receive *zakāt*) are specified later in the coming chapter.

However, and according to the legislations set in Quran and by the following Prophetic sayings, "no *zakāt* is to be imposed on wealth until it has been in the possession of its owner for a period of one full year"[15]. According to Zayas, in the terminology of Islammic jurisprudence, the minimum limit to be taxed is called "*niṣāb*" (11) indicating that *zakāt* applies to surplus wealth only. Thus to be a giver of this kind of zakāt, which is known as monetary *zakāt* or *zakāt al māl*, one must possess at least a "taxable" minimum upon which one year has passed. The exception of zakāt that must be given even without reaching the *niṣāb* is the *zakāt* to be paid on agricultural products, the product of gold and silver mines, treasures gained in war and finally to what concerns *zakāt al fitr* which is a fixed amount given right after the end of the holy month of Ramadan.

1.5.1.1 Specific Conditions of Zakāt

In light of this study, I would like to highlight certain conditions of *zakāt* that are of great relevance to encouraging organized philanthropy and the establishment of community foundations serving a specific geographical area in a developmental approach.

1.5.1.1.1 Give to Enrich and to Achieve the Basis of Social Justice

Give to enrich is a condition that calls for the distribution of *zakāt* in a way that meets the receivers' needs to enable them to live in dignity without having to ask for assistance. *Zakāt* should enable the poor to "stand on their own feet" as Chapra[16] puts it. He continues that *zakāt* should a permanent source of income to those unable to work and it also should be a source of support to economic projects of small and micro enterprises (SMEs) to encourage self-employment to reduce inequalities between people (83). Hence, by giving to enrich, the society adopts a system of redistributing incomes in a way that attempts to fight stagnation of excess capital by providing opportunities to the poorer members to catch up. From here, the concept of *kifāya*, or sufficiency is

---

14 Yaseen Ibrahim Al Sheikh. Zakat: The Third Pillar of Islam. Lebanon: Al Maktab Al Islami in Beirut, 1998

15 Farishta G. de Zayas. The Law and Instiution of Zakat. Kuala lumpur: The Other Press; 2003

16 Ibid.

a significant condition of *zakāt*. According to Ibrahim[17], unlike what common people think of *zakāt* as being simply a means to meeting basic immediate needs of the poor from food, shelter, medicine, etc (which is a significant role by itself), but the role of *zakāt* is far more important than that. *Zakāt*, as he explains, is a tool to combat poverty from its roots by enforcing a system of redistribution of resources. Accordingly, it encourages work for those who are able to, and guarantees that *ḥadd al kifāya*, or subsistence level is met for those who are poor and unable to work. *ḥadd al kifāya* in this context is not the minimum level of survival, which is called *ḥadd al kafāf*; but it is the level that guarantees a decent living status, taking into account the time and the place. Hence, zakāt is to be used for meeting basic needs like food and shelter but equally important is to meet the peoples' psychological needs like enabling him/her to get married with all the needed support, and to also meet his/her moral needs like the need to education and tools to enhance his/her mental capabilities, etc. All these needs are the basics for *ḥadd al kifāya* that should be granted to every human being. *Ḥadd al kifāya* condition is one of the priorities of Islamic economy and it is not only a human right, but it is a divine right that rises beyond all rights. (157–158). Accordingly, fixed rates of payments for *zakāt* were imposed on each Muslim and in case of zakāt al māl, on those whose wealth reaches a certain amount or *niṣāb*. According to the Quranic verses 24 and 25 of Surah LXX, "And in whose wealth there is a **right acknowledged** for those who beseech (for aid) and for the destitute" (LXX: 24–25). Accordingly, zakat is the right of the needy and it is not a simple voluntary act of charity, but a legal right with set values and conditions.

According to Sayyid Qutb[18], *zakāt* is the right of those who receive it as much as it is the duty for those who give it. He explains that God granted nobility to the humankind; "We have given nobility to the sons of man, and and have carried them by land and sea; We have given them provision of good things, and have given them great preference over' many of the things, which We have created" (17:72). Hence, Qutb argues that Islam disapproves the status of suffering from poverty and need, as He has given the human beings, the vicar of Allah on His earth, nobility through their minds, emotions, spiritual yearnings and intellectual abilities. Accordingly, if the human beings have only their basic physical needs and only the bare necessities of life met and accordingly have to strive for their daily survival, they are deprived of enjoying their spiritual longings and far behind exercising their intellectual abilities. In that case they are robbed of their nobilities and degraded to the level of animals (163). Hence, give to enrich is a vital condition in zakat payment, which should enrich and not simply meet the basic essential need, but enrich in the sense of providing a decent living that allows for social mobility and the acquisition of opportunities to excel.

---

17 Medhat Hafiz Ibrahim. Dor al Zakat fi Khedmat al Mujtama'. Cairo: Dar Gharib lel Nashr wal Tiba'a.
18 Ibid.

Following this logic, Ibrahim[19] denounces limiting *zakat* to cash money to be directly consumed, but he argues that a good sum of *zakāt* money must be allocated for investment. He also explains that investments in this context could take two forms: The first is by supporting artisans seeking to expand their businesses and in need of production tools, or merchants, bakers, tailors, and any small business owner in need to expand his/business. The second form he elaborates is by investing *zakāt* in ways that bring regular income to support those who are unable to work, either because of their old age or their severe illness. Investing in tools and in enabling people to rely on themselves and encouraging their businesses is meant to increase ownership among people to eventually bridge the gaps between them and ensure a better distribution of resources (160–163).

1.5.1.1.2 *Zakāt* Ownership or *Milkiyatul Zakat*: The Need for Clarification

Drawing on the previous point discussed above, which encourages enriching people by investing *zakāt* in production tools to enable people to work and expand their businesses, there is the condition of ownership by *zakāt* recipients that causes uncertainties by some and disputes by others. This condition of ownership for *zakāt* recipients is by all means a significant condition as it implies that *zakāt* must be owned by the receiver and is accordingly interpreted as the direct money or material to be given to the receiver, and accordingly indirectly denouncing efforts to invest *zakāt* in businesses that generates money or in establishing factories to absorb the jobless for instance. Similarly, investing zakāt in revolving loans to the poor through small and micro enterprises is also denounced by many religious philosophers as the capital is not owned by the receiver. Philanthropic organizations in Egypt wishing to invest *zakāt* money in building a factory to absorb unemployment in their villages for example are not allowed to, because Al Azhar University[20] would not give a *fatwa*[21] for religiously legitimizing such an operation. In several cases the Azhar's division responsible for releasing the *fatwa* to allow or denounce certain behaviours, clearly denounced investing *zakāt* money in income generating projects, in building factories or in funds providing good loans (*qarḍ ḥasan*, i.e. loan without interest). This kind of *fatwa* (plural: *fatāwa*) is a big obstacle for directing *zakāt* towards developmental

19 Ibid. Medhat Hafiz Ibrahim. Dor al Zakat fi Khedmat al Mujtama'. Cairo: Dar Gharib lel Nashr wal Tiba'a

20 Al Azhar University is Egypt's oldest degree-granting university that was founded around 970 in the 10th century as a center of Islamic learning. It is considered one of the strongest pillars for Islamic legislations in the world.

21 Fatwa is a non-binding legal opinion given by a religious authority or reference on a point of Islamic Law (sharia'a).It is usually answering questions asked about the Islamic legalities of certain issues and situations.

activities and limits the expenditure of *zakāt* to direct charitable activities that circuate from person to person and often ad-hoc and unorganized.

On the other hand, many prominent religious thinkers and philanthropists such as Dr Mohamed Shawky Al Fangary argue differently. As Al Fangary[22] argues, zakat must be given in the form of services and not only financial assistances. This goes in accordance with the idea of enabling someone to fish (by training and equipments) rather than giving him/her a fish to eat. Therefore, he suggests that part of *zakāt* resources must be invested in desert reclamation for instance and by distributing these lands among the poor, or by building houses and distributing them on those without shelter. He also proposes building factories that absorb jobless to allow them to develop and allows for their social mobility. He also refers to the good loan, (*qarḍ al ḥasan*) which is a loan of no interest (*ribā*) and suggests that *zakāt* institutions should take on the responsibility of providing such loans as it becomes a necessity of life. He advises that loans as such are to be given to the needy, for production or consumption purposes in order to prevent them from resorting to banks that lends them with interest or from undertaking illegitimate endeavors due to their desperation

(106). Similarly, Umer Shapra[23] stresses on the importance of Small and Micro Enterprises (SMEs) and quotes Dr. Mohamed Yunus who emphasizes that financing people to be self-employed is the most significant and main right to be granted to them and upon which all other human rights will follow. Thus, Shapra continues that since in poorer Muslim countries there is a surplus of labour, yet scarcity of capital and foreign exchange as well as lack of educational infrastructure that allows for technological advancement, there is a higher potential for them to rely on SMEs than on large-and medium-scale capital-intensive industries especially if they wish to expand employment and self-employment opportunities. Accordingly Shapra refers to *zakāt* as the" social self-help program" and argues that since Islam obliges people to earn their livelihood, it is evident that preference should be given in *zakāt* disbursements to the objectives enabling the poor to stand on their own feet. *Zakāt*, as he argues, should accordingly become a permanent income supplement only to those unable to work, but otherwise should be invested in socio-economic projects to expand self-employment opportunities and combat injustice among people (82–109).

From the above, it is vital for religious persons in charge of providing *fatwa* on issues as such to be well informed about the possibilities of *zakāt* investment in income generating projects and the possibility of selling shares of factories to workers to meet the condition of ownership for instance. Clarification and clarity in reference to this point is crucial, especially that *zakāt* is the basis of social solidarity (*taḍāmun*) and

---

22 Mohamed Shawqy Al Fangary. Al Islam wal Tadamon al Ijtima'i. Cairo: Al Hay'a al Misriya al 'amma lel Ketab, 1990.

23 M. Umer Chapra. Islam and Economic Development: A Strategy for Development with Justice and Stability. Pakistan: The International institute of Islamic Thought and Islamic Research Institute, 1993

interdependence (*takāful*) among people and is one of the five pillars of Islam. *Zakāt* could be either used as a tool to create independence among the poor and hence a tool for development, or a tool that creates dependence on charitable assistance; a condition leading to more poverty and further injustices and inequalities among people

1.5.1.1.3 The Localization of Zakāt Spending: Decentralizing Development

Another condition worth highlighting applies to the disbursement of *zakāt*, whether *zakāt al māl* of all its different kinds or *zakāt al fitr*, and prioritizes its giving within the geographical area of the giver unless the needs of all the poor, the needy and those entitled to receive *zakāt* are entirely met in this geographical area. From the premise that people of each geographical area or neighborhood are more worthy of their resources, and accordingly the needs of the poor or needy in one geographical area are to be met in priority before transmitting *zakāt* to people in other areas. According to Al Fangary[24], in the premier Islamic states, *zakāt* was collected by the state's employees to feed the Money Fund or House (*bayt al māl*), which is the entity responsible for distributing *zakāt* thereafter. Thereafter, *zakāt* collected was to be distributed in the same area of its collection as it was considered a local tax, allowing each branch of the *zakāt* institution to be independent meeting the needs of its defined geographical area. In case of excess or low resources, branches are allowed to feed and support each other (84–85).

Al aqrabūn awlā bi al maʿrūf is a citation from the Quran and a well repeated verse by most Muslims indicating the importance to give to those related to you whether by kin or by geography. This actually paves the way, at least theoretically, for the establishment of a form of community foundations that is responsible for developing a fund that serves the development of a specified geographical area and to meet its needs before moving to serve other places.

1.5.1.1.4 The *Zakāt* Institution and *al* ʿāmilūn ʿalayha (the *Zakāt* Officials)

It is noteworthy that the third deserving entities of the seven outlets of *zakāt*, right after the poor and the destitute come those *Zakāt* Officials who are responsible for collecting and distributing *zakāt* known as *al ʿāmilūn ʿalayha*. By including their salaries from sums of the *zakāt* given, this form of philanthropy is institutionalized in a solid perpetuate philanthropic system. According to Makhzangy[25], those are the *zakāt* workers, who work on its collection and distribution in honesty (174).

---

24 Ibid.

25 Alsayed Ahmed al Makhzangy. Al Zakat wa Tanmeyat al Mujtama'. Saudi Arabia- Mekka: League of Islamic World; 2005

As Zayas[26] elaborates, those officials include the collectors (*al muṣādiqūn*) who collect zakāt dues, the distributers (*al qasimūn*) who brings the *zakāt* to those who deserve, the custodians (*al ḥāfiẓūn*) who make sure that the *zakāt* funds reach the lawful beneficiaries, the measurers (*al kayyalūn*) who measure or weigh agricultural products due for *zakāt* or those responsible for *zakāt* calculation in specific, the scribes or clerks (*al kātibūn*) responsible for maintaining *zakāt* files and records, the accountants (*al ḥāsibūn*) who hold the duty of keeping accounts of *zakāt* revenues and expenditures, the informers (*al ʿārifūn*) who are in charge of reaching out to those who deserve *zakāt* and inform respectively the *zakāt* officials of their conditions, the assemblers (*al ḥāshirūn*) who hold the duty of assembling *zakāt* payers when required and finally the officers in charge (*ruʾasāʾ al ʿāmilūn*) who are responsible of managing the different *zakāt* centers and who are directly responsible to the State of the proper functioning of their concerned centers (289).

From the above, one notices the magnitude of the *zakāt* clergy assigned for this significant task. This system implies the institutionalization of *zakāt* and for a considerable number of religious thinkers, this is a task to be performed by the State and not to be left to individuals as the case in many countries and also in Egypt. However, this point of view varies according to the thinkers' conviction whether a secular state, or a corrupt state, or whatever other form than an Islamic one, is entitled to undertake this mission of *zakāt* collection and disbursement. The purpose here is not to legitimize nor deny the State's right in managing the *zakāt*, but it is noteworthy to indicate that such an organized system is also manageable through non-profit civic organization that is capable of gaining trust and credibility to undertake such a role in an organized manner. However, the purpose of this discussion is to show that through enrolling the *zakāt* officials on the payroll from the *zakāt* money, this legislation strengthen the functioning of the Institution of *zakāt*, let it be governmental or non-governmental.

1.5.2 Al Nudhūr, al Kaffārāt, al Aḍāḥī, and Emergency Aid

These four forms of giving, *al nudhūr, al kaffārāt, al aḍāḥī*, and emergency aid, in addition to *zakāt* in general and *zakāt* al fitr in specific, are considered compulsory giving in Islam.

Al nudhūr (singular: *al nadhr)*, is an obligation that the person undertakes upon him/herself to be paid for God's sake. For instance, *al nadhr*could be a promise to sponsor an orphan student's education in case my child succeeds or to sponsor a sick person's treatment in case my child survives his/her sickness. A promise to demonstrate gratefulness to God is free willing and optional, yet it is obligatory giving once

26 Ibid.

promised. As to *al kaffārāt*, it is also due as an obligation if a person commits any error in the legislation of the fasting, the pilgrimage, etc, or simply to wipe off a sin as it is generally understood. Among the *kaffārāt* in the old days was to release slaves for instance, a way that contributed to the abolition of slavery starting from the early Islamic era and onwards. *Al aḍāḥī*, which indicates slaughtering an animal (sheep, cow, goat and their sorts) in the days of religious festivals to distribute food on the needy, people of kin and friends, is also compulsory on those who could afford it. Finally, emergency aid is also compulsory as in the Islamic legislation, it is unacceptable not to help a neighbor who is in need or to go to bed knowing that she/he is hungry. In a condition of such, assistance or giving becomes obligatory.

1.6 Voluntary Giving

Voluntary giving varies and is importantly interrelated in the Quran as all other '*ʿibādāt*or worshops. As written in Quran, "The likness of those who spend their wealth in Allah's way is as the likness of a grain which growth seven ears, in every ear a hundred grains. Allah giveth increase manifold to whom He will. Allah is All-Emracing, All-knowing" (The Cow, 261). This indicates that spending for a good cause is like a plant that gives birth to more and more plants and God awards in multitude any single good act. From these good acts is also a good word, made with an analogy in the Quran to a good trea with a solid origin and a branch in heavan: Do you not see that God has cited the example of the good word as a good tree whose root is firmly fixed, and its branches are high in the sky? It produces its crop every season, as designed by its Lord. GOD thus cites the examples for the people, that they may take heed.[27]. A smile, a good word or a compliment to boosts one's spirit is considered a ṣadaqa or a voluntary philanthropic hehavious that will be rewarded generously by God. In addition to voluntary expenditures to the needy, assistance, a good word or a smile to bring happiness in peoples' hearts and soul, these are other forms of voluntary giving: writing the Will before death and allocating sum to charity, hospitality to strangers and wayfarers, *iʿāra* or lending goods to others (in-kind lending), gifts or *hiba* (pl. *hibāt*). However, the form that is most sustainable and institutionalized is the *ṣadaqa jāriyya* or the sustainable and ongoing *sadaqa*that is synonymous to waqf or endowment building that benefits others. For the purpose of this dissertation, I will focus in my theoretical framework on this form of voluntary giving and present it as follows in this coming section:

27 See Quran, *surat* Ibrahim (14), 24–25.

1.6.1 Waqf (Endowment Building) or Ṣadaqa Jāriyya (Sustainable Giving)

1.6.1.1 An Overview on the Origin

The *waqf* or civic pious endowment building to tie-up capital and allocate profit or interest for social causes as a *waqf khayrī* (charity waqf) or to family heirs as a *waqf ahlī* (Family Waqf) is an Islamic religious voluntary act seeking the consent of *Allah*, God. It is not only a *ṣadaqa* by which one gives assistance to the needy, but it is a *ṣadaqa jāriyya* that is continuous and sustainable (*jāriyya*) due to the fact that the capital endowed is tied-up to support the cause that the endower specified and allocated this waqf to serve in perpetuity. A *waqf* adds up good deeds to the endower even after his/her death adding sustainability to the spiritual, intangible world of *ḥasanāt*, or good deeds. The waqf was defined by the Shafi'i scholars as follows "the alienation of revenue-generating property by the founder (wāqif), with the principle remaining inalienable, while its revenues are disbursed for a pious principal, in order to seek God's favor"[28]. Thus, literally, *waqf* means tying-up and legislatively it means sustainable giving or *ṣadaqa jāriyya*. Legally and over the course of history, three types of waqf models have taken shape: the charity *waqf* (*waqf khayrī*), the family *waqf* (*waqf ahlī*) and the mixed *waqf* (*waqf mushtarak*) that combines those two in one *waqf*. In brief, the charity waqf are these endowments supporting charitable or developmental causes of individual or public benefit. The family *waqf* is those endowments supporting family heirs, and the mixed *waqf* is one that supports both, general charity and family members.

The *ḥadīth* (Prophet's saying) that is quoted to explain what *waqf* is states the following: "when a human being dies, his deeds cease except three: perpetual almsgiving (ṣadaqa jāriyyaor *waqf*), knowledge which is beneficial, or an upright offspring who prays for him" (*idhā māta ibn ādam inqaṭa'a 'amaluhu illa min thalāth: ṣadaqa jāriyya, aw 'ilm yuntafa'u bihi, aw walad ṣāliḥ yad'ū lahu*).

Although profoundly legislated in Islam, humanity has known *waqf* or endowments before Islam. Ever since the existence of human beings the search for God has prevailed and houses of God took different shapes and people of religions dedicated their lives to their services. Hence, means to sustain these worship places took the form of endowed properties allocated by devoted endowers. As explained by Al Dessouki, in the civilization of Babel, there was a similar system of endowment that kings allocated for the widowed and the poor without transferring property to them. Ancient Egyptians knew *waqf* properties and allocated their profits in the service of their Gods, their temples and to sustain the graves of their kings. Ramses II allocated for the temple of Abidous a wide range of properties and a big celebration took place to witness the transfer of these properties to the temple, which encouraged many people to follow his act and endow properties to the temples and their workers. Ancient Egyptians have

28 Al-Nawawi, Rawdat al-talibun. Beirut, AH 1385, v. p. 314

also known family endowments and endowed properties to their offspring without giving them the right of ownership and usually these endowments were run by the elder son (33–35). As to Romans, they developed the concept of religious endowments and considered endowed properties in support of temples a divine ownership that forbids the interference of human beings. Endowments were not only limited to serving religion and the impoverished, but also extended to serve education and culture like the school of Plato that lived longer than six centuries due to the endowments that were allocated to sustain it by its founders. Same applies to the library of Alexandria in Egypt that was supported by plenty of endowments that enabled it to enlighten people for centuries and centuries until eaten up by fire in year 48BC.

1.6.1.2 An Overview on the Form and Legal Structure of Waqf: A Historical Brief

In the Islamic history, the first waqf was attributed to either Abu Talha Al Ansary or to Omar Ben Al Khattab, the second Caliph. It is said that Abu Talha endowed a well called "Bir ‘aa" that he allocated for his offspring and cousins. As to Omar Ben Al Khattab, it is said that he owned a land in Kheiber and consulted the prophet Mohamed what to do with it. The prophet (mpbuh) advised him to endow the land in the sense that it cannot be sold, bought or inherited, and allocate its profit to the poor, those close in kin and geography (dhūou al qurba), liberating slaves, and to hosting wayfarers and strangers. Omar Ben Al Khattab did endow the land of Kheiber, which is known to be the first charity endowment or *waqf* in the history of Islam. After the death of the Prophet, many of his companions established endowments, whether charitable or in support of family members. In the Omayad period the *waqf* prospered in Egypt and in the Sham region, and during the rule of Hisham Abdel Malek in Egypt, as elaborated by Abu Zahra, the grand jury Tubah Ben Numair, created the first government entity administered by the judicial authorities called *dīwān al aḥbās*to supervise and regulate endowed properties (12). This *dīwān*took the responsibility of registering the endowments to protect the rights of the beneficiaries and is considered the first organizational structure to supervise endowments, not only in Egypt but throughout the Islamic countries. From there, endowments became under the jurisprudence of law and judges took the responsibility of supervising the endowments, issuing the tie-up procedures of the principle and allocating the profit according to the conditions of the endower. In the Abbasid period the endowments grew further and began to support not only the impoverished but also schools, students, llibraries, hospitals and almost all aspects of life including the support of infrastructure like paving streets and services to the general public not excluding care for animals and birds.

Throughout history the founder of the *waqf* used to appoint a comptroller (*nadhīr*) to be in charge of administrating the *waqf* in respect of the will of the endower (*wāqif*); in other incidents the *wāqif*itself or his/her descendants managed the *waqf*; and in many instances the endowments were placed under the direct supervision of the Chief Judge.

However, with the beginning of what is referred to as Modern Egypt realized by the Ottoman ruler Mohamed Ali Pasha[29] in the 19th century, the *waqf* structures began its deterioration. Mohamed Ali Pasha enforced taxes on endowed properties and confiscated all the endowments in Egypt, whether charitable or family *awqāf*. As Abu Zahra indicates, Egypt became like a farm owned by Mohamed Ali, who was the sole provider of services and the sole distributer of land to those he admired (28). With the coming of *Khedewi* Said following Mohamed Ali things began to change and ownership of land to the Egyptians re-appeared in 1891 together with allowance to endow properties to charity and offspring. This brought again some of the draw-backs or the abuses of family *waqf*, which permitted those, who wish to deny some of the heirs their inheritance rights (especially girls in many instances) to allocate family *awqāf* to their preferences denying others their heritage rights.

From its part, and in an attempt to organize charity *waqf* and make sure the conditions of the endower (*sharṭal wāqif*) is respected, the government created *dīwān* al *awqāf* in 1895, a government body that became a Ministry or a *Wizāra*in 20 November 1913. This *dīwān* was responsible to manage those charity endowments that do not have a *nadhīr* or a comptroller, those *awqāf* that juries think should be referred to the *dīwān*, the *awqāf* that do not have known beneficiaries, and also those *awqāf* that their beneficiaries together with their *nadhīr* voluntarily wish to refer its management to the *dīwān*. This Ministry began in Egypt and with the unity between Egypt and Syria in the United Arab Republic, the Ministry of Awqaf was responsible for the *awqāf* in the two regions with two administration units in each province. However the ills of the previous independent system remained with the inauguration of the Ministry: those who wish to deny family members their inheritance right continued to do so, the system of supervision varied from one *nadhīr* to the other depending on his honesty and management, and a degree of dependency existed among those beneficiaries who got used to being supported by the *awqāf* and hence did not strive to work. To face these problems, in 1926 the Egyptian Council voted to reform the *waqf* system and among those suggesting reform was a wave calling for abolishing the *awqāf*. Their reasoning for it referred to the fact that one-eighth of the land in Egypt was endowed and hence this constrained buying and selling of these lands in addition to the mal-management of the *nudhār* (plural of *nadhīr*) that led many beneficiaries to lose their rights. Other reasons include the constant disputes and legal suits between the *nudhār* of the different *awqāf*; the decreasing shares from the profits of the *awqāf* due to the long periods of sustainability of these *awqāf* that benefited generations after the others and hence the individual share in the *waqf* itself has become far greater from the tiny profit distributed on a great number of beneficiaries; the management of the *waqf* was not as good as private business management because the *nudhār* did not care for the long-distance benefit of the waqf and its sustainability and often took

29 The ruler of Egypt and father of Modern Egypt from 1805 untill 1848.

decisions that led to the deterioration of the business or the properties at hand. Many writings and meetings have followed and in 1946, law48 was issued to organize *waqf* and it focued on three major objectives: One, adding flexibility to the *waqf* system to allow changing it any time and using it in different ways. This opened the door for legislations that permits the *wāqif* (endower) to regain its *waqf* during his/her lifetime (except for *awqāf* on mosques); family endowments became limited to 60 years or to benefit two generations at most; the condition of the endower or *sharṭal wāqif* (which is the core value in the original legislations of *waqf*) is not to be respected if it contradicts with the present needs. For example if the endower conditions that beneficiaries receive bread, it became possible to give them money instead and not necessarily bread as indicated by the *wāqif*. In addition, it was permitted to abolish the *waqf* completely if the beneficiaries agree to sell it and obtain their shares of the principle. The second major objective of this law was to protect the heirs from the injustices of the endowers, concerning family *waqf*. Without getting into details, just to give an example, the court had to look into the reasons that led endower to exclude family members from the *waqf* and it was up to the court to decide the legitimacy of these reasons. The third objective of the law was to protect the rights of the beneficiaries. Here, a wide range of clauses were issued to limit the authority of the *nadhīr* or the comptroller and put him under strict judicial control. Also without going into details but just to give an example, the *nadhīr* was now restricted to invest a sum of the profit from the agrarian land to buy new machinery without obtaining an approval from the court. In sum, this law brought considerable reform to the previous legislations; yet the very same clauses that aimed to organize and enhance, became those who led to further deterioration (Abu Zahra, 31–40). This law, in my opinion, legalized the deterioration of the condition of the endower, which is the essence of civic *waqf*. In addition, it allowed more interference by the part of the authorities with regard to the *nadhīr* and influenced the way business was done by introducing more bureaucracy like obtaining permissions that usually take long time. Finally, this law paved the way for further isolation from the essence of the *waqf* as a civic act to which the will of the endower is to be completely respected and signaled the downfall of the *ahlī waqf* (family waqf) by limiting its life cycle.

With the coming of the socialist regime in Egypt and the spread of this wave in other parts of the region, the government became the sole provider of goods and services, again like the time of Mohamed Ali. In 1952 the family *waqf* was abolished by law in Egypt and Syria (where it is called *waqf sūrī*). This law 180 of year 1952 in Egypt was followed by another law 342/1952 which was reformed further to transfer the *nidhāra* or the function of the comptroller to the Ministry of Awqaf making in that sense the Minister of Awqāf, which is a government employee appointed by the President of the Republic, the *nadhīr* of all the existing *awqāf*. Christian *awqāf* by this law were excluded and remained under the jurisprudence of law, not that of the Ministry. The *awqāf* under this law could also fall under the direct *nidhāra* of the endower if s/he wishes during his or her lifetime. The same law which was reformed to be law

547/1953 gave the Ministry of Awqaf the absolute right, in approval of the court, to change the *maṣārif al waqf* or the outlets and conditions that the endower has once expressed for his/her *waqf* to support; in other words, the disbursement of the profit followed the government or the Minister's will, and not that of the original endower. Furthermore, it was necessary, under the socialist regime to facilitate land reforms, to abolish the family *waqf* because it goes in line with the structural adjustments that took place. Abolishing feudalism, limiting land ownership, the nationalization of land and the distribution of lands on farmers could not take place with the existing endowed lands. Abolishing family *waqf* was a logical consequence of this era and its nationalization policies and an end result of of previous consecutive legal reforms, as presented above.

Finally, with putting an end to the family *waqf* and the powers granted to the Ministry of Endowment with regard to the charity *waqf*, this system completely failed and vanished. The family or *ahlī waqf* vaninshed by the force of law, and the charity *waqf* by two major factors, the obvious cut between the endower and its offspring, because after the endower's death the *waqf* becomes a property of the Ministry of Awqaf , and second is this absolute power to manage the *waqf* by the part of the Ministry, which makes people prefer to practice other forms of philanthropy that makes them in control, not the government.

1.6.1.3 An Overview of the Significance of the Waqf

The *waqf* system is an old rooted civic form of institutionalized philanthropy that throughout history played a major social, economic and political role not only in Egypt but throughout the Arab and Islamic World for centuries and centuries.

Every individual *waqf* or civic endowment followed an independent vision for the *waqf* management and the allocation of its resources conditioned by the endower. In practice, endowments took the following forms: One, distributing the interest from the *waqf* or *rīʿ al waqf*, monetary or in-kind, to directly or indirectly spend on certain beneficiaries following a set management of the *waqf* determined by the endower to continue also after his/her death. Second, providing services that are not subject to the market supply and demand policies, either free of charge or with symbolic fees. This includes educational services, health care, housing and shelter, etc. These services take place by the support of the *waqf* to specific institutions like hospitals, schools, etc. These institutions could be endowed or not. Third, endowments tended to provide vocational training through enhancing the capacity of the *waqf* beneficiaries to learn skills in order to allow for economic, social and cultural mobility. This also manifests through specific foundations like vocational training centers, etc. Fourth, many endowments were established to meet the spiritual needs of the beneficiaries through supporting the maintenance of mosques and churches. Those endowments meeting the spiritual needs and are directly related to mosques for Muslims and churches for Christians are among the primary forms of *waqf*. These kinds of awqāf were also those influenced the least by the government policies and by the confiscation of *awqāf* under the Minsitry of Endowments. Those civic *awqāf* supported the establishment of religious institutions, their maintenance and renovations, as well as payed the salaries for the *Imāms* leading the prayers, the *mu'dhins* calling for the prayers, the cleaning personnel, religious classes, libraries and all other services and facilities needed like water, electricity, etc. Many of these awqaf supported the maintenance of ancient mosques and also the beneficiaries coming to obtain sustainable *ṣadaqa* or charity from the mosques. The endower would specify the names of the mosques that he/she wishes to support and calculates from the *awqāf* allocated what guarantees that all the expenses are met in perpetuity. This allowed, first, a financial independence to the religious institutions guaranteeing their continous function, and second, it granted these religious institutions managerial independence through the management of the endower or the *nadhīr* he appoints.

The other major area of support by the *waqf* was education. Education remained for centuries a significant attraction to *waqf* and in many instances in history the civic *awqāf* were the sole provider of education in this region. Amongst the many *dīwāns* or *dawāwīn* (plural of dīwān), there was no *dīwān* for education as this was a civic-funded affair, completely independent from the government. The *waqf* institutions played a significant role in funding education and especially Islamic education in the Islamic Middle Period with many students of higher education depending on stipends for continuing their studies. The *madāris* (schools) funded were not primarily targeted to serve the poor, but some endowers intended to serve orphan students and those whose families cannot afford to pay for them. Only with the rule of Mohamed Ali Pasha in the 19th century education became a government responsibility after centuries and centuries of belonging to the civic sector. In 1836 a school advisory council was developed and soon turned into *dīwān al madāris* in 1837, or what in our epoch corresponds to the Ministry of Schools, which in return signaled the emergence of government education. Needless to say, civic *awqāf* used to fund the *katātīb*, which were indigenous schools decentralized all over the country to teach students and fight illiteracy. With the rule of Mohamed Ali and the introduction of modern education, these *katātīb* started to vanish and western education and culture started to take over. However, conscious of the importance of traditional education and the significance of guarding local culture, mid 19th century witnessed a rise in *awqāf* supporting the *katātīb*. Among the major *awqāf* supporting education and the creation of *katātīb* was that of khedewi Ismail who endowed two big pieaces of lands in 1865 and 1876 and allocated one of his palaces in Upper Egypt for the educational purposes. In 1882 with the British invation in Egypt, one of the major forms of fighting foreign interventions was the creation of *katātīb* as a social wave that continued progressively until the libration. However, with the increasing involvement of the government in education the *waqf* for *katātīb* lessened[30]. Same applies to the schools, azhari institutions, public libraries, and vocational training schools that were heavily funded by civic *awqāf*. Among the most famous in modern time is the Cairo University, the major Egyptian University up this time that was established in 1908 through full civic funding and plenty of endowments or *waqfiyyāt* supporting it. The most considerate endowments for the university is that of Princess Fatma who, in 1913, endowed immense amounts of lands to support the university, in addition to donating jewelry and money for the construction costs[31]. In 1914, a total of 1028 *feddans* of land supported the university; however, from this time and after the government's taking over the university and putting it under the Ministry of *Maʿārif* (knowledge), endowing properties seized almost completely[32]. It should be noticed that at the time, Egypt was under the British occupation, which had made its finances under the control of the occupation forces; hence, the civic *awqāf* by building the university and supporting all the wave of education and culture in the country, have kept a strong social and economic resistance. Not only by preserving the cultural identity, the language and the curricula, organized philanthropy has succeeded, but also by this civic will to build and invest independent of the position of the government.

Civic *waqf* income also invested heavily on providing medical care, which was a source of great attraction to philanthropists throughout the Islamic history; this involved endowing huge amounts of properties, markets, and income-generating projects to support the construction of hospitals and health care center and their maintenance. There were individual *waqfiyyāt* specified to support the salaries of doctors, researchers, and also social workers who bring hope to people to help them overcome severe maladies or to endure fatal ones. One of the most notable hospitals in modern Egypt in the Delta area was endowed by Ahmed al Minshawy Pasha in 1903 to offer free treatment for the poor; and for those who could afford; they had to pay for medicine and doctors. The interesting thing about this civic *waqf*, is the fact that al Minshawy allocated another *waqf* for medicine to fund foreign hospitals like that of the German, Italian, Russian, French and Austrian hospitals in Egypt in order to have local contributions in the foreign medical attempts of the country[33]. Hence, also in the domain of health care, endowers were aware of their national role to enhance the country and contribute to its development through mobilizing local resources. It is also noticeable that a strong degree of civic-government partnership took place where individuals endowed properties to fund public hospitals and health care centers using the power of *sharṭal wāqif* or the condition of the endower to guarantee the proper allocation of his/her resources in the areas he/she specifies. After 1952 the legal and

30 Ibrahim al Bayoumi Ghanem. Al awqaf al Siasiya fi Misr.Cairo: Dar al Sherouk, 1998

31 Tarich Insha' al jami'a. Al Hilal Newspaper.

32 Ibid.

33 Ibid.

legislative power of *sharṭ al wāqif*lost ground, but still *waqf* to fund health issue in the Ministry of Endowment has remained relatively more alive than other domains of philanthropic attraction to endowers.

Throughout history, there has been *waqf* institutions focusing on charity supporting the provision of food and water to the poor, the impoverished families and the crippled, insane, or unemployed who depend on charity to eat. The *waqf* provided these people with a sustainable source of basic need supplies saving their fortunes from the moods of potential almsgivers. Of course the allocation of the permanent *waqf* outcome depends on the wish of the endower, and even for funding food and water, there were *awqāf* sponsoring food and drinks only for prisoners, like the famous *waqf* of Fatima bent Sudun which provided bread and fresh water all year round for four prisons in Egypt in the mid fifteenth century. In the 19th century Egypt *waqf* heavily founded orphanages and what was known as *takāyā* or those places established for the elderly, the windows, the poor and the strangers who could not afford to work; the *takāyā* (singlular: *takīya*) provided them with shelter and food. There were also *takāyā* established for students and people going on pilgrimage passing by different countries like al Minishawy *Waqf* in Gharbeya Governorate in Egypt, serving those passing by Tanta on their way to pilgrimage[34]. Needless to say, the endowers were very meticulous in determining the daily management of the *waqf*; for example for hosting men and women, the endower specifies the amount of food served, the montly pocket money given to each, and new dresses to women in celebrations of religious and happy occasions, in the fasting month of Ramadan, etc. In addition to these characteristics, *waqf* in many cases were transnational institutions, in the sense that they supported not only people of one country but in the region. One of these examples are the two *takāyā* established by Mohamed Ali in Makkah and al Madina al Munawara and for their support he had endowed in 1844 a great *waqf* in Egypt (2877 feddan of Egyptian agrarian lands). These *takāyā* fed around 4150 person yearly and were further annexed by other *takāyā* by khedewi Said and a medical care center, a pharmacy and the famous ‘Abasia water fountain in Mena supported by the endowments of khedewi Abbas in Egypt. After more than 150 years of function, the Egyptian Minister of Awqāf closed these takāyā down in 1996[35].

Before the modern epoch, the *awqāf* used to play a leading role in public work, like in funding the paving of streets, digging of canals, constructing bridges, building public bathes (traditional bathes, steam rooms and saunas), establishing commercial markets, hostels, and funding religious fiests and public parades to celebrate cheerful occasions. In a country like Turkey civic *awqāf* used also to fund the army. Another common area of support by the *waqf* is burial of the dead which was considered a public safety and sanitation, especially during famines and epidemics in the epoch

34 Hujat Waqf Ahmed Pasha al Minshawi, page 47
35 Ibid.

of Medieval Islam; during occasions as as such, the streets of Cairo for instance were filled with corpses. Modern sanitation methods did not exist and unburied bodies posed a danger health-wise and were psychologically burdening to the living; especially that people strongly believe in the importance of not leaving a Muslim body unburied. The first Sultan concerned about this issue was Sultan al-Dhahir Baybars in the Mamluk Egypt (in spite of his trials to confiscate agricultural lands endowed by others, as indicated in a number of history books). He had founded a fountain where strangers who die (thus have no families to take care of their bodies) could be washed according to Islamic ceremonies and be buried in dignity. However, this service extended to poor Cairenes who died and were left unburied for whatever reason[36]. In modern times, *waqf* for health and public benefit continued and took a civilized shape like the building of beautiful public bathes all of the country and the region to accommodate men and women's quest for clean and healthy bodies. Yet with the time this type of *waqf* in support of public bathes diminished and more popular was the *waqf* supporting the *sabīl* (plural: *asbila*) or the water fountains to offer fresh water to people. Water fountains were also less costly to construct and maintain than public bathes. However, since the beginning of the twentieth centuries, both forms of *asbila* and public bathes deteriorated and gradually disappeared. Only in recent years in Egypt in the 21st century, a new wave of *sabīl* creation started to take shape as an individual civic attempt to revive what is refered to as *ṣadaqa jāriyya* or sustainable form of giving, i.e. the essence of *waqf*. These newly constructed *asbila* or water-fountains lack fundamentals that the traditional ones enjoyed; first they lack the beauty in construction, as the new *asbila* take the form of small metal boxes or refrigerators lacking any kind of attractive or aesthetic taste as the previous ones. In addition, any maybe more importantly, the new ones lack any form of sustainability like that granted through the *awqāf* to the *asbila* in the previous ages. Thus, these kind of asbila became individual efforts lacking any form of institutionalization and done in most cases as a *ṣadaqa jāriyya* by family members for their dears who passed away. This could be seen as desperate attempts to revive what the successive governments have destroyed.

Hospitality also manifested in al *maḍāfa* (plural: *maḍāyif*) which was a location constructed and maintained by civic *awqāf*. Al madaief existed all over Egypt and throughout its villages. As believers in the Prophet Mohamed's *ahadith* on the importance of hospitality and care to strangers and guests, these *maḍāyif* were constructed to accommodate strangers and guests to the cities or villages. There was a post funded by the *waqf* for the host who welcomes people coming to the *maḍāfa* in a pleasant way and his job also entailed taking care of them and trying to meet their requests as a sign of generous hospitality. In addition there was usually a cook, the

36 Adam Sabra. Poverty and Charity in Medieval Islam. Mamluk Egypt, 1250–1517; Cambridge Studies in Islamic Civilization; UK: Cambridge University Press, 2000.

catering team, the cleaning team, and all the facilities that guarantees good hospitality in serving food and drinks. This whole business was sustained by small, middle or high class endowers. In addition to hospitality, *waqf* also funded religious celebrations by providing new clothes and money for the poor to make people of all levels enjoy the feast as well as facilitate the equipments and the parades needed for the. Among these celebrations were also those transnational in nature, as they travelled between countries[37].

To sum, many of the *takāyā* as well as orphanages that the Ministry of Awqaf managed in Egypt were handed over later to the Ministry of Social Affairs that was established in 1936 to do similar activities, yet it was not concerned with *waqf* management or supervision. From here a clear line was drawn between the old system of civic mutual interdependence manifested in *al awqāf* and the new model of civic institutions manifested in the Non-Governmental Organizations (NGOs) that respond to Western civic models and which started to take rise in Egypt and all the countries of the region. In a way that was a signal of the takeover of this model vis à vis the *awqāf*, which gradually became smaller in size and turned into old monuments guarded in secrecy by the Minister of *Awqāf*. More ironically, civil society became connected to the West who exported this concept to Egypt and the Arab and Muslim worlds, which to Western eyes did not have any civil society movements before the civic movement in the West that exported in return this concept to other parts of the world!

Finally, the *ahlī* or family *waqf* which was primarily constructed to preserve the family structure and to keep it solid and together in order to maintain its social standard and protect the properties from falling into strangers' hands; this form too deteriorated until completely prohibited in 1952.

1.6.1.4 Concluding Remarks

In sum, motives behind *waqf* creation varied but one common feature remained unchanged: *waqf* remained one's preparation for the afterlife; a connection that was highlighted even in the *waqf* deeds. *Waqf* deeds accordingly stated that the *waqf* should be perpetual, from the moment they are made to last forever. However, although *waqf* were meant to be perpetuate, not all attained this goal. Many lasted for centuries and centuries, others not, and currently many are managed by government officials and conditions originally put by the endower are no longer respected. It must be also noted the government, throught the Ministry of Endowment, confiscated all the *awqāf* under its control and management; much of the profits generated was channeled to serve other things irrespective of the will or the condition of the *wāqif*.

37 See: Ilhab Mohamed Zohny. Misr fi kitabat al ra'alah wal qanasil al firinsiyin fi al qarn al thamin 'ashar; Cairo: 1992

The government became the sole *nadhīr* of all awqāf and the one and only who knows how this is managed and where the money is spent.

In 12 May 1967, the Council for Awqāf Affairs issued a verdict to change all the *maṣārif* or profit allocations of all the charity awqāf in Egypt and limit the expenditure in two domains only: Spreading Islamic *Da'wa*, i.e. support all what concerns spreading Islam in the World; and charity in its general sence while keeping priority to those related by kin to the original endowers[38]. This law was like the straw that broke the Camel's back. It was a further confirmation of the government's control and ownership to the civic *awqāf*. It gave the government the full authority to allocate *awqāf* resources, which were a considerable source of wealth that had been accumulating since centuries and centuries, to whatever the government's own will on the expense of the civic will. In addition, and with changing the *maṣārif* of the awqāf spendings, the Ministry went also under a structural reform. It became one of the government's mobization tools, especially through the role its Imams played in mosques. Due to the importance of this mission to the government's security, the Ministry of Awqaf had to give away its inherited responsibilities and handed over hospitals, schools, orphanages and all social institutions to the related Ministries, whether health, education, etc, or to the Ministry of Social Affairs. This trend cut completely the connection between the Ministry of Awqaf and the civil society as represented by individuals and organizations and which is referred to in this part of the region as the ahlī or family community, *al mujtama' al ahlī*.

1.6.1.5 Monetary *Waqf*

Although the forms of *awqāf* that existed in Egypt and that are run by the Ministry of Awqaf are mostly agrarian lands and buildings, it is not a condition to limit *awqāf* in these domains of income generation. Monetary *awqāf* is another form of endowments that have and are still existing and excelling in Turkey since the 15th and 17th centuries[39]. Endowments in Banks, endowing stocks, endowing bonds are all means of monetary *waqf*.

This domain is relatively new in Egypt and is unfolding. Fortunately it provides another venue of *waqf* and does not fall under the domain of the Ministry of Awqaf, whose inheritance of *waqf* does not include monetary ones. Hence conditions and shape of this form could be legislated and applied independently from the Ministry of Awqaf , however these legislations have to be done in conjunction with the Ministry of Social Solidarity which is the government supervisory concerned with the third sector in Egypt.

38 Ibrahim al Bayoumi. Ibid., p (470)

39 Nizam al Waqf wal mujtama' al madani fi wattan al 'rabi. Markaz dirasat al wihda al 'arabeya wal amana al 'ama lil awqaf fi dawlat al Kuwait. Beirut: 2003.

1.6.1.6 Specific Conditions of Waqf

In this coming section, I would like to sum up the three vital conditions for the establishment of *awqāf* and which, in my opinion, form the legislations encouraging *waqf* creation and the formation of perpetual independent civil bodies serving the community. The motive of this coming brief demonstration is to strategically shed the light on the cornerstones on which a solution for a reform to revive the waqf structure could be attained.

1.6.1.6.1 Ownership of God (*Milkiyyat Allah*)

One of the conditions that are agreed upon by most theology schools is that once *waqf* is established, its ownership is transferred to God and the endowers cannot reclaim it. Hence, it should not be timely but perpetuate as a gift that cannot be repossessed. Hence, ownership becomes divine and in exchange the endower gains good deeds during his/her life and after; i.e. a perpetual *ṣadaqa* that adds to one's good deed until dawns day.

This condition reflects the importance of owner transfer, which makes the *waqf* independent and not subject to mood changes by the endower or those who follows him/he, whether people of kin or governments nationalizing properties and distributing them. '

1.6.1.6.2 The Independence and Autonomy of Waqf

Most of the religious scientists of the four *madhāhib* of the Islamic Law (*sharīʿa*) agree that the *waqf* is an autonomous institution in the sense that its ownership becomes that of God's as soon as endowed by the endower. This legislation granted the *awqāf* a civic character because it is an individual act seeking the consent of Allah or the consent of one's consciousness, and their management remained subject to the choice of the endower by either taking over the *nidhāra* or by appointing a *nadhīr*. This civic independence and autonomy from government's ownership allowed these structures to spontaneously emerge in a decentralized manner enjoying stability and a degree of perpetuity away from any political or governmental command, unrest or corruption. It has been a venue for the community to support the government and not to challenge it; autonomous *waqf* structures characterized a strong civic sector but not one that was a buffer between the state and the people like in the Western context, but as a "family community" or *mujtamaʿal ahlī* that symbolizes the civil sector but that of the Arab and Islamic region context.

1.6.1.6.3 Respecting the Conditions of the Endower (*sharṭ al wāqif*)

The conditions of the *waqf* is what the endower registers in the endowment *waqf* document (*wathīqat al waqf* or *hujjat al waqf*) to specify the management structure, the division of the *waqf* resources and to which channels they are to be spent. This is one of the primary conditions of the *waqf* legislations. Unfortunately, and as previously demonstrated and as indicated by al Fangary[40], the Ministry of Endowments in Egypt violate the condition of *sharṭ al waqif* and the Minister of Awqāf became the "*Nadhīr al Waqf*" who by the force of the new law 247 issued in 21 May 1953 have the following rights:

1. Put all the charity *waqf* under the *nidhāra* of the Ministry of Awqaf , who in return will manage, reclaim and spend profit on charitable causes.
2. Provide the Minister of Awqāf with the full authority to change the *maṣārif* or outlets conditioned by the original endowers.

These two clauses had serious implications; the first clause the independence and autonomy of the *waqf* were abolished and hence this whole system was put in the service of the governing authority. The second clause implied that the core of the function of any waqf according to all previous *fiqh* legislations, which was *sharṭ al waqif* is no longer respected. This not only destroyed the civic will behind the creation of awqāf, but also centralized the decisions in the hands in one person representing the Ministry and all the previous and coming endowers.

1.7 Introduction to the Study at Hand

As a concept, the term "philanthropy" is not commonly used in Egypt. However the general perception when the concept is discussed reveals an understanding of "giving". In the context of the research, philanthropy will be referred to in Arabic as "social giving" *or al i'ṭa' al ijtimā'ī* [41]. This includes all acts that involve giving, whether material or non-material, as well as the different mechanisms of social interdependence (*takāful*).

For many centuries, Muslim traditions contributed enormously to shaping cultures of social interdependence that grew and flourished upon solid foundations of philanthropy and civil society institutions. These traditions beautifully diffused within cultures of diverse beliefs, and within different countries and nations bonding people and bridging diversities, not only through charitable giving but also through institutionalized philanthropic mechanisms that enjoyed legal and financial autonomy and sustainability.

Throughout history many factors affected motives and forms of giving, as well as the philanthropic nature and structure of civic organizations. In the world of today, a

40 Mohamed Shawqy Al-Fangary. Watha'ik 'an Awqaf Al Fangary.

41 A workshop on the perception of philanthropy was prepared by Marwa El Daly as part of her MA Thesis on: Private Philanthropy in Egypt. The workshop organized by the Institute of Cultural Affairs and funded by the Ford Foundation in Cairo, demonstrated different perceptions of the term philanthropy, and the Arabic concept *al al i'ṭa' al ijtimā'ī* was agreed upon to mean philanthropy and was first introduced as such by the researcher.

portion of the Muslim societies are impoverished and many of them rely on international aid programs to finance development programs that local philanthropic structures do not address. On the other hand, in the Arab region with a predominantly Muslim population, earlier social policies, the solidarity inherent in the culture, and the traditions of philanthropy helped reduce dire poverty in comparison to other regions[42]. Studies reveal that the Arab world today has suffered a twenty-year growth slowdown. Nonetheless, poverty levels in the Arab world are not as bad as in countries with similar levels of income. A main reason given by the recent Arab World Competitiveness Report 2002–2003 is the "cohesive system of private social responsibility" that distinguishes the Arab region, and within which families help their disadvantaged members through religious giving systems (24). However, and according to the same report, reduction of poverty over time can be best achieved through increasing the growth rate of the economy, currently associated with inefficient investments, political instability, a weak business environment, low quality of human capital, primarily education and knowledge advances (25–31). Can private philanthropy be mobilized towards achieving growth and innovation? Can it be understood in this context? Can the concept of public benefit, social justice, social development and social innovation gain ground in the mind-set of a donor, big or small? In sum, could we set the tone for philanthropy for social development, where social justice is integrated in systems of giving that are modern in nature, traditional in principle?

1.7.1 Significance of the Study

In Egypt, which is the focus of this study, philanthropy dates back to hundreds of centuries and has been enrooted not only in traditions of giving, but also in the sustainability system of social interdependence of the Egyptian society. Over centuries, indigenous philanthropy in the form of *awqāf* played a major role in funding public utilities, hospitals, schools, universities, infrastructure projects, research institutions, and supported salaries of workers in civil society formation[43]. Nevertheless, post-colonial Egypt (mid 20th century) witnessed many changes in the philanthropic structures, which greatly affected them as channels of social and cultural interdependence. It is worth mentioning that at times in history, philanthropy and its institutions were solely under the jurisprudence of law, and at times it was under strict government control. At other times, certain forms of philanthropic establishment were banned or modernized to take the form of semi-state structures. This long his-

42 UNDP: Arab Human Development Report. July 2002

43 Marwa El Daly. Private Philanthropy in Egypt: Institutionalized Private Philanthropy as a Mechanism for Sustainable Community Development. MA Thesis: The American University in Cairo, Dec. 2000.

tory with all its external, internal, cultural, economic and social influences affected people's perceptions and practices of philanthropy, as well as the shapes and structures of philanthropic organizations that exist in Egypt today.

Thus, it was significant to explore and attempt to understand current philanthropic practices, whether giving or volunteering, current structures, whether religious or secular, and the forms of the organizations through which local philanthropy are channeled. There are three reasons behind the necessity of our study interventions: First, in a world of global political instability, it is not advisable, let alone feasible, to rely on external donations to develop a country and achieve social justice. It is of vital importance for Egyptians to re-build their country, and to engage the different and diverse civil society members by depending on variant local resources to achieve the desired social change. Second, in the last twenty years, Egypt has witnessed a growth in civil society movements, resulting in an increase in the number of NGOs, reaching around 18,600[44] NGOs in 2005 and doubling over a period of 15 years to reach 40,000 NGOs in 2020[45]. This includes civic formations, corporate philanthropy initiatives and new private foundations as evidence for new upsurge of social responsibility. Many of these organizations are charity-oriented, and so are many of the private initiatives that contribute with a large amount of money and effort in social services and charity work. These form a great potential to institutionalized philanthropy that aims to achieve development and social work. Many of these organizations and initiatives are untapped potentials, or in other words not efficiently used sources of support to development, which can be mobilized, organized and geared towards social, economic and cultural growth. Third, as a society where religion is an important aspect of its thinking and functioning, it would be of value to complement this with information that could help guide philanthropy to allow for the development of a just society. All these factors, in addition to the lack of a comprehensive data on local philanthropy, its challenges and potentials, were crucial to carry out this pioneering study as a leading step that looks into the core of the development problem: local assets; where are they, and how can they be best utilized?

1.7.1.1 Research Objective

This study aims to explore philanthropic practices at the individual and institutional levels in Egypt. The overall objective is to understand current philanthropic perceptions, practices, structures, and activities in Egypt and come up with recommenda-

---

44 This figure is given by Mahmoud El-Sherif head of the General Union for Local NGOs in a personal interview on 2 August 2004. The published figure is 14,774 NGO, which might be due to relatively older references.

45 Dr. Talaat Abdel Kawy: President of the Federation of NGOs in Egypt (Personal Interview in January 2020)

tions and propose means that spark change-driven philanthropy to achieve development and social justice.

1.7.1.2 Research Questions

1. What are philanthropic traditions and resources upon which philanthropic institutions are founded? This will include the nature, structure and management of these institutions, their means of distributing funds and how accepted they are among diverse members of civil society?
2. What is the legal, cultural and economic environment that surrounds philanthropic organizations, and what is it internally or externally that affects transparency, accountability or trust in their interventions among their counterparts and vis-à-vis civil society members and the State?
3. What are the models of integrating religious and cultural legitimacy with modern structures that conform to social justice and human rights?

The analysis of this study is based on a national representative survey of 2000 Egyptian publics and 1200 NGOs operating in the field of social giving. In addition to these samples, 200 people combining NGO board members, donors and recipients were intensively interviewed in a 2-hour face-to-face intensive qualitative interview. While the first section of the report deals with the structure of institutions, their sources of funding and interaction with the State and other local NGOs, the second section focuses on the analysis of the socio-cultural aspects of philanthropic behavior and tradition among the Egyptian public. The goal behind the two components of the study is threefold:

- To explore the nature and practice of philanthropic institutions in Egypt to assess their contribution in mobilizing their sources of funding for enhancing social justice and to show how they ascertain public trust and accountability.
- To explore the ways by which the Egyptian public perceives religious philanthropy and to what extent they are motivated by religious and secular traditions.
- To analyze to what extent the philanthropic practices of both the institutions and individuals lead to collective orientations that may promote a social justice form of philanthropy

1.7.1.3 Research Output

This research is expected to generate a clear picture of the nature of philanthropy in terms of its resources, potentials and limitations. The main output will be concrete recommendations for bringing about a consensus on institutionalizing philanthropy in the Egyptian society and channeling it through innovative business models towards sustainable development that would eventually lead to social change and social justice. In addition, the researcher will attempt to develop a model of institutionalized philanthropy that goes in line with the results and recommendations generated by the research. So the output is summed up in two envisioned productions: An exploratory study and a community-based philanthropic model.

1.7.2 Exploratory Study with a Representative Sample Design

This is an exploratory study that aims to explore and identify philanthropy as a practiced phenomenon in Egypt. This goes to the fact that studying philanthropy, which involves perceptions, motives, practices, etc, is of a complex nature and brings up interrelated issues together in a vast topic. It is also worth mentioning that local philanthropy has not been thoroughly studied before, and hence this study is a pioneering initiative and a preliminary source in this field.

Thus, the quantitative study took place in 2004–2005. It is designed to have 95% confidence interval and a permissible error that should not exceed 5%, whereby two units of analysis are employed, the publics and the philanthropic organizations in Egypt at large. These two criteria were employed to provide the basis for determining the appropriate sample size for each study. From the Master Sample Plan of the Central Agency for Population Mobilization and Statistics (CAPMAS) at that time that includes Nine Hundred Thousand (900,000) families representing the Egyptian Public, we drew our sample for the public with 2000 interviewees. And based on a list containing 14,774 civil society organizations (representing NGOs in 2005) in all geographical regions in Egypt, a probability proportionate to size (PPS) sampling method was employed and 1200 NGOs from different fields were interviewed. The qualitative methods involved intensively interviewing 10% of the publics sample mentioned above and hence highlighted the views of 200 individuals representing NGOs' Chairpersons of Board of Directors, religious *Shaykhs* and Priests, as well as individual donors and aid recipients from secular and religious bodies.

Elaboration on the research methodology and sample design is to proceed in the coming chapter on the research methodology.

1.7.3 A Philanthropic Community Development Model: Waqfeyat al Maadi Al Ahleya – Maadi Community Foundation

The model initiated by the researcher lies profoundly on the results of the research and involves the mobilization of community members towards investing in change-driven philanthropy and the establishment of a community foundation that simultaneously and primarily attempts to revive the concept of *waqf* endowments.

Waqfeyat al Maadi Al Ahleya Community Foundation was the result of this field work and it was founded by the researcher, Marwa El Daly, and registered in 13 May 2007 to make what the research preach a tangible reality to prosper and grow.

2 Research Methodology

2.1 Introduction

This chapter deals with the methodology on which the field study was founded. As the methodology encompasses both a quantitative and a qualitative approach, this chapter is divided into two sections. The first section discusses the selection of the sample for the surveys as well as for the intensive interviews, and a brief on the content of the surveys and interviews in reference to the objectives of each set of questions or discussion themes. It also sheds light on the research teams that were involved in the study, those of the qualitative as well as the quantitative interventions.

The second section of the chapter deals with the geographical characteristics of the sample, such as the gender, age, education, occupation and income, due to the significant role these variants play in affecting the philanthropic culture and practice. As an example, the monthly income, as one variant, reflects the economic condition and in return indicates how the economic conditions and environment affect philanthropic practices; the same applies for other variants, such as age and its effect on the type of giving or volunteering.

Thus, a detailed description of the methodology and the demographic characteristics of the sample are the core of this chapter and are described thoroughly below.

2.2 Methodological Approach

The present research uses both qualitative and quantitative approaches. As this study is the first of its kind in Egypt, it was important to rely on qualitative methods to explore trends and explain findings that were to be studied on the national level using quantitative methods.

In the quantitative research, a questionnaire was designed to collect information from the heads and board members of 1200 institutions distributed over 10 governorates (out of a total of 26) in Egypt as a representative sample of the nation-wide philanthropic institutions. A national list of these institutions functioned as a sampling frame, and a probability proportionate to size sampling design (PPS) was employed. The other unit of analysis was the public at large, where a representative sample covering 2000 adults was employed.

Throughout the research, it was realized that both qualitative and quantitative methods are not only appropriate but they complement each other in studying a topic of such a complex nature. The quantitative study, through the surveys on the Egyptian public and on philanthropic institutions, has wider access to respondents, and helps us study national trends in philanthropic attitudes and practices. The qualitative component with its intensive interviews to various key figures is the verification tool that was used to explain reasons behind the quantitative indicators. The qualita-

https://doi.org/10.1515/9783110697032-002

tive analysis was important in revealing data on significant issues that could not be tackled in the quantitative research due to its close-ended nature. These issues include perceptions and understanding of some concepts encompassing social justice, human rights, development and civil society. It also includes some of the factors that affected the philanthropic environment that were revealed thoroughly through the in-depth interviews. These factors reflect aspects that shape motives, preferences, and relationships between partners and stake holders in philanthropy. This is in addition to the religious institutions represented by mosques and churches which the in-depth interviews dealt with comprehensively through interviewing *shaykhs* and priests as well as beneficiaries and donors of these institutions.

The qualitative component of the present investigation addressed not only the Board members, Directors and Staff of philanthropic institutions, but also donors and recipients as well, covering six governorates in Egypt. In addition to non-governmental bodies, the qualitative analysis has studied religious institutions engaged in social work, interviewing leading figures of these institutions, as well as their donors and beneficiaries. In-depth interviews were organized using a random sample of board members, donors and recipients affiliated with 57 institutions in the six governorates. The institutions in these governorates represented 3% of the total institutions that were included in the quantitative survey. A total of 120 in-depth interviews were conducted with around 200 NGO board members, leading figures of religious organizations, as well as recipients and donors of secular and religious bodies.

It is worth mentioning, that both quantitative and qualitative methods targeted the Egyptian population, Egyptian NGOs, as well as religious organizations at large, irrespective of their religious affiliation.

2.3 Preparation for the Fieldwork

In preparation for the fieldwork, training for qualitative and quantitative interviewers took place. Special considerations were observed in training our interviewers for field research, be it a qualitative or a quantitative field research. The following has been taken into account during the training of field interviewers.

2.3.1 Training for the Qualitative Field Researchers

For the qualitative field research, the following was discussed with the interviewers:
- The role they are going to play in conducting the in-depth interview and their relationship with the people they will encounter during the interview. They were oriented with the importance of identifying themselves to the respondents as researchers. For this reason, interviewers were advised to read carefully the concepts and the objectives of our study to give to the respondents the impression

that they are well informed. This was an important consideration since almost all of the NGOs' directors, staff and board members are very sensitive in dealing with interviewers who might represent the State or foreign institutions. If interviewees incorrectly thought that the interviewers were undercover governmental agents, their answers may have been different. This also applies to incorrectly sensing that the interviewers represented foreign organizations seeking to harm Muslim and Arab civic organizations.

- The language of the questionnaire and how to ask the questions had to be flexible. Interviewers were trained to use a simple language with respondents of modest educational background and a higher level of language with Directors of organizations or certain donors. This point has proven its significance in the pilot test of the interviews.
- Another important issue that discussed within the field interviewers is to relate to the general direction of the conversation and the specific topics that will be raised by the respondent. As it was relied on interview guides and structured interviews, interviewers were trained not to miss additional information and issues raised; however, it was important that each interview guide is carried out fully by each interviewer. The documenter, who assisted the interviewer in documenting as well as setting the tape-recorder, was also instructed to act as "another mind" with the interviewer, write personal observations and remind as well as alert interviewer if an answer needs further elaboration by respondents.
- The qualitative research component of the present investigation also called for utilizing the focus group discussion method to assess the recipients' attitudes towards the services being offered by the CSOs. Those who undertook discussions among the recipients were instructed to act as moderators only. They were instructed not to let any member of the group dominate the discussions for fear that this may affect group participation. Letting one interviewee dominate the interview may generate the problem of what is called "mentality of the herd", the tendency for people in a group to conform to the opinion and decisions of the most outspoken members of the group. Focus group discussions followed the in-depth interview guide.

2.3.2 Training for the Quantitative Field Researchers

A detailed plan for the training of the field interviewers was put before data collection. Such training has specifically dealt with the following subjects:

- A discussion of general guidelines and procedures about how to apply the questionnaires in a face-to-face setting.
- A general discussion of the specifications accompanying the structured-interview questionnaire.

- Special attention was given to the contingency question format and special training was directed to the proper presentation of contingency questions.
- A thorough revision of the questionnaire has taken place to answer any comments that interviewees may raise concerning the questions.
- A simulation using the actual questionnaires involving pairs of interviewers was conducted.
- The final stage of the training for interviewers involved some "real" interviews with people not included in the sample. Every effort was made to check interviewers' performance during training and over the course of the study as well.

It is worth mentioning that proper control and management of the interviewing operations are as important as the training sessions themselves. Two supervisors were recruited to handle the everyday operations of the fieldwork. One person was assigned the responsibilities for overseeing the field survey, help the interviewers find the assigned addresses, and make sure that the interviews were appropriately conducted at the respondent's place of residence. This person was also responsible for verifying that all the questions were answered consistently according to questionnaire' specifications during the interview.

Another supervisor was assigned to handle the logistics of the operation, coordinating with the project director, to recruit and train additional interviewers, and monitor the field supervision.

2.4 The Research Teams

The Lead Researcher has selected distinguished research teams and these were divided into two main fronts: one responsible for the qualitative component and the other for the quantitative.

1. The main researchers are:
   - Marwa Ahmed El Daly (Lead Researcher and Program Manager)
   - Marlene Kanwati (Research Advisory Board Member)
   - Abdel Hamid Abdel Latif (Quantitative Research Consultant and Director of the EMAC center for Training)

   The major tasks of the main researchers were the following:
   - Developing the quantitative and qualitative interviews
   - Implementing the pilot quantitative and qualitative interviews
   - Supervising the field research
   - Implementing the quantitative and qualitative research
   - Analyzing the quantitative and qualitative results
   - Report development.

2. The main assistant researchers of the qualitative research are:
   - Radwa Abdel Wahab Al Gaaly
   - Areeg Al Badrawy Zahran

   The major tasks of the main assistant researchers of the qualitative research were:
   - Implementing and documenting the qualitative interviews
   - Emptying and cleaning data from the cassette recorders and the documentation booklets used during the intensive interviews.
   - Revising (by exchange among reviewers) each documented cassette.
   - Rewriting/coordinating and organizing the contents of the qualitative interviews.
   - Extracting qualitative results and taking part in their analysis.
   - Assisting in the preparation of the draft and final report
   - Integrating the Academic Committee's comments during the colloquium on the study.

3. Assistant researchers:
   - Ayman Abdallah Shehata
   - Dalia Sabry Abdel Rahman
   - Mary Sabry Hana
   - Mohamed Magdy Bakr

   The major tasks of the assistant researchers of the qualitative research were:
   - Implementing and documenting the qualitative interviews
   - Emptying and cleaning data from the cassette recorders and the documentation booklets used during the intensive interviews
   - Revising (by exchange among reviewers) each documented cassette
   - Rewriting/coordinating and organizing the contents of the qualitative interviews
   - Extracting qualitative results and taking part in their analysis
   - Assisting in the preparation of the initial draft report

4. The secondary researchers of the qualitative research are:
   - Mohamed Tharwat Shahim
   - Talha Hassan Tawfik
   - Noha El Shoky
   - Mostafa Thabet Abdel Baset
   - Yasmine Mohamed Hassan
   - Shaimaa Qadry

   The main task of the secondary researchers is:
   - Implementing and rewriting some interviews.

5. The main assistants of the quantitative research are:
   - Ibrarhim Hassan Ibrahim
   - Fatma Gaber Abdel Kerim
   - Mohamed Mostafa
   - Noha Hassan Mohamed
   - Wessam Mahrous Ibrahim
   - Mohamed Bayoumi Ahmed
   - Asmaa Bayoumi Ahmed
   - Rehab Salama
   - Hanaa Abdel Maboud
   - Shaimaa Hassan Ibrahim
   - Shaimaa Mohamed Mohamed Tawakl
   - Marwa Abdel Hamid
   - Mohamed Khairy Mohamed
   - Hesham Abdel Naby
   - Mohamed Hamza Amin Abdallah

   The major task of the main assistant researchers of the quantitative research was:
   - Implementing the questionnaires with the public and the philanthropic organizations.

   The Desk-Researchers Team:
   - Doaa Hassan Ibrahim
   - Asmaa Ahmed Abdel Ghafar
   - Nashwa Ahmed Wedn
   - Sally Salah Eldin Mohamed
   - Asmaa Ahmed Wedn

   The major tasks of the main desk-researchers included:
   - Revising the data
   - Closing the open-ended questions in the quantitative research
   - Entering data on the computer
   - Data cleaning

6. In the early phases of the study, Mostapha Yosry Khalil assisted in the linguistic revisions, while Heba Heleil, Yasmine Ahmed, Niveen Badawi and Ramy Moftah participated in the final revisions.

2.5 Research Methods

2.5.1 The Qualitative Research Component

The qualitative approach includes, in addition to the bibliographical research on the nature of philanthropy in the Egyptian society, the analyses below.

A macro and micro level descriptive analysis of religious and non-religious philanthropic institutions as well as places of worship that implement social activities in six Governorates in Egypt, using in-depth interviews with the chairpersons, board members or religious authorities of these institutions. In addition, in-depth interviews are carried out with recipients and donors of these institutions to give an assessment of each institution as a whole. Each organizational interview set, apart from its implication on the overall study, reflects a comprehensive picture of the work of the institution and could be an independent case study. Thus, the institution under study included:

- Religious institutions:
  - Mosques (privately run, or those under the management of the Ministry of Awqaf)
  - Churches and monasteries – none are subject to the management of the Ministry of Awqaf and are independently run.
- Non-religious institutions:
  - NGOs including community development associations (CDAs) and other forms of local associations according to the sample framework of NGOs in Egypt given by the Ministry of Social Affairs (MoSA).
  - Philanthropic foundations

The qualitative interviews targeted the following respondents:

- In-depth interviews with one of the NGOs' principals (the results of these interviews complement the results obtained from surveying the 1200 civil society organizations (CSOs).
- In-depth interviews with mosque or church head authorities.
- In-depth interviews with those who have donated funds to the selected CSOs.
- In-depth interviews and focus group discussions for recipients of the services provided by the selected CSOs.

To complete the above qualitative interviews, our field researchers were instructed to follow the seven stages suggested by Steiner Kvale (1996:88) in the complete interviewing process:

- Thematizing: clarifying the purpose of the interview and the concepts to be explored.
- Designing: laying out the process through which the interviewer will accomplish the purpose of the interview.

- Interviewing: conducting the interview.
- Transcribing: one of the two interviewers should be assigned to creating a written text of the interview. In all interviews (with an exception of three, who refused), a tape-recorder was used to record the interview with the respondent's consent.
- Analyzing: determining the meaning of gathered materials on the spot in relation to the purpose of the interview.
- Verifying: checking the reliability and validity of the materials.
- Reporting: telling the other team members what he/she has learned from the interview.

2.5.1.1 Interview Guidelines

Four different sets of "interview-guidelines" were developed and applied to each of the targeted respondents as outlined above:

1. In-Depth Interviews with Chairpersons of the Board of Directors (BoD) and Board Members of CSOs[46]

   To complete this qualitative interview guide, a prior contact was made with the chairpersons of the BoD of the selected CSOs. Two members of the research team took the responsibility of holding one intensive interview according to the guidelines prepared in advance. The following topics were covered during this qualitative intensive interview:
   - History related to initiation of the CSO
   - Ideas and traditions behind the establishment of the CSO
   - Financial resources mobilized
   - Who are the recipients? What are their relations with the institution?
   - Discussion on what is meant by terms, such as philanthropy and social justice
   - Relations between concepts, such as development and social justice.
   - The concept of human rights and how concepts as such are integrated in the institution's programs
   - The CSO's impact on the community
   - Issues of transparency and trust and their effect in building relations and in the CSOs's work in general
   - The administrative and structural principles in institutional building
   - Relationship of the institution with the state and religious organization
   - The social and cultural environment surrounding the institutions
   - The image of social giving as presented in the media
   - The culture of social giving and how to increase knowledge of it among the public

46 Appendix 1: In-Depth Interview with Chairmen and Board Members of NGOs

- Religious motivation for philanthropy
- The legal environment as it is emphasized in the new NGOs' law
- The economic environment and its impact on philanthropy
- The respondents' future perspective

2. In-Depth Interviews with figure heads of Mosques and Churches[47]
   This type of qualitative interviews was arranged by leaders of mosques and churches (with shaykh/priest) who are widely known in the community for a history of philanthropic activities. Some of these mosques and churches are part of well established religious organizations at both the local and national levels. The interview guide discusses the following topics:
   - Background information related to the management, volunteering, and sources of funding
   - Types of social activities in the religious institutions
   - Ideas and concepts that guide the activities in the religious institution
   - Types of financial resources available to the institution
   - Relationships with recipients
   - Perspective on the concept of social justice
   - Perspectives on the concept of 'development' as it relates to social giving (*al iʿṭaʾ al ijtimāʿī*)
   - Perspectives on the concept of human rights as it relates to philanthropy
   - The impact of the social activities on the local community
   - Perspectives on issues related to transparency and trust
   - Relationship between the state and the CSOs
   - Surrounding socio-cultural environment
   - Images of social giving as they are displayed in the media
   - Cultural and religious motivations behind philanthropic behavior
   - The legal and economic environment as direct influences affecting philanthropy

3. In-Depth Interview with Donors[48]
   To arrange these qualitative interviews with donors was not an easy task. Special efforts were made with the chairpersons of the BoD of the CSOs to recommend members of the local community to us who had donated to the ongoing operations of their institutions. Efforts were made to locate these persons particularly those who are known in each community as socially responsible businessmen. Luckily interviews with some of the old Egyptian aristocracy who have contrib-

47 Appendix 2: In-Depth Interview with Leaders of Religious Institutions: Sheikhs/Priests
48 Appendix 3: In-Depth Interview with Donors

uted a lot to the betterment of their local communities have been arranged. The qualitative interview guide has dealt with the following topics:

- Background information
- Motivation for social giving
- Inherited ideas and traditions that explain reasons behind philanthropic behavior
- Perspectives on social justice
- Perspectives on development and *ṣadaqa jāriyya*
- Perspectives on human rights
- Perspectives on transparency and trust
- Socio-cultural environment as encouraging force to philanthropy
- Perception of social giving as presented in the media
- Cultural and religious forces affecting philanthropic behavior
- Economic environment and social giving

4. Individual and Focus Group Discussions with Aid Recipients[49]

   A quota sampling technique was used in connection with the focus group discussions organized to explore recipients' experiences and how they relate to the concepts of social justice and human rights. To conduct these focus group discussions, up to seven recipients who receive any kind of services or assistance from each selected CSO were brought together in the qualitative sample. It was realized that it was appropriate to also assemble several groups of different kinds of aid-recipients, varying according to the type of assistance they receive. The topics that were raised during the discussions were organized along the following issues:

   - Background information on the aid recipients
   - Issues that are related to the recipients' experiences with the institution(s)
   - Recipients' perception of what social justice means to them
   - The connection between development and charity
   - Recipients' perception of human rights
   - Recipients' perspectives on transparency and secrecy
   - The impact of the socio-cultural environments on the recipients' lives

2.5.1.2 Numbers Accomplished

A total of 120 in-depth interviews with around 200 individuals ranging from chairpersons and board members to donors, recipients, and religious leaders in six different governorates in Egypt were completed. Transcribing the interviews took almost two months. This time was necessary to verify the reliability and validity of the materials. A list of donors and beneficiaries from selected institutions in selected communities

49 Appendix 4: In-Depth Interview with Aid-Recipients (beneficiaries)

were compiled and used as sampling frames. These sampling frames were used as the basis for the selection of a sample to carry out focus-group discussions. This qualitative part of the study complements the quantitative analysis of the philanthropic organizations. The emphasis here is placed on motives, practice, and perception of philanthropy traditions of both donors and beneficiaries.

2.5.1.3 Quality Measures in the Interviews

The qualitative study task force was distributed as follows: eight persons make a group of four researchers, where each two members constitute a group of one documenter and one interviewer. In addition to the documenter, a cassette recorder was used to guarantee full coverage of information (this was used upon interviewees' consent). The duration of the quantitative interview ranged between 45 minutes and one hour, while the duration of the qualitative interview reached an average of two hours. Each documented interview was subject to revision by another person, who fully reviews the documentation of each single interview; a time consuming process, yet one that guarantees accurate reflection of the fieldwork.

2.5.1.4 Case Studies

The qualitative analysis involved the development of case studies of local interventions that show distinguished philanthropic engagement. The objective of this portion of the qualitative component in our investigation is to provide an assessment as to how resources are mobilized to achieve development and social justice. It is expected that the case studies of a selected number of philanthropic institutions will yield explanatory insights into the structure of philanthropic institutions and the philanthropic process of and practice of the private sector and other supporters/donors. It was also expected that the case studies will show the potential and limitation to mobilizing efforts, which might have policy implications.

2.5.2 The Quantitative Research Component

This part of the study utilized the methodology of survey research to collect the required information on both the institutional and individual levels. Original data for describing the philanthropic practices from both institutions and individuals using probability sampling techniques was collected. This was necessary to arrive at general characteristics which may reflect that of the larger population of Egypt. To achieve this goal, standardized questionnaires were constructed to provide data that follows similar form from all respondents.

The quantitative research component consists of two main surveys:

2.5.2.1 Surveying Philanthropic Organizations

A sample of the institutions[50] operating in the field of social services was used as a unit of analysis. A national list of these institutions functions was used as a sampling frame. A probability proportionate to size sampling design (PPS) was employed for the purpose of institutional assessment focusing on managerial systems and activities according to their types, programs, and means of distribution of funds. The utilized questionnaire also deals with questions related to institutional conformity to the promotion of transparency and public accountability.

The questionnaire designed to collect information from the 1200 institutions is thoroughly described below. It consists of questions and statements that were carefully phrased to reflect the particular attitudes and perspectives of these institutions mobilize their sources of funding for enhancing social justice and how they ascertain public trust and accountability. Open-ended and closed-ended questions were used in the questionnaire. In the case of closed-ended questions, respondents were asked to provide their answer to a set of questions that contain exhaustive categories. Most of the response categories were constructed as mutually exclusive and respondent was compelled to select only one answer. On some questions, however, respondents were asked to solicit multiple answers.

The questionnaire also contains contingency questions as some of the questions are relevant to some of the respondents and irrelevant to others. The contingency questions are designed to facilitate the respondents' task in completing the questionnaire, so they can avoid answering unnecessary questions.

The research team has spent a considerable time arranging items in the questionnaire. The debate on the ordering of questions in both the institutions' and the public's questionnaires involved other philanthropy group team members. Everybody agreed that the appearance of one question could affect the answer given to later one. This is particularly true when respondents were asked to assess their overall religiosity, their knowledge about the conditions that are applied by the Muslims in the case of zakat, for example. In ordering the questions, the team was oriented that if respondents are first asked specific questions about certain attitudes and practices, their subsequent overall assessment will reflect the earlier answers.

The institutions' questionnaire was structured into three main sections:

1. The Nature of Philanthropic Organizations in Egypt: Objectives, Mission, and Scope of Activities:
   - Main objectives
   - The nature of organizational activities
   - Classification of philanthropic organizations
   - Reasons for donations and voluntarism among the founders
   - Assessment of organizational objectives

50 Appendix 5: The Institutions' Survey (Quantitative Study)

2. Organizational Resources and Deployment of Charity:
   - Organizational resources and system of disbursement
   - Types of charitable activities
   - Recipients and outreach programs
   - Assessment of organizational activities in promoting societal development and social justice
   - Mechanisms for achieving transparency within the organization
   - Points of strength and weakness in philanthropic organizations

3. Philanthropic Organizations and Socio-cultural Issues in Egypt:
   - Legal, social, and economic environments
   - Relationships with other civil society structures and local communities
   - Relationships with the state
   - Relationships with local religious organizations
   - Extent of transparency with donors
   - Perceptions of the state's responsibilities towards NGO's in respect of the New NGOs Law
   - Perceptions on reasons behind the public reluctances to donate to NGOs
   - Legal change that is necessary to improve organizational activities.

2.5.2.2 Surveying Philanthropic Practices and Activities among the Egyptians Public

A cross-sectional survey was used to assess the philanthropic attitudes and practices of the Egyptian public[51]. A questionnaire was constructed to derive information on the ways the Egyptian public perceives Islamic philanthropy in order to assess the extent to which they are motivated by religious or secular traditions. In order to achieve this purpose, a probability sample was designed to be able to generalize our findings to the Egyptian population from which the sample was selected. Sampling procedure will be discussed in the next section.

The same procedures that were adopted in the construction of the institutions' questionnaire were applied in the construction of the public's questionnaire. Since the public's questionnaire contains several statement measuring individual attitudes and orientations towards certain issues, a 5-point scale was used employing carefully chosen words or verbal qualifiers. The questionnaire also contains instructions on how the respondent can use the 5-point scale rating. By offering him/her two-step decision i.e., "If you are in favor of.... Please reply with '4' or '5', depending how strongly you agree (mostly or fully). If you are not in favor of this view, reply with '2' or '1', depending how strongly you disagree (mostly or fully). If you stand somewhere

51 Appendix 6: The Publics' Survey (Quantitative Study)

in the middle, please reply with '3'". The pretest has proved that this format is less ambiguous, particularly in cross-cultural setting.

Since the topic under investigation requires that respondents must be willing to answer the questions addressed to them, it was significant to maintain their complete anonymity. The Egyptian cultural context was also considered during the face-to-face interviews. In rural areas, for example, interviewers were instructed not to enter the household that was included in the sampling frame if a male is not present in this household at the time of interview.

The public's questionnaire was constructed into three main sections:

1. Philanthropic Orientations among the Egyptian Public: Concepts and Practices
   - The public's perception of social giving (philanthropy)
   - Philanthropic motivations and feelings
   - Forms of social giving (philanthropy)
   - Reasons for and factors that encourage donations among the Egyptian public
   - The public's perceptions of the relationship between philanthropy and social justice
   - Responsibility of helping the needy
   - Prevalence and types of philanthropic donations among the Egyptian public
   - Donations and volunteering preferences by type of organizations
   - Charitable donations: individuals or institutions?
   - Implications of philanthropy on beneficiaries

2. Religious Philanthropy among the Egyptian Public:
   - Concepts of Islamic philanthropy among the public
   - Disbursement of *zakāt* (almsgiving, *zakāt al fitr*) and *ṣadaqa*.
   - Motivation behind Islamic philanthropy among the public
   - Collective orientations in Islamic philanthropic practices

3. Determinants of Philanthropic Behavior:
   - Religiosity and philanthropic behavior
   - Socio-economic determinants
   - Gender differences in philanthropic behavior
   - Rural-urban differences in philanthropic behavior

2.5.3 Pre-testing the Questionnaires

Since there is always a possibility of error in the development of questionnaires, it was essential to pre-test the instruments among selected number of subjects. It is not usually essential that the pre-test subject comprises a representative sample, but people for whom the questionnaire is at least relevant were interviewed in the pre-test. Every attempt was made to ensure that guidelines for questionnaire construction were met. Recoding of responses as a critical aspect of questionnaire design has been adopted to facilitate the quantitative data processing.

The aim of pre-testing was:

1. Targeting the nature and type of problems and obstacles that might hinder the field work.
2. Testing the questionnaires' effectiveness, the relevance of the questions and their variables.
3. Testing the interviewers' ability to understand the questionnaires and the way they ask the questions.

The pre-testing of the questionnaire helped shape the questions in their final forms, including revising and deleting some phrases and words to avoid ambiguity and repetitions.

2.6 Sampling Design

Multi-stage probability sampling methods were used to develop the sampling frames for the present investigation. Two separate sampling frames have been developed for the purpose of collecting information from the civil society organizations and from Egyptian households. It was decided that the required sample size should give an accurate estimation of the true value of the universe with 95% confidence interval and a permissible error that should not exceed 5%. These two criteria were employed to provide the basis for determining the appropriate sample size for each study.

Two sampling methods were utilized to develop the sampling frames from which a probability sample was selected:

- Based on a list containing 14,774 civil society organizations in all geographical regions in Egypt, a probability PPS sampling method was employed.
- Based on a master sample of 600 rural-urban census blocks representing the entire Egyptian population and designed by the CAPMAS, an initial sampling of 125 census block, a representative sample of 2000 households were selected. In estimating the households' sample, a 5% margin error was allowed.

A detailed account of the steps that were followed to estimate the sample size for the above two surveys is as follows:

2.6.1 Civil Society Organizations (CSOs)

The Egyptian MoSA has compiled a list of 14,774 social institutions that are registered to provide services in the field of philanthropy in Egypt. These institutions are cross-listed by the type of services they provide all over Egypt. This list constitutes an excellent sampling frame for the purpose of philanthropic organizations in Egypt. If a random sample is selected from this list, the data that will be collected from that sample could be taken as representative of all institutions operating in the field of social giving.

The 14,774 institutions are listed by their geographical location in 26 governorates and by the type of services they provide according to the Ministry of Social Affairs' Directory for the year 1997/98. Since these institutions vary according to the services they provide, a PPS sampling method is employed. Each cluster is given a chance of selection proportionate to its size in the distribution.

Multi-stage probability sampling methods were used to develop the sample frame for this study. The primary stage sample consists of governorates, followed by a second stage sampling of administrative units within sample governorates divided into rural-urban. The final stage of multi-stage sampling design involves sampling of associations within rural-urban administrative units.

2.6.1.1 Stratification of Primary Stage Units

The primary stage of sampling registered associations was divided into 26 Governorates based on boundaries in the Egyptian local governance system. Because these Governorates are not homogeneous, the 1996 Census divide these Governorates into four areas:

1. *Urban Areas* include Governorates, which are urban as a whole, Cairo, Alexandria, Port Said, and Suez.
2. *Northern Urban/Rural Areas* include the northern part of the Nile Valley: Damietta, Isma'iliya, Daqahliya, Sharqeya, Qalyoubiya, Gharbeya, Menofeya, Kafr El-Sheikh, and Behiera.
3. **Southern Urban-Rural Areas** include the southern part of the Nile Valley: Giza, Beni Soweif, Fayoum, Assiout, El Menia, Sohag, Qena, and Aswan.
4. **Border Areas** include desert outside the Nile Valley governorates: North and South Sinai, Red Sea, New Valley, and Matrouh.

In Urban-Rural Areas each Governorate has some small towns but most inhabitants live in villages and work in agricultural activities. Table 1 shows the distribution of the CSOs according the four different areas. As this table indicates, the share in each area in the two samples is proportional to the total CSOs and Population in the area. Because of the small size of the borders area sample, its share was increased for both the CSOs and the populations:

Table 1: Population Areas (1996 Census) and Representative Sample Size of Philanthropic Associations for the Quantitative Research Component

Region	Governorate	N_h	n_h	p	Q	SQRT(PQ)	N_h SQRT(PQ)	n_{hi}
Urban areas	Cairo	3747	392	-	-	-	-	392
North	Alexandria	997		0.33	0.67	0.47	468.6	197
	Gharbiya	472		0.16	0.84	0.367	173.4	73
	Sharqiya	832		0.27	0.73	0.444	369.4	156
	Menofiya	718		0.24	0.76	0.427	306.6	129
SUM			555				1318	555
South	Giza	1421		0.53	0.47	0.499	709	138
	El Menia	741		.027	0.73	0.444	329.9	64
	Qena	355		0.13	0.87	0.336	119.3	23
	Aswan	174		0.07	0.93	0.255	44.4	9
SUM			234				12.2	234
Borders	South Sinia	40		0.44	0.56	0.496	20	8
	Marsa Matrouh	50		0.56	0.44	0.496	25	11
SUM			19					19
			1200					

2.6.1.2 Primary Stage Sample of Governorates

1. Cairo has been chosen separately as a self-represented governorate since it is a unique area in itself.
2. Northern urban–rural areas: Alexandria was randomly selected to represent the urban stratum that also includes Port Said, Suez, Isma'iliya, Gharbeya, and Sharqeya.
3. Menofeya is selected to represent Daqahliya, Behiera, Kafr El–Sheikh, Damietta Governorates. These governorates have a "V" shape, meaning that it is narrow in the south and wide in the north. Since most of these communities are similar, Alexandria was randomly selected to represent cities in the North, West, and East and Menofia to represent the southern part.
4. Southern urban-rural areas have a stripe shape along the Nile River. Giza was randomly selected to represent the northern area. El Menia and Qena governorates were randomly selected to represent the middle area, and Aswan was randomly selected to represent the southern area.
5. Border governorates. This stratum is represented through a random selection of the Southern Sinai Governorate.

Including the self-representing selection of Cairo, ten governorates were selected in the primary stage of sampling to represent the Egyptian CSOs.

2.6.1.3 Second Stage: Sample of Rural-Urban Areas

One town and two villages in each urban-rural governorate have been randomly chosen while four districts have been randomly chosen in urban cities.

2.6.1.4 Third Stage: Classification according to Types of Services

Dividing sample according to types of social services offered, the CSOs were chosen proportional to the type of services provided.

2.6.1.5 Fourth Stage: Choosing the CSOs to be included in the Survey

In each selected urban district, town, or village, directors of the CSOs or one of the board members have been selected and interviewed for the purpose of institutional assessment using the questionnaire prepared for the study. As for institutions that were not found due to change of address or that were meanwhile closed for any reason, alternate CSOs were identified with the help of the local Ministry of Social Affairs officials.

2.6.1.6 Calculating the Expected Confidence Interval Range

$$n_h = \frac{n \times N_h P_h \sqrt{Q_h}}{\Sigma N_h P_h \sqrt{Q_h}} \quad n \times N_h P_h \sqrt{Q_h}$$

$$n_1 \text{ (Urban Areas)} = \frac{1200 \times 2207}{6767} = 392$$

$$n_2 \text{ (Alex \& Lower Egypt)} = \frac{1200 \times 3131}{6767} = 555$$

$$n_3 \text{ (Upper Egypt)} = \frac{1200 \times 1321}{6767} = 234$$

$$n_4 \text{ (Border Areas)} = \frac{1200 \times 107}{6767} = 19$$

Since the derived sample statistics should be considered a good estimate for the characteristic it represents in the population, it is possible to measure the difference between the true value and the estimated one with 95% confidence, therefore the expected confidence interval range is:

$$\hat{P} = \text{P} \neq \text{Z} \sqrt{(1\text{-F}) \left(\frac{\text{PQ}}{N}\right)}$$

$$= 0.32 \neq (1.96) \ 1\text{—-} \ 0.0812 \times \frac{0.32 \times 0.58}{1200}$$

$$= 0.32 \neq 0.25$$

Therefore E is < 0.03

2.6.2 Egyptian Households

The proposed sampling design for the selection of 2000 households involved an initial sampling of 125 Census Blocks from a master sample containing 600 Census Blocks. This master sample was designed by the Central Agency for Public Mobilization and Statistics (CAMPAS), divided into 360 Urban Census Blocks and 240 Rural Census Blocks. Our sample was designed on 3 stages:

2.6.2.1 Stage 1

The 125 census blocks were selected from the two main stratified census areas: Urban and Rural. The sample units in each stratum followed the probability proportionate size sampling (PPS). This involved the distribution of primary units into the following categories:

1. The distribution of administrative units into urban governorates and its district capitals, urban administrative units, and all villages in Lower and Upper Egypt.
2. A random selection of an urban Governorate to represent urban sector: Cairo Governorate.
3. A random selection of 2 Governorates to represent the governorates in Lower Egypt: Gharbeya and Sharqeya.
4. A random selection of 2 Governorates to represent the governorates in Upper Egypt: El Menia and Aswan.
5. Border Governorates were dropped due to their small numbers.
6. Random distributions of the selected 125 Census Blocks over the entire area sample according to their proportionate size has been selected.

2.6.2.2 Stage 2

At this stage, a selection of sampling segments from each census block determined the number of households to be selected for each sampling segment. Each segment contained from 200 to 300 households.

2.6.2.3 Stage 3

Sixteen households were selected from each census block, which yielded 2000 households. A systematic sampling technique was used to select this sample of households from a list containing the names and addresses of the head of households. This list represents the sampling frame for the present study. From these households, individuals 20 years of age and over were selected for the intensive face-to-face interviews.

2.6.2.4 Method of Choosing Respondents

The method of choosing respondents for the intensive face-to-face interviews was determined to fulfill some requirements as follows:

1. A random sample of households stratified according to the two main strata (i.e. rural-urban). The sample was further divided according to the internal strata that would represent the Egyptian society very well.
2. A household-questionnaire was completed at the beginning of each interview for all members in the households. Basic information about all members of the household was recoded including age, gender, work status and other social conditions.... etc.
3. Members of the households who were 20 years of age and over were asked to complete the remaining of the questionnaire's items as discussed before. Question related to individuals assessment of the feasibility of social giving programs either within philanthropic organization or outside, and whether or not they have participated in such activities were addressed to these individuals.

Calculation for obtaining the sample size of 2000 households with 95% confidence intervals and a permissible error of 5%:

The statement was made earlier that the required sample size should give an accurate estimation of the true value of the universe with 95% confidence interval and the permissible error should not exceed 3%. For obtaining a representative sample of 2000 households, a 5% margin error was allowed:

Let us assume that coefficient of the squared variance and $(CV)^2 = 0.1$ and $N = 600$, we can therefore calculate

$$(CV\bar{Y}) = \frac{S\bar{Y}}{Y} = \frac{E/K}{\bar{Y}}$$

$$= \frac{0.03 \times \bar{Y}/1.96}{Y} = \frac{0.03}{1.96} = 0.015$$

$$N = \frac{(CV)^2}{[CV\,(\bar{Y})]^2 + \frac{(CV)^2}{N}}$$

$$= \frac{0.10 \times 600}{.000225 \times 600 + 0.01} = \frac{60}{.235} = 255 \text{ census blocks}$$

If the permissible error is increased to 0.05%, the obtained census blocks would be 125. In this case 6 households from each census blocks will have to be randomly selected in order to provide 2000 households:

$$16 \times 125 = 2000 \text{ households}$$

In order to provide an assessment of the performance of philanthropic institutions at the Governorate level, in-depth interviews were organized using a random sample of donors and recipients affiliated with **57** institutions in 6 Governorates. The institutions in these Governorates represented 3% of the total institutions that were included in the quantitative survey.

Table 2 reflects the qualitative sample undertaken: In each organization an interview with the head or a member of the board, donor(s), and recipient(s) took place.

Table 2: Sample Size of the Philanthropic Organizations Serving the Qualitative Research Component

Governorates	**NGOs**				**Religious Institutions**				**No. of cases**
	Muslim		**Christian**		**Mosque**		**Church**		
	Urban	**Rural (slum)**	**Urban**	**Rural (slum)**	**Urban**	**Rural (slum)**	**Urban**	**Rural (slum)**	
Cairo	3	1	1		2	2	1		10
Giza	3	2		1	2	2		1	11
Alexandria	5	4	1		1	1	1		13
Gharbiya (Tanta)	3	3		1	1	1		1	10
Minia	2	2	1		1	1	1		8
Aswan	1	1			1	1		1	5
Total	17	13	3	2	8	8	3	3	57

2.7 Fieldwork

Fieldwork was conducted using the sample frames that were prepared for both the public and the institutions. The interviewing was conducted face-to-face. Field supervisions ensured the quality and consistency of this. Interviewers were trained to, as much as possible, ask every respondent the same questions, in the same words, the same sequence, the same setting, etc. This was done in accordance with Oppenheim's suggestions (1992:67) or what he has labeled as the 'equivalence of stimulus.'

Table 3: summarizes the number of interviews that were conducted in the ten governorates

Governorates	Public' Interviews	Institutions' Interview
Cairo	700	392
Alexandria	-	197
Giza	-	138
Menia	300	64
Qena	-	23
Aswan	100	19
Menofiya	300	129
Sharqia	600	156
Gharbia	-	73
South Sinai	-	9
Total	2000	1200

The actual fieldwork of the quantitative research commenced on the January 13, 2004 and ended on April 20, 2004. Approximately two weeks before going to the interviews, two groups of interviewers were selected to handle the households' (public) and the institutions' questionnaires separately. On the day of the interview, the field supervisors made all the necessary arrangements and guided the interviewers to follow the day's agenda. The same arrangements were repeated daily until the fieldwork came to an end.

2.8 Data Processing and Analyses

2.8.1 The Qualitative Data Analysis

After bringing the data from the field, field researchers were engaged in emptying the data recorded on cassette recorders as well as documented by the documenter in each interview. An exchange revision was applied to guarantee that data was accurately emptied on the computer. Thereafter a participatory process began, whereby researchers were engaged to categorize and code topics. As mentioned in the previous sections, qualitative data analysis tends to be inductive as it allows researchers to organize data into categories and to identify patterns (relationships) among the categories. Although there is no standard procedure for qualitative analysis, some systematic techniques were followed in order to analyze our field notes as obtained through the in-depth interviews with the head officials of religious and non-religious institutions, donors, and recipients. Each of these groups of interviews was carefully examined. This process involved the following steps:

- Coding: our aim was to discover patterns among the data of each group of interviews. Coding is the key to this process. After reading notes developed through the in-depth interview, search for coding units had to be searched, such as concepts, or mission and size in the case of organizations. Codes that were generated from the field notes not only allowed us to understand the evolved patterns among the data but also enabled us to retrieve data appropriately as needed.
- Memoing: besides coding, the technique of memoing was also used, which is, writing memos or notes to one-self and others involved in the qualitative analysis. It was essential to the analysts to write down a clear account of what they mean by the codes used in their analysis.
- Cross-case analysis: the transcripts looking for patterns appearing across several observations or cases in order to understand the cross-cutting issues among the interviewees were examined. The focus here would be on interrelations between their perceptions, behaviors, and motivations that relate to philanthropy. The cross-cutting issues rely on what is known as variable-oriented analysis. The aim here is to achieve a partial, overall explanation using a relatively few number of variables or issues that describe, for example, the donors' philanthropic behaviors and attitudes.

2.8.2 The Quantitative Data Analysis

2.8.2.1 Data Processing

After the completed questionnaires were received from the field, the research assistants were involved in the process of converting the responses to the questionnaire items into numerical format. This involved converting the responses to a machine readable form a form that can be read and manipulated by the computers. This process involved several steps:

- Checking the pre-established coding schemes that were assigned to the questions on each questionnaire
- Open-ended questionnaire items were coded before analysis. Code categories were generated from individuals' responses to open-ended questions and were quantified for data analysis.
- Data entry into SPSS data matrix was performed by data entry specialists.
- Data cleaning: this was done in order to eliminate errors. This was achieved through two processes: (1) checking errors as the data were being entered, and (2) examining the distribution of responses to each item in the two data sets.

2.8.2.2 Data Analysis

Having obtained the data from the completed questionnaires, it was necessary to analyze them. The analysis of our quantitative data has been conducted through the use of the computers utilizing a version of the statistical analysis software called SPSS (Statistical Products and Service Solutions)[52]

A set of descriptive statistics have been used to present the findings of the present analysis. These descriptive statistics also involve Figureical and numerical techniques for summarizing the data for the present investigation.

2.9 Demographic Characteristic of the Sample

The survey that was conducted among the Egyptian public yielded informative data on the socio-demographic characteristics of the sample. The sample included 2000 adults selected randomly, considering the following criteria: gender, age, educational level, residence, and other socio-economic indicators such as occupation, family-income from each household, and household's possessions. Only one subject who is 21 years of age and over was selected from each household for the interview.

2.9.1 Overall Description of Respondents

The sample of the survey that was conducted among the Egyptian public included 2000 adults in the quantitative surveys and 200 adults in the qualitative in-depth interviews. They were selected randomly for the quantitative interviews. For the and in respect to whether they were heads of organizations, donors or recipients in the qualitative component, and putting into consideration the following criteria: gender, age, educational level, residence and other socio-economic indicators such as occupation, family-income from each household and household's possessions, especially for the public survey. Only those starting from 21 years of age and over were selected for the interview covering ten governorates in Egypt. The in-depth interviews covered six governorates from all over Egypt. The sample of the 2000 members of the public reflected a concentration of (71.8%) in urban areas and (28.2%) in rural areas. In the in-depth sample the respondents from urban areas were double those from rural areas, and those from rural doubled those living in slums and shanty areas.

---

52 The SPSS is a system that was developed to assist social science researchers to analyze quantitative data that is collected in the field by facilitating the statistical analysis involved. A good reference on the use of SPSS is a publication by Abdel Hamid Abdelatif, the Sociology Professor at Ain Shams University and consultant on the quantitative component of this study. His publication is entitled "Using SPSS Program through Windows: Statistical Package for the Social Sciences" (2001).

The gender of the respondents surveyed was balanced, as 44.8% were male and 55.3% were female. However, in the in-depth interviews women outnumbered men by 3:1, especially among the beneficiary group. They included married and single females. When it came to donors, the number of male donors outnumbered female donors by 2:1.

The majority of the 2000 surveyed sample of the public falls under 45 years of age with a relatively modest concentration in the categories between ages 36 and 45 making 24.3% of the total sample. This suggests that our findings reflect, with a reasonable degree of certainty, the opinions held by most adult Egyptian population. The in-depth interviews started with age ranges of 14 to 75 years old, as the survey team interviewed a group of elderly males from a hostel for elderly males. The 14 year old age group; are boys from an orphanage, and the 15 year old age group; are girls from another orphanage in a different governorate. Interestingly, the age of donors started from 20 years old, however, the donors falling between 40 and 69 years of age doubled those falling between 20 and 40 years.

A significant number (27%) of the 2000 respondents reported that they received college education, while 17.4% were illiterate and 32% had secondary education. This diverse sample is very positive in terms of representation.

As to the socio-economic status of the respondents, most households interviewed possess the necessary appliances to keep their life going. A total of 25% of the sample surveyed earn between LE[53] 500 to LE 999 per month, while 21% fall between those earning less than LE 300 per month. Their occupation characteristics reflected that the majority of the answers given, making 17.1% of the respondents are professionals (teachers, lawyers, physicians, etc), while the remaining sample is highly concentrated with administrative and manual workers. The in-depth study respondents among donors revealed that they varied between a majority of employees, followed by businesspersons, housewives and people on pension.

An Illustration of the above is as Follows:

2.9.1.1 Gender

A large proportion of our respondents (55.3%) were females. This may be due to the fact that the interviews were conducted during the day while most of the male heads of the household were at work. Given the cultural context in Egypt, most of these females are housewives who are well aware of the financial situation of their households. This makes them good candidates for participation on any decisions related to allocations of financial obligations such as zakat or sadaqa.

---

53 Exchange rate against USD$ is 6.15; i.e. USD$1 = LE 6.15. This was the average exchange rate of the year where the study took place and it was not subjected to fluctuations.

2.9.1.2 Age Categories

The majority of respondents fall under 45 years of age, and there is a relatively modest concentration in the categories between ages 36 and 45. The data seems to represent a wide spectrum of the Egyptian population. This suggests that our findings may reflect, with a reasonable degree of certainty, the opinion held by most adult Egyptian population.

2.9.1.3 Educational Levels

As you can see in Figure 1; nearly a third (32.8 %) of our respondents appeared to have completed their high school education. The second largest category represents those who have completed their university education (26.9%). Thus, a significant number of our respondents reported that they received either university or college education. This should be taken as a good indication of the ability of our respondents to answer the questions posed to them by our interviewers. Only 17.4% of the sample was illiterate.

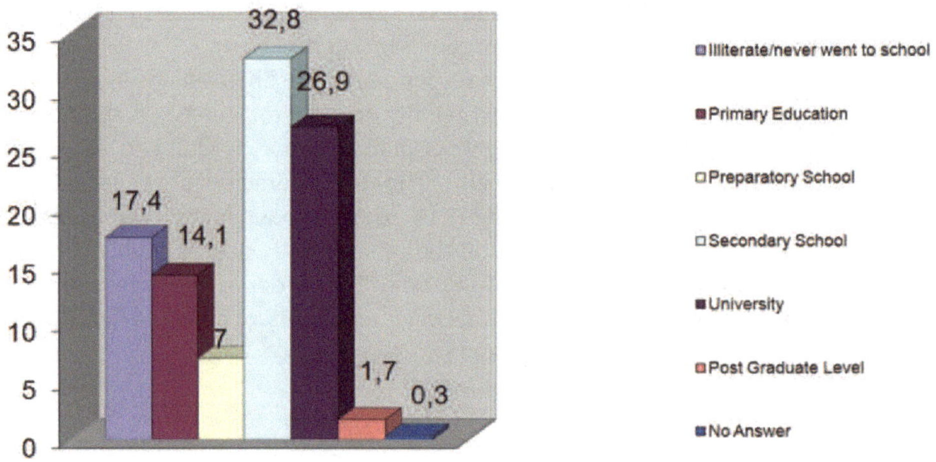

Figure 1: Educational *level of the sample*

2.9.1.4 Rural-Urban Residence

Almost 72% of our sample lives in urban areas. This seems to be a logical conclusion since the master sample from which our sample was first drawn, represents about 60% of the Egyptian population at large who live in urban areas.

2.9.1.5 Employment Status

Figure 2 shows the employment status of our respondents where 45% of them are employed and 13% indicated that they are unemployed. The housewives represent 30.7% of those who completed the questionnaire.

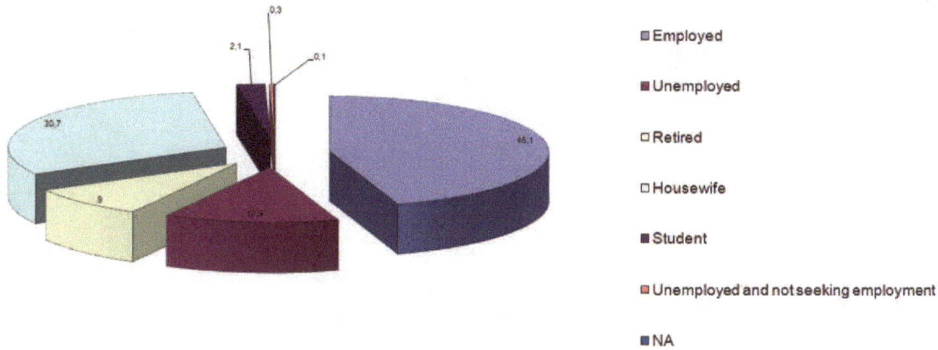

Figure 2: Respondents' Employment status of the sample

The findings in Table 4 appear to be consistent with the educational levels reported by the respondents. There are 17.1% of those who reported to have an occupation define themselves as being professional.

Table 4: Occupation Characteristics of Respondents

Occupation	Frequency	Percentage
Professional (Doctor, Lawyers, Teachers...)	341	17.1
Owner of Private Project	102	5.1
Administrative Occupations	175	8.8
Salesman	28	1.4
Services Worker	49	2.5
Social Development Workers	14	0.7
Agriculture	35	1.8
Skilled Workers	138	6.9
Army or Police Officer	19	1.0
NAP	1099	55.0
Total	2000	100.0

The majority of our respondents appear to engage in urban-oriented occupations. Only 1.8% of all respondents are engaged in agricultural activities.

2.9.2 Marital status of the sample

Figure 3: Marital status of the sample

Most of our respondents are married and having children as it is presented in Figure 4:

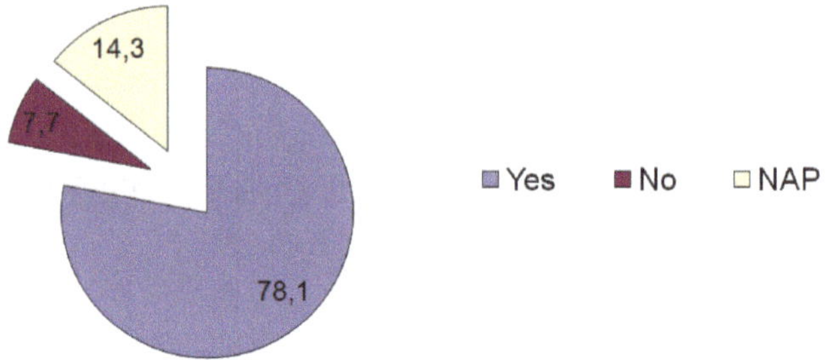

Figure 4: Those who have children within the sample

2.9.2.1 The Number of Household Members

The average number of persons living in the sampled households is almost 5 individuals. There is almost a balance in the sex ratio since the average numbers of males and females are 2.6 and 2.5, respectively.

2.9.2.2 Socio-Economic Status

The data reported in Table 5 clearly indicate that households do possess the necessary appliances to keep their life going. The only indicators which can be used as indicative of high socio-economic status are automatic washers, air conditioners, mobile phones, and cars.

Table 5: Family Possessions as Indicator for their Socio-Economic Status

	Frequency	Percentage
Owns TV	1906	95.3
Owns Car	283	14.2
Owns Taxi	25	1.3
Owns Video	636	31.8
Owns Mobile	771	38.6
Owns Computer	389	19.5
Owns Air Conditioner	200	10.0
Owns Satellite Dish	409	20.5
Owns Automatic Washer	892	44.6
Owns Refrigerator	1757	87.9
Owns Dishwasher	88	4.4
Owns Deep Freezer	186	9.3
Owns Oven	1823	91.2

Family possessions also appear to be consistent with the educational level and occupations as reported by the respondents. Cars, air conditioners, dishwashers, and deep freezers are still less prevalent in the Egyptian households.

2.9.2.3 Monthly Family Income

From the table above it is noticeable that the family income in general is very low, with 42% of the respondents making less than LE 500 a month and only 25.6% having a monthly income ranging between LE 500 and LE 1000. This reflects a weak economic condition, which would possibly affect the philanthropic practices.

Table 6: Monthly Family Income

	Frequency	Percentage
Under 100	72	3.6
100–199	125	6.3
200–299	221	11.1
300–399	239	12.0
400–499	164	8.2
500–999	515	25.8
1000+	261	13.2
Missing	403	20.2
Total	2000	100.0

2.9.2.4 Sources of Family Income

Figure 5 reveals that the majority (76%) of our respondents are salaried employees. Very few of them are landlords or owners of agricultural lands. The second source of family income comes from operating small workshops by some heads of the households.

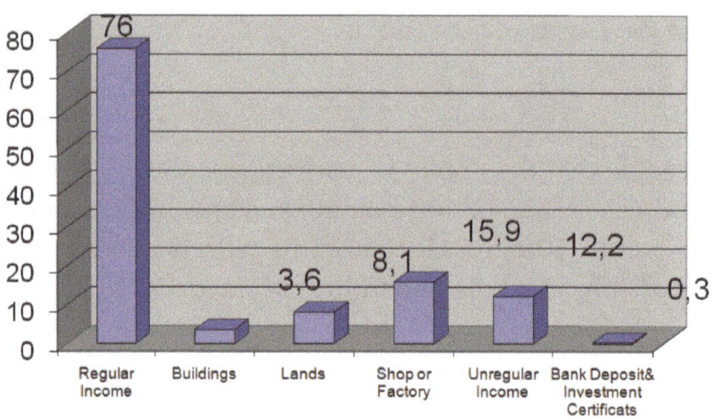

Figure 5: Family Income Resources

2.10 Framework of the Study

The study on philanthropy in Egypt is an action-based study that combines scientific research methods with on-the-ground development of means to learn and share learning about local giving, its challenges and potentials.

The premises that underlie this intervention are the following three:

First, philanthropy as a phenomenon is an old practice known in Egypt and the Arab and Islamic region for centuries. Hence, understanding its dynamics is a learning process for this region and others. It is also an important step towards building on and reviving civic philanthropic structures that construct cultures of knowledge and carries out project of public benefit.

Second, philanthropy for social development, not for charity, is a significant component of Islamic jurisprudence (*sharīʿa*) and of sunna through the Prophet Mohamed's sayings (*aḥādīth* pl. and *ḥadīth* sing.). Development-oriented philanthropy becomes an important change that is needed by the Egyptian society.

Third, the concept of social justice is an integral part of social development. According to the Arab Human Development Report[54] for instance, the distribution of income and wealth and hence power, has an effect on economic growth, as well as on the allocation of resources to be invested in knowledge acquisition, which eventually leads to development (138). Thus, philanthropy, development and social justice are closely interrelated. Understanding the prevailing perceptions of the three concepts, their practice, interrelation, potential and challenges is the hallmark of our study.

The approach to explore philanthropy in relation to development and social justice must be examined in their cultural contexts as well as in comprehension of the prevailing economic and political circumstance. Understanding what affects cultural development, through influences that shape beliefs, behaviors, practices and perceptions, is a first step toward overcoming the hindering factors that diminish the developmental effect of local philanthropy. This approach does not only need to start from within, but it must be founded upon solid cultural grounds that legitimizes this appeal, and gives credibility and strength to any attempt that seeks changing current conditions and practices. If this approach can gain support from religion, which is a significant attribute to culture in this region, a potential for its success is higher than if it is imposed from outside. It is also stronger if it is civic, rather than if government-initiated.

2.11 Summary

This chapter discussed the methodology used and explained the processes of selecting the samples for the quantitative and the qualitative research components and presented the demographic characteristics of the interviewees. It provided a detailed description of the research approach as a whole and the interview guidelines and surveys of the public and institutions.

54 Arab Human Development Report 2003: Building a Knowledge Society. United Nations Development Programme; Arab Fund for Economic and Social Development

3 Environments Affecting Philanthropy in Egypt

3.1 Introduction

Various stimuli influence philanthropic practices in Egypt. Cultural and economic factors as well as the general legislative environment have their proven effects on patterns of giving. Relationships among civil society organizations themselves and between them and the government also affect the size, form and trend in philanthropy. These factors can act as either a catalyst or a barrier to philanthropic activities. This Chapter presents; study results in light of such aspects and the role they play in promoting or hindering social giving, solidarity and volunteering.

3.2 The Cultural Environment

The cultural environment has a significant influence on philanthropic practices. Distorted concepts lead to distorted actions. It is the environment of concepts that decides what people understand, and that of learning, whether religious or popular, that shapes people's awareness of their surroundings, beliefs, ethics, values and everything that determines their behavior. In this view, the role of all learning institutions and players, whether family, school, role models, etc., become a vital determinant to shaping the cultural environment and in return the positions and behavior of the peoples towards the different aspects of their lives.

3.2.1 Concepts and Perceptions

The study dealt with a number of concepts to explore the understanding and awareness of philanthropy among the population. This aspect of the study revealed the relatively low awareness among many of the respondents of concepts frequently used by the media and development practitioners. This signals a gap in communication. A number of reasons can explain this low awareness; however, one must not forget the low education levels, especially among the beneficiary interviewees. Additionally, concepts that are not derived from Egyptian cultural heritage, such as "civil society" and "transparency" by the mass media, are not understood by the public.

3.2.2 Public Awareness-Level of the Main Concepts

3.2.2.1 Philanthropy

Philanthropy is defined as the good will to assist fellow men and the active effort to promote human welfare. It stems from a number of theoretical and practical factors

https://doi.org/10.1515/9783110697032-003

including love towards fellow human beings, but as a concept it involves an understanding of giving and volunteering with clearer strategies, organization and systematic thought as a mature professional act of social responsibility.[55] According to Burlingame,[56] philanthropy is voluntary giving to help the community either by material or non-material means. It involves a social relationship between at least two parties who interact in the form of donors and recipients. This partnership is flexible and interchangeable as donors can become recipients and recipients can become donors.

In the Arabic language, there is no literal translation of the philanthropy concept, however, the term that was used to describe philanthropy to respondents is *al iʿṭaʾ al ijtimāʿī* or "social giving" in literal translation[57]. The following table shows the Egyptian public's answers when asked about their understanding of the term philanthropy. The question asked was the following: "What does philanthropy mean to you?"

Table 7: What does Philanthropy mean to you?

Answer	Frequency	Percent
Financial or material assistance to the poor and the needy	1805	26.8
Paying *zakāt/ṣadaqa/ʿushūr* (tithes), or establishing a *waqf* (reflecting faith-based philanthropy)	1726	25.6
Mutual support/*takāful*	1589	23.6
Volunteerism and community service	1580	23.4
Emotional Support	15	0.22
Implementing projects to solve social problems to serve development	12	0.17
Sum	6727	100

3.2.2.2 Philanthropy as Charitable Giving

The majority of respondents (26.8%) see philanthropy as charitable acts in the form of monetary or material assistance given to the poor and the needy. Intensive inter-

55 See: Marwa El Daly. Private Philanthropy in Egypt: Institutionalized Private Philanthropy as a Mechanism for Sustainable Community Development. MA Thesis: The American University in Cairo, Dec. 2000; p.5.

56 Burlingame, Dwight F. "Altruism and Philanthropy: Definitional Issues". Indiana University Center on Philanthropy, pp.6–7.

57 A workshop on the perception of philanthropy among Egyptians was prepared by Marwa El Daly as part of her MA Thesis on Institutionalized Private Philanthropy in Egypt at the American University in Cairo. The Institute of Cultural Affairs (ICA) and Ford Foundation sponsored this workshop in 1999. The workshop demonstrated different perceptions of the term philanthropy, and the term *al al iʿṭaʾ al ijtimāʿī* as a translation to philanthropy was first introduced.

views consolidated this point, and revealed that chairpersons of NGOs' BoD, religious figures, donors as well as beneficiaries relate philanthropy as a concept to the assistance and aid given to the needy, people with special needs, orphans and those deprived of vital services with no relevance to any organized, systematic act of giving or volunteering geared towards solving social problems in a professional manner.

3.2.2.3 Philanthropy as Faith-Based Giving

Philanthropy as a concept in peoples' minds proved to be strongly connected to religion (25.6%) and to the duties of paying *zakāt*, *ʿushūr* (tithes) and *ṣadaqa*. This was very clear, in particular among chairpersons of the BoD of organizations and religious figures. In defining what philanthropy means, respondents preceded with quoting the Quran or the Bible and the Prophet's sayings (*aḥādīth*) on giving, as well as God's rewards or punishments to those who do not help others. As the head of the board in one NGO operating in a run down area of Cairo said, "Philanthropy for me is what the Prophet Mohamed said in his *ḥadīth*: 'None of you will have faith until he wishes for his brother what he wishes for himself.'" Another affirmed "Philanthropy is important in every civilized society, because it takes the poor and marginalized into account. The NGO facilitates philanthropy: the rich people give through donations and the not-very-rich volunteer their effort. Religion asks us to do this, whether Islam or Christianity. We are asked to give *zakāt* and *ṣadaqa jāriyya*." Confirming this point, a head of board from a Muslim Sufi Order pointed out that "Philanthropy is every good offered by the NGO, without focusing on nationality, religion, tendencies or principles. We offer our philanthropy to whoever accepts it, materialistic, spiritual, tangible and non-tangible for those who seek guidance for example." It is worth highlighting that smiling and spreading good words were perceptions of the *ṣadaqa*, reflecting the understanding and awareness, in some people's minds, of the importance of non-material assistance. Hence, philanthropy from a faith-based perspective is understood to be a material, non-material and highly spiritual act.

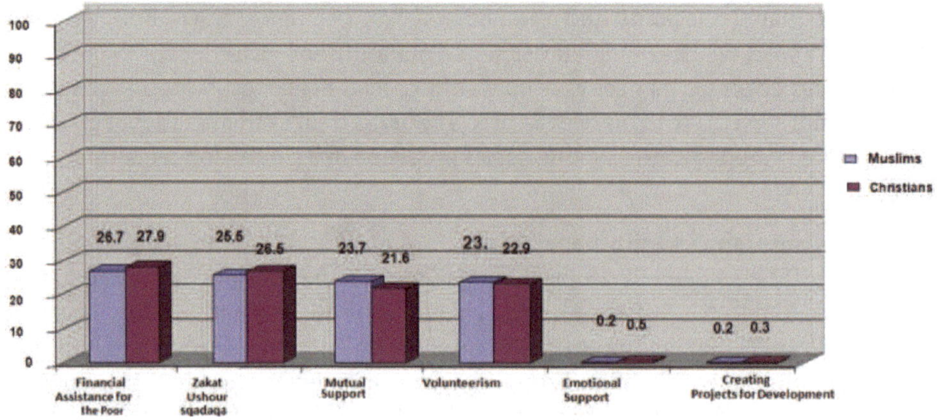

Figure 6: Individual's Perception of Social Giving. What Philanthropy means to People (Muslims and Christians)

3.2.2.4 Philanthropy as Social Solidarity

Among the interesting results is the apparent relevance to people of philanthropy as *takāful* or social interdependence, a concept deeply rooted in the Egyptian culture. As one of the donors described, "Philanthropy for me represents social balance, where the competent support the incompetent in the form of *takāful*." Especially among religious figures, philanthropy was related to the concept of *takāful*. Their understanding of *takāful* is summarized by the following quote given by a shaykh: "Philanthropy is the giving of a helping hand by the wealthy to the poor to enable him/her to satisfy his/her basic needs in terms of food, shelter, clothing, medical care, and education for their young. This way, the latter's suffering is alleviated, the social gap between the classes is narrowed, any feeling of spite and envy in society is done away with, and a general spirit of love and respect through '*takāful*' (interdependence) is spread." This idea of intrinsic tendency to live in *takāful*, together with compulsory giving imposed by religion, shapes the perception of philanthropy among Egyptians of all faiths. The importance of *takāful* as a concept was strongly asserted throughout the whole study. This highlights that it is a traditionally and religiously significant concept that's social acceptance indicates mutual help among the public.

3.2.2.5 Philanthropy as Volunteer Effort

A considerable percentage of the respondents (23.4%) see philanthropy as the volunteer effort to assist others. Many of the respondents elaborated that faith-based philanthropy in the form of sadaqa involves non-material giving such as a smile to cheer up a sad person, a kind word that boosts a spirit or any voluntary act of assistance. This perception towards volunteerism promises a positive impact of volunteer effort if organized and directed towards development.

3.2.2.6 Philanthropy is not linked to Development in People's Minds

As most respondents related philanthropy to charity, only a small fraction (0.6%) of the respondents related it to development through the implementation of projects that target social problems. People appeared to comprehend philanthropy from a non-developmental point of view, where direct assistance and charity prevails in their perceptions.

In an attempt to explain this tendency which cognitively relates philanthropy to charity and not to development, Neamat Mashhour believes that philanthropy is regarded as an act that reflects the voluntary will of the giver (out of *tafaḍḍul* or courtesy), while it is actually not a voluntary act, nor should it be out of courtesy; it is a duty and should be understood as such. Therefore, according to Mashhour, there must be clarity about what is termed "sufficiency" or "subsistence" or *ḥadd al kifāya* in Islam, which determines the right of the recipient to receive what allows him/her to live in subsistence-or-sufficiency level. She then questions, what the substance level in our society today and explains that it differs between Cairo and Aswan for instance, and varies according to personal circumstances. There are people who are physically or mentally not capable to work, and others who are at an age that does not allow them to seek a job, yet need to live in substance. Therefore, in cases such as these, Islam calls for monthly sponsorship or kafāla to provide them with their basic rights as human beings. In this case, what Mashhour's explanation hints at, is the fact that understanding concepts such as *ḥadd al kifāya*, which is synonymous to the economic term subsistence-level, is a way of educating people and shift thinking towards social responsibility to achieve a clear goal and help alleviate the status of the impoverished in the long run.

3.2.3 Zakāt and 'Ushūr (Tithes)*Zakat*

Zakāt[58] is the third pillar of Islam and its importance is reflected not only in being a pillar of Islam but by its repetition in 82 verses or *ayāt*[59] in the Qur'an. There are eight types of zakat, and if one possesses any of the following eight properties (briefly discussed below), he/she should pay *zakāt*according to the quantity of the property when it reaches a certain amount (*niṣāb*) after one year has passed. Thus, after reach-

58 For details on Zakātand its legislations, see: Yousef El-Qaradawy. Fiqh al-Zakat: Dirasa mokarena le a'hkameha wa falsafatiha fi do' al-Qur'an wal Sunnah. Cairo: Maktabet Wahba (publishers), 23rd edition, 2003; and Naguy Al-Sherbiny. Kayfa tokaddir wa to'adi zakat amoalak. Cairo: 1986; and Ahmed Yehia Ismail. Al-Zakat: Ibadah maliya wa idarah iqtisadiya. Cairo: Dar El-Ma'aref, 1986; and Mohamed Kamal Ateya. Halat tatbiqiya fi mohasabat al-Zakat wa 'ard lehalat tatbiqiya. Alexandria: Monsha'at al-Ma'aref, 1988.

59 Ahmed Babay. Sa'adat al-anam fi al-sa'i ila al-zakat wal siyam. Al Sharika Al-Tunisia lel Tawzi' (Publishers): Tunis: 1981; p. 23

ing a set amount, value, size or number, i.e. *niṣāb*, *zakāt*is due. However, *zakātal-fitr* or *fitra* as some Muslim countries refer to it, is an exception, as it is a duty or a fard on each Muslim to pay immediately after the holy month of Ramadan to bless his/her fast, irrespective of how much property he or she owns. It is obligatory for the rich and the poor and is estimated in monetary terms to be paid for each member of the family, old and young. Following is a brief description of highly detailed legislations that concern *zakātal māl*.

3.2.3.1 Zakāton Money (*Zakātal Māl*)

The *niṣāb*or quantity on which *zakāt*must be paid is equivalent to 85 grams of gold and 600 grams of silver. This applies to gold and silver properties as well as banknotes equivalent to this value in gold or silver. If one year passes on the money that reaches the *niṣāb*or more, a value of 2.5 percent must be paid as *zakātal māl*. Gold and silver jewelry used are not subject to *zakāt*, however when they reach more than the *niṣāb*equivalent of 85 grams of gold, the additional grams are subject to the 2.5% *zakāt*. However, if the purpose of the jewelry is investment, collection or trading, and exceeds the equivalence of 85 grams of gold, the total of the value is subject to *zakāt*and 2.5% of total must be paid in *zakāt*.

1. Articles of Merchandise and Industry
   The *niṣāb*is also equivalent to 85 grams of gold after the passing of one year. A percentage of 2.5% of the capital, savings and profit on which one year has passed should be given in the form of *zakāt*. Fixed capital used for merchandise and industry are not subject to *zakāt*as they are essential for running the business, however current assets in merchandise on which one year has passed undergo the *niṣāb*rule and are subject to *zakāt*after deducting essential living costs and any outstanding debt if the person is indebted.

2. Plants and Fruits
   Agricultural lands, plants and fruits are fixed assets. The *niṣāb*for plants and fruits applies to the profit they derive and according to the quantity and weight of the harvest or the rent in case the land is rented. To reach niṣāb, the produce should weigh a minimum of 50 kila (a weight measuring unit), which is about 653kg. As for plants that are difficult or impossible to weigh, if their value equals or exceeds that of 50 kila of the average price of agricultural yields, then the nisab is complete. There is also a difference between agricultural lands irrigated by machines and those irrigated without; whereby those irrigated by machines are subject to a 5% *zakāt*, while those without a machine are subject to 10% *zakāt* as there was less investment incurred. These percentages could be given in the form of the harvest itself or in monetary terms if it is of better interest to the receiver.

3. Livestock
   Livestock raised for breeding are subject to *niṣāb* when the animals reach a certain number, from 30–40 depending on the type of the livestock. One year has to pass before *zakāt* is required upon livestock. Livestock raised for dairy products usually require higher costs to prepare them for milk production and therefore, only when the profits (after deducting cost and essential living requirements) reach the *niṣāb* of 85 grams of gold, is 2.5% of the total subject to *zakāt*.

4. Mining
   Metals and stone that are extracted from the land do not have a specific *niṣāb* to reach; however, 20% of all extracted resources are subject to *zakat* after deducting the cost incurred in the extraction.

5. Stocks and Shares
   Zakāt applies to stocks and shares used for the purpose of investment or trading and its *zakāt* rate is 2.5% on the profit they make. As to shares for trading, its *zakāt* encompasses its price when being sold in addition to the profit it generated (if more than what is equivalent to 85 grams of gold) after deducting debt, necessary living expenses out of this business and what was paid as taxes to the government.

6. Bonds and Securities
   For both bonds and securities, *nisab* should reach an equivalence of 85 grams of gold and its value is 2.5%.

3.2.3.2 Zakāt al fitr

Zakāt al fitr is one aspect of *zakāt* that is an obligation on both, the rich and the poor alike and is not limited to the individual grown up and sane giver, but it is a small amount of money that must be paid for each member of the family, even children and the completely disabled. In that case the head of the household, whether male or female, calculates the amount that should be paid by each of his or her family members to pay *zakāt* on their behalf.[60] Thus, it is compulsory on male, female, the free or the enslaved, the healthy and the disabled, and even on children, and their share is to be paid by their parent as indicated. In first day of the feast ("*ʿīd*) after fulfilling the holy month of Ramadan and before the *ʿīd* prayer, every Muslim becomes a giver of *zakāt* and everyone shares a responsibility towards the other who might be less fortunate. This makes *zakāt al fitr* a considerable source of social solidarity deriving a source of income to the community in the occasion of end of Ramadan.

60 Anwar ʻAli Ashour: Quabs Min al-Fiqh al-Islami fi Alzakah, Al-I'tisam library, 1980. Pages5, 6.

3.2.3.3 *'Ushūr* (tithes)

'Ushūr [61] (tithes) means "tenth", i.e. the paying tenth of every Christian's income to charity. *'Ushūr* incorporates any income one receives. Types of *'ushūr* include:

1. Money and Gifts
   It is all the income a person owns whether it is in a salary form or income from a project either industrial, commercial, services or anything else. One tenth of any income throughout the year is subject to go as *'Ushūr* according to the Coptic Orthodox Christian faith.

2. Property
   This is any property one receives as inheritance, gift or any other means

3. Time
   Every Christian should give one tenth of his/her time to God, whether in the form of prayer or in helping the poor

4. Harvest and animals
   Any harvest one gets or any animal one slaughters to eat or sell is subject to 'Ushūr as well.

Thus *'Ushūr*, like *Zakāt* for Muslims, should be part of a Christian's life, and they should give a percentage of their income for the sake of God.

After this brief theoretical orientation about Zakāt and 'Ushūr, a description will follow to highlight how they, as concepts, are perceived and accordingly practiced by the Egyptian public in light of the field study.

3.2.3.4 Zakāt and 'Ushūr in the Eyes of Muslims and Christians

Muslims and Christians share closely their perception of philanthropy and associate it in a similar degree to faith-based giving. Like Muslims relate philanthropy to *zakāt* and ṣadaqa, Christians speak of it in reference to *'ushūr* (tithes) and other forms of giving mentioned in the holy books.

It was observed throughout the study that even the most concrete concepts like *zakāt* or *ṣadaqa* could have different meanings to different people. People vary in their perception of even the most basic terms that drive their faith-based giving. The majority (40.6%) could identify *zakāt* as a religious obligation, equivalent to that segment representing Christians (8.2%) identifying 'ushūr as a religious duty, and as Table 8 suggests, more than 70% define more or less correctly what *zakāt* is.

61 For further information on 'ushour see: *Al'ata' wa kayfa yakoun*. Bishop Jacobos; Bishop of Zakazik and Minia el Qamh. Egypt: Virgin Mary Church and Mar Johanna, 1998

Table 8: The Meaning of *Zakāt* and *'Ushūr*

	Frequency	Percent
Zakat is a Religious Obligation Dictated Upon Us	812	40.6
Things Given out Based on what the Individual Owns	482	24.1
Charitable Giving Either in Material or in Kind	103	5.2
Assistance Given to Relatives, Orphans, and the Poor	127	6.4
Assistance Given Either Secretly or Openly	7	0.4
To Maintained Social Interdependence (takafol)	7	0.4
Anything that the Individual can Give in the Cause of God	37	1.9
'Ushour Means that the Individual Gives a Portion of his Income to Charity	164	8.2
DK	96	4.8
NA	166	8.3
Total	2000	100

Whether or not the idea of *takāful* is related to *zakāt* in people's minds is debatable. It came out that as little as 0.4% of the sample viewed *zakāt* as a means to maintain social interdependence, which indicates that the relationship between *zakāt* to *takāful* is not as strong in people's minds as relating it to a religious obligation.

In our in-depth interviews, it was also noted that to a significant extent, religion legitimizes giving. An example given by a board member highlighted that in order to attract female volunteers to the NGO, religious logic was used to persuade their family. After this, it became a custom. Among female board members, in particular, it was noted that the understanding of what philanthropy means goes beyond this material assistance, and extends to non-material and psychological help to people in need, to "make them feel like the others", as one female board member in Upper Egypt said.

Last but not least, it was noted that the beneficiaries of services are ignorant of most, if not all concepts, which began with their confusion to what philanthropy or al i'ṭa' al ijtimā'ī means. Even when asked about their perception on philanthropy in the most simplistic language, a quarter of those intensively interviewed did not know what it means. Half of them understood it as help from the rich to the poor, or from NGOs to them, relating it to their own very specific cases and not in general terms.

3.2.3.5 Awareness of the Types, Conditions, and Outlets of Zakāt

The intensive interviews revealed that the majority, starting from NGO board members to donors and beneficiaries, are aware of *zakāt al fitr*, and a lesser percentage is aware of *zakāt* al mal. As to other forms and percentages of *zakāt*, such as that on agriculture, animal husbandry, gold, etc., they are not well known by the respondents. The reason why the majority, whether rich or poor, knows of *zakāt al fitr* is that it is the form of *zakāt* that is compulsory to every Muslim, who affords to feed him/herself and his/her family for one day. This makes the vast majority of Muslims givers of this *zakāt*, as a compulsory giving and the third pillar of Islam. Generally, *shaykh* Al Azhar (the highest religious authority) gives an annual estimation of *zakāt al fitr* ranging between LE 5 to LE 8 to be given by each Muslim person. A family of five in that case, will multiply the *zakāt* amount by their number and pay it before the prayer of the ʿīd (the small feast after the fasting month of Ramadan).

Most are eligible and hence obliged to pay *zakāt al fitr*, and accordingly the vast majority is well aware of it. As to *zakāt* al māl, the intensive interviews revealed that the majority are not aware of its percentage and conditions. One reason is due to the fact that it is compulsory for those who own money equivalent to 85 grams of gold, on which one year has passed, a condition not applicable to people living in poverty. Another reason is the lack of deep religious education in relation to philanthropy and its conditions and practices among the rich and the poor alike. Many of those who give *zakāt al māl* are not aware of its outlets (who the money should go to) and its conditions (*shurūṭ al zakāt*). It must be noted though, that conditions and outlets of *zakāt* are thoroughly described in detail in the Quran and hence should be strictly held to by *zakāt* givers as an integral part of their faith, which is not currently the case according to our study.

In addition, there are urban/rural differences that determine awareness. Mainly farmers and respondents who live in rural areas are aware of forms of *zakāt* that concern animal husbandry or agriculture, its conditions and percentage, while those living in urban areas are less aware. This lack of awareness could be among the main reasons behind the unorganized and scattered giving habits.

3.2.3.6 Effect of Distorted Knowledge of Zakāt

Mashhour[62] believes that the reason behind lack of awareness of these concepts and the distorted knowledge about *zakāt* or about the *ṣadaqa jāriyya* or waqf could be explained by the following observation. As she notes, and according to the findings of the study, *zakāt* al fitr is the only concept that people shared consensus about with regard to its clarity and hence was the most observed and practiced. This goes back to the fact that it is the only type of giving that when its due date comes, the media highlights it tremendously and the shaykhs explain it thoroughly in their preaching and emphasize the timing and amount. Accordingly, people start asking and seek further knowledge, whether those who give or those who are entitled to receive it. As to the other form of *zakāt*, these are not publicized in the media and nor are they men-

62 Neaʿmat Mashhour is Professor of Islamic Economics at al Azhar University. She contributed with her opinion during a workshop organized by Marwa el Daly to collect the academia's reading to the results of the survey and the qualitative analysis.

tioned by shaykhs in detail. Even in educational books in schools, *zakāt* does not receive particular attention, although it is an obligatory and not a voluntary act and is highly associated to praying in the Quran. Praying as compulsory worship on the other hand is highly stressed upon and explained in utmost details by religious figures and schools' curricula. Hence, this contributes to people dealing with *zakāt* as a voluntary act, not as a compulsory act (*farḍ*). Mashhour continues that even the preaching held by the religious figures (*al khuṭāb*) to the public must include information to the poor to enlighten them about their rights in receiving *zakāt*. During the times of the Caliph Omar Ben Abd Al Aziz[63], *zakāt* resources used to reach ḥadd al kifāya or sufficiency levels. Thus, when it reached abundance, *zakāt* administrators responsible for its distribution used to go to people who are in the process of getting married to give them *zakāt* and assist them in their marriage arrangements. Some of the beneficiaries are documented to refuse taking the *zakāt* asserting that they have already received *zakāt* from other individuals and that they need no money from the "House of Money" or *bayt el māl*, where *zakāt* money of the whole nation used to be collected and distributed. Mashhour explains that back then, people knew their right (*ḥaqq*) and knew when to stop receiving what might exceed these rights. However nowadays, the giver and the receiver lack knowledge about the rights and duties of both parties and the limits and rules, thus, it becomes impossible to administer *zakāt* effectively and in many cases *zakāt* is even paid to those who are not eligible.

Finally, Mashhour stresses upon the important resources behind developing a healthy and constructive cultural environment, namely the family, the school, media, the mosques and all religious institutions.

Supporting Mashhour's point of view, Mohamed Kamal Imam[64] affirms that the absence of awareness with regard to where *zakāt* should be spent (*maṣārif al zakāt*) lies in the weak education that students receive right from their primary education until they graduate. Imam adds that when religious figures only talk about the veil for women (*al ḥijāb*), genies, magic, etc, and neglect major details that concern an essential pillar of Islam as the *zakāt*, lack of awareness spreads and this leads to significant cultural illiteracy about the core of the religion.

3.2.3.7 Awareness about Outlets of Zakāt (Maṣārif al Zakāt)

There are eight outlets for *zakāt*; which, together with *zakāt* rules, distinguish *zakāt* from other forms of giving, as *ṣadaqa*, *nudhūr*, *aḍāḥī* or *waqf*. The following Quranic

63 Omar Ben Abd el Aziz is the fifth Caliph according to the Sunni belief ruling from 717 to 720. His governance mark his Omayad era of great integrity and prosperity granted to all members of the society. It is said that during his time, it was difficult to spend the zakat money because there were no people in need of it.

64 Mohamed Kamal Imam is Professor of Islamic Shari'a, Faculty of Law, Alexandria University

verse declares:[65] "Alms (*zakāt*, i.e. contributions of cash, merchandise, animals, etc) are for the poor and the needy, and those employed to administer the (funds); for those hearts have been (recently) reconciled (to truth); for those in bondage and in debt; in the cause of Allah; and for the wayfarer: (Thus is it) ordained by Allah. And Allah is full of knowledge and wisdom." (9:60)

Thus, there are eight categories of people according to Quran, who are entitled to receive *zakāt*. The poor (*al fuqarā'*), the needy/impoverished (*al masākīn*), whether thy express their need or are too dignified to do so. The third group is the *zakāt* collectors (*al 'āmilīn 'alayha*) who are appointed to collect the *zakāt* including shepherds and clerks who administer the process. The fourth group includes those who need to be reconciled (*al mu'allafāt qulubuhum*), which according to scholars include Muslims and non-Muslims whether to strengthen their faith and/or make them compassionate to Islam. The fifth group represents the enslaved and those who are not free (*fī al riqāb*). In the days of slavery, *zakāt* money was to be paid to the master to free the slave as a means of gradually abolishing slavery. Presently and as slavery has long since been abolished, this category includes the imprisoned who cannot afford to pay the fines imposed on them, and any person facing slavery in any form – some believe that illiteracy is a form of slavery. The sixth group is the overburdened debtors (*al ghārimīn*), which opens the channel of paying off the debts of the indebted persons as *zakāt*. The seventh group is paying *zakāt* for people following the cause of Allah (*fī sabīl Allah*). This includes *zakāt* to be paid for *jihād*, or fighting for the cause of Allah. This includes *jihād*for the sake of Allah in all its forms, whether seeking knowledge and education or fighting those who fight Muslims and force them to leave their homes. Finally, the eighth group is the wayfarers (*ibn al sabīl*), which describes those travelers who are away from their homes and need money to return home.

As listed here, these are the outlets of *zakāt*, other causes that one wishes to donate to are encouraged by the many verses of Quran and sunna, yet they go under the other different forms of voluntary giving, such as *ṣadaqa* for instance. It was important for the sake of this research to understand how people in Egypt perceive the difference between *zakāt* and other forms of giving, which would reflect how they are bound to the rules and percentages of compulsory giving. The study revealed that, although these outlets of *zakāt* together with the conditions, are an integral part of this compulsory act of giving, the respondents in the intensive interviews could only distinguish between *zakāt* and *ṣadaqa* to what concerns their intension (*al niyya*), but not according to the outlets and conditions.

65 Yasseen Ibrahim Al-Sheikh. Zakat: The Third Pillar of Islam. Beirut: Al Maktab Al Islami (publishers), 2nd edition, 1998

One of the donors who completed his education in Al Azhar University explained to us that he recalls Shaykh Mohammed Metwally Al Sha'rawy[66] indicate that *zakāt* money is only 2.5%, and although it is not much, people use this money on causes that are not strictly *zakāt*. As a result the poor and the needy and the other categories of people entitled to receive *zakāt* with certain conditions, such as reaching sufficiency or ownership of *zakāt* lose out. From here there are arguments about whether one could give *zakāt* to build institutions that provide services to the poor and the needy, for example the Mufti Nasr Farid Wasel has issued that contributing to building the New Cancer Hospital 57357 in Egypt is a form of *zakāt*. Some scholars tend to consider such contributions *ṣadaqa*, not *zakāt*, because they do not meet the condition of ownership (*al milkiyya*).

3.2.3.8 Tolerance to Give People of Different Faith

An interesting finding is the readiness of almost 40% of the sample to give *zakāt* and *ṣadaqa* to people of different religions. When we cross-tabulated the data by religion, we found out that 37.3% of the Muslim community compared to 34.3% of Christians reported to have no objections to giving to charities of people of other faiths. This reflects the tight fabric of the Egyptian population, as Muslims and Christians, where even faith-based philanthropy, by a large percentage, is seen to serve those of a different faith.

3.2.4 Waqf (Endowment)

3.2.4.1 Overview of Waqf

Waqf (plural: *awqāf*) is a major Islamic form of institutionalized philanthropy, which supported Egyptian civic life for centuries. The concept waqf is derived from the Arabic word meaning "to tie-up", and refers to tying-up profit to a social cause. For centuries, people in Egypt, as in many Muslim countries, tied-up properties by establishing a *waqf*, either directed to support charitable purposes, to support projects of public benefit (*waqf khayrī*), or to the heirs and successors (*waqf ahlī*) of the *wāqif* (the person who established the *waqf*), or mixed *waqf* (*waqf mushtarak*) which supported both, charitable purposes as well as family members (*heirs*). This act of giving and establishment was considered a *ṣadaqa jāriyya*, or a sustained giving that is derived from Prophet Mohamed's (pbuh) hadith indicating that, "when the human being dies, his life duty ceases (stops) except for three things: a sustainable giving (*ṣadaqa jāriyya*, or *waqf*), useful knowledge, and a faithful offspring who prays for him."This

66 Sheikh Mohammed Metwally Al Sha'rawy (1911–1998) is a famous Egyptian Quranic analyst who graduated from Azhar University and became Minister of Endowments in the 70s. He is given the title "Imam of Preachers" (imam al du'ah) to symbolize his worldwide importance as an Islamic Preacher.

ḥadīth indicates that the good deeds of a human being continue to grow in his/her favor even after his/her death if the three factors he/she did during his/her life are adhered to: raising good offspring, leaving behind good education that people benefit from, and a *ṣadaqa jāriyya*, i.e. a *waqf* that sustains community projects of public benefit. The origin of the *waqf*[67]is also related to the story of Omar Ben Al Khattab[68] (the second Caliph), who acquired groves and fields as booty after the Arab's conquest of the oasis of Khaibar. He approached the Prophet to ask him about the best use of this property. The Prophet advised him to tie-up the land, devote its income and harvest to the poor.[69] In Egypt and over the course of history, many factors affected the *waqf* structure, and many government policies hindered the establishment of *waqf*. During the beginning of the 19th century, the government established a ministry for Awqaf (*dīwān al Awqāf*) that confiscated all privately owned *waqf* putting it under the ministry's control. The deterioration of waqf as an institution gradually took place until the *ahlī waqf* was banned in the 1950s by the socialist regime in Egypt. In the present time, the Ministry of Awqaf administers all the awqāf and most of the mosques in Egypt.

3.2.4.2 How People Perceive Waqf in Egypt Today?

In spite of the long history and significance of *waqf* as a form of philanthropy and a solid civic institution in Egypt for hundreds of centuries, results of the public survey show that around 30% of the respondents did not understand what *waqf* means at all and 58% of the respondents could not define or identify any waqf in Egypt, except the Ministry of Endowments, which was identified as a *waqf* institution by only 28.4% of the respondents. When asked what they knew about "waqf", 46.4% believed that "waqf" is just a property inherited from ancestors and that it is subject to *zakāt al māl*.

In-depth interviewees revealed ignorance of the term *waqf*, notably more than *ṣadaqa jāriyya*, a concept more utilized recently. In our discussions with donors, who were the most educated of the sample, comprising professionals, employees and businesspersons, the ignorance of the meaning of *waqf* was striking. Some of the respondents tried to guess. An example is when one donor said, "I heard people talk about *waqf*. At work for instance, when somebody overspends government's money, people tell him 'shame on you' (*ḥarām ʿalayk*), this is *waqf* money (indicating that it should be protected and treated with care). I don't know what this word implies, I never thought about it and I don't know what it really means."

---

67 Gregory Kozlowski, C. Muslim Endowments and Society in British India. NY: The Press Syndicate of the University of Cambridge. 1985

68 The second Caliph ruling from 634 ti 644 and was one of Prophet Mohammed's close companions. He was given the title "al farouq" to symbolize his justice.

69 El Daly, Marwa. Islamic Philanthropy: Institutionalized Giving in the Muslim Perspective. City University of New York; The Center for the Study on Philanthropy, 2001

Some other donors have limited or distorted understanding of what *waqf* means. However, one could undoubtedly deduce that people relate it to the government. For example, a significant number believed that "*waqf* is the property of the government" as one respondent, explained, "Everything the government owns is *waqf*," a view held by another, or "it is the government's capital and it is the only entity that that should manage it" according to another respondent. Some with the same understanding related *zakāt* that goes to mosques to *waqf*; stating that "even the *zakāt* that we give to mosques enter the domain of *waqf*, and it becomes unacceptable to disburse it without the approval of a government body, like the Ministry of Awqaf." Another female donor said, "*waqf* is anything that goes for something related to the government or to Azhar Mosque."

Those who could identify what *waqf* meant mainly related it to the past, and they mostly complain that the Ministry of Awqaf is monopolizing the management of *waqf*. This contradicts their understanding of the origin of the concept as a civic act of institutionalized philanthropy, autonomous in nature, and independent from the state.

One donor said, "A pasha from the past established a *waqf* of land to support a mosque, an orphanage and a hospital. This act of *waqf* followed certain rules, but nowadays, I can't establish a *waqf* because I don't believe that it will not be robbed. The Ministry of Awqaf is robbed and its employees abuse its resources." In general, it was evident throughout the study that the perception of the public towards the Ministry of Awqaf varies between mistrust, ambiguity, and indifference. The reasons behind this mixture of perceptions will be discussed in later parts in the study where the relationships between the government and other philanthropic partners, including donors and mosques are thoroughly addressed.

Because of the results of this study and due to the work of Waqfiyyāt al Maadi Community Foundation (from 2007 until 2020) lobbying for a policy change that allows *waqf* revival and innovation, *waqf* as a concept has seen considerable advancement. After the Arab Spring in 2011 in Egypt, a new Consitution[70] was passed in a referrundum in 2014. El Daly, as she is a member of the Board of Directors of the Federation of NGOs (appointed through a presidential decree) lobbied to introduce a clause on *waqf* in the constitution, which in deed happened and Article 90 was successfully introduced to the constitution. This Article reads as follows: Article 90: Charitable Endowment (Waqf). The state shall encourage the charitable endowment system to establish and sponsor scientific, cultural, health, and social institutions and others and to ensure their independence. Its affairs shall be managed in accordance with the conditions set by the person who created the endowment. This will be regulated by law (28).

70 https://www.constituteproject.org/constitution/Egypt_2014.pdf

3.2.4.3 The Reason behind Deterioration of Waqf as a Concept

It is clear from the above that over the course of history due to governments' confiscations of *awqāf* and due to the gradual disappearance of this civic act, whether because of legal bans or lack of trust to do a waqf that would be part of a governmental structure, *waqf* as a concept became a forgotten term. It has lost its strengths and meaning as an idea, and accordingly deteriorated as a social act.

From a legal point of view, Kamal Imam attributes the deteriorating conditions of the status of the *waqf* today to the absence of the idea of "the condition of the endower" (*sharṭ al wāqif*) from the Egyptian endowments due to the shift from a waqf that is used to be managed by an individual to the *waqf* managed and controlled by the government. Imam explains that re-imposing the idea of the condition of the endower or *sharṭ al wāqif* will revive the Islamic *waqf*; there will be a *waqf* for taking care of the animals, another for education, and another for helping young people with marriage arrangements, etc. All the variant *awqāf* that used to exist are established upon the idea of the condition put by the endower to guarantee that his/her *waqf* would serve a specified purpose(s) dictated by the endower and cannot be changed. That is why legal theologists (*al fuqahā'*) give this condition a primary importance as it is a means to limit the authority of the government or the caliph from changing where the waqf money goes and makes any impositions subject to the decision of the judicial authorities only.

Therefore, Imam relates the problems facing *waqf* in Egypt today to what concerns *waqf* as a whole and as a part. As a whole, the *waqf* supervisor (*nadhīr al waqf*) who used to be chosen and appointed by the endower no longer exists and instead the government, in this case the Ministry of Awqaf, has become legally the new supervisor.

According to Imam, the *awqāf* underwent different phases: The first phase involved the *waqf* that had a supervisor or *nadhīr* appointed through the endower, while supervision of him came from the judge and the legislative authorities that all *waqf* supervisors had to follow and submit all accounts to. Any changes that the supervisors wanted to enforce on the *waqf*, such as changing beneficiaries for instance, required the judges approval. This was the system followed. However, after the establishment of the Ministry of Awqaf, the government started to partly interfere in managing these awqaf and limit the role of the judge, or the legislative authorities. Thus, gradually the government substituted these supervisors and the legislative authorities as well. In the 1950s, after the revolution, the government even abolished the ahli *waqf* and when it became the supervisor it left the *awqāf* resources to the Land Reform Institution which became the owner, instead of the Ministry of Awqaf. The Christians in Egypt on the other hand have established a Christian *awqāf* Institution and received their *waqf* land back to manage independently with no governmental interference or supervision as in the case of the *waqf* owned by Muslims within the same country.

As to the *waqf ahlī*, or the *waqf* that used to be endowed by parents to guarantee that their heirs will not sell or waste their properties when they inherit them and also to eliminate the possibility that the government might confiscate them, these, according to Imam, were abolished and its social role seized. This, as he continues, was one of the implications of the foreign banks that opened in Egypt and which demanded real-estate security deposits. As *waqf* institutions could not be used as such, a war against endowed properties was launched. Imam highlights in his book on Islamic *Waqf*[71] that the legislative development in Egypt was accompanied in actual implementation by major problems, which led to many legislative violations. Only legislative interventions are capable of solving thee problems according to Imam.

Going back to what people in Egypt today understand of what remained out of the *waqf* system, we found out that the types of waqf that people have in their minds are basically related to buildings and lands as well as mosques. Those who knew about *waqf*, referred to it as inheritances of lands and buildings from ancestors. They also see mosques that are known for their affiliation to the Ministry of Awqaf as waqf of certain properties, and accordingly correlated the mosque to this concept.

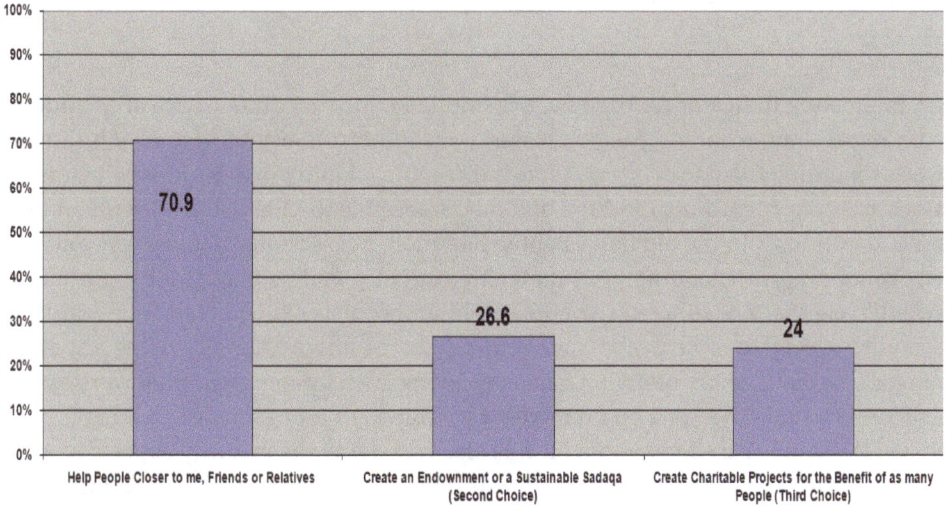

Figure 7: Preference in Charitable Giving When Money is Available

As shown from Figure 7, establishing a *waqf* or a *ṣadaqa jāriyya* comes as a second choice (26.6%) among respondents.

71 Mohamad Kamal Imam. Al Wasaya wal Awqaf fi al-Shari'a al-Islameya: Dirasa Fiqhiya wa Tashri'iya. Alexandria: Monsha'at Al-Ma'arif, 2002 (page 212)

The study shows that (97.9%) of respondents did not establish any *waqf* and only (1.9%) did attempt to establish one. This reflects further the deteriorating condition of the waqf in Egypt and the reluctance of the public to establish any. This is a logical consequence for the factors mentioned above from the lack of awareness to what waqf means to the harsh economic conditions that deter people from establishing a *waqf*. From those who did establish a *waqf* or who wish to do so, the following table reflects the reasons they gave.

Table 9: Did You Ever Establish *Waqf*?

	Frequency	Percentage
No	1957	97.9
Yes	38	1.9
Total	1995	99.8
NA	5	0.3
Total	2000	100

An interesting indicator for the future is implied by the fact that 67.2% of the public who understand what *waqf* is, expressed their interest to establish a *waqf* if the obstacles banning them to do so are removed. Yet the majority of this group who understood the concept of *waqf* doubted that it was possible to establish a *waqf* under current conditions. "In the old days, people had more possessions to give away and the environment was encouraging, financially, morally and religiously. People had a strong base that encouraged them to be philanthropists. Now, if someone wants to establish a *waqf*, people would accuse him of being a fool. Nobody makes any *waqf* nowadays; the Ministry of Awqaf makes its living from former *awqāf* that were established in the old days" one board member affirmed.

In the public's understanding, it was also noted that the majority expects *waqf* to serve individuals, which also reflects the purpose of waqf as being an institution of a public-benefit nature.

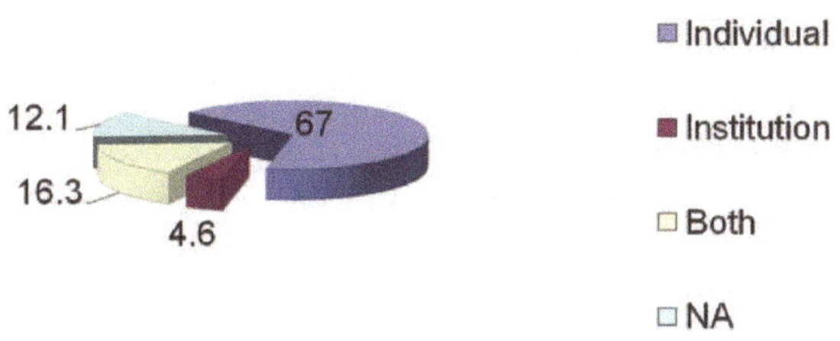

Figure 8: Who Would Benefit from Establishing a Waqf?

Finally, the motives that would probably drive Egyptians to establish a *waqf*, if obstacles are removed, would primarily be religious motives based on extending the good-doing after ones' death as the Prophet's hadith on the *ṣadaqa jāriyya* indicated.

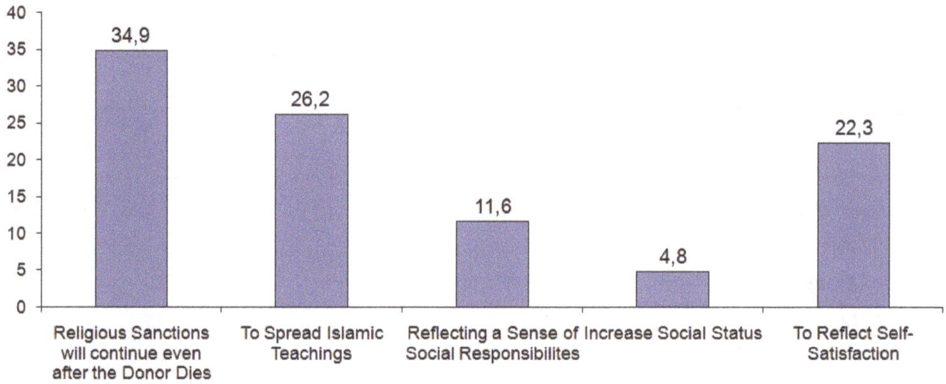

Figure 9: Motivation behind Establishing *Waqf*

3.2.5 ṣadaqa jāriyya (Sustainable Giving)

Ṣadaqa jāriyya in the literature is synonymous to *waqf* and implies the institutionalization of giving that aims at perpetuity. *Ṣadaqa jāriyya* in the minds of the people is connected to charity work and public services with no relation to development work. It is mainly limited to building a water-fountain, issuing a booklet of Quranic verses, or donating to a mosque. Most of these are also related to a *ṣadaqa* one does for the spirit of someone who passed away.

3.2.5.1 How People Perceive Ṣadaqa Jāriyya?

Our survey revealed that 20% of the public do not understand or do not want to answer the question regarding what they understand about *ṣadaqa jāriyya*. The respondents' first choice was a sustainable reward for the individual after his/her life.

Our data reflects that around 40% of the public understand that *ṣadaqa jāriyya* is a *ṣadaqa* you give for the purpose of preserving ones good deeds after death.

The in-depth interviews revealed a limited understanding among the respondents to what *ṣadaqa jāriyya* implies. Most relate it as a concept to a *ṣadaqa*done for the spirits of those who passed away. One donor pointed out, "I thought about *ṣadaqa jāriyya*, and did one for my father who died by donating monies to build a mosque."

From the donors' limited awareness to *ṣadaqa jāriyya*, most of their giving towards it goes to making modern water-fountains (*sabīl*) for people to drink (referred to as Coldeir in reference to the refrigerator's brand name), and to building mosques. For them, these are the only forms of *ṣadaqa jāriyya*, unlike previous generations in Egypt where the *ṣadaqa jāriyya*was understood in a much broader sense and in connection with establishing a *waqf* of public service nature.

Table 10: What is Ṣadaqa Jāriyya?

	Frequency	Percent
Paying money to a charitable project to benefit people	149	7.5
Establishing a charitable project or investing in one	287	14.4
Offering sadaqa secretly and openly according to religious teaching	91	4.6
A sustainable reward for the individual after his/her life	781	39.1
A sadaqa that will benefit both the individual and others	125	6.3
Any assistance given to the needy, poor, families in need	143	7.2
Sadaqa can also be achieved through the good deeds of man	20	1.0
DK	160	8.0
NA	244	12.2
Total	2000	100

It was obvious that those who were aware of *ṣadaqa jāriyya* were those speaking about what their fathers have done; "*ṣadaqa jāriyya* is to plant a tree, or make a water fountain. Our fathers and the elderly have done a health unit, all from local resources. They also did a cooperative that offered goods for the community with good prices. The government took its management over, yet it did not do any renovation or maintenance to the health unit, and ventilations and all the renovations that we are currently providing are supplied through local resources considered as *ṣadaqa jāriyya*.".

Although some donors deal with NGOs that enjoy a long history of institutionalized philanthropy, and which have projects of public benefit nature, this culture of institutionalized giving and *ṣadaqa jāriyya* is quite lost. As one donor to an organization dating back to the 19th century said, "I tried to do a *ṣadaqa jāriyya*but all that I could think of is to do a water tap (she refers to a water-fountain) or put something in the mosque, but I think this is not of great importance. I couldn't think of something else." There is an obvious quest for ways to revive *ṣadaqa jāriyya* among many respondents, yet this search for a new model that allows a sustainable giving mechanism to flourish and meet donors' expectations is not available.

The following example consolidates this dilemma of some donors who do not have the proper information about what *ṣadaqa jāriyya* really means. One donor in Aswan explained, "They (referring to a commercial in the media) claim that *sadaqa jariya* is this animal husbandry project that Nasser Bank and the National Council of Women are doing; they make people buy a cow for others to take and make a project. In my understanding, *sadaqa jariya* is to plant a tree to make a space of shade to people, or to get a carpet for the mosque, but to give a cow or a buffalo to someone; this is insane, it is not possible! However, thank God, I participated in building a mosque and I held the building materials by myself and also supported it financially until the Ministry of *Awqaf* took it under its control."

However, it is not always the case that people insist on their traditional thinking without accepting new ideas of *ṣadaqa jāriyya*. That was revealed from positive examples mentioned by several respondents, including one donor who said, "We collected money from our community. One paid LE 100, another paid LE 200 and a third contributed with LE 300 and so on, until we built an educational institute related to Al *Azhar*." Also the TV commercials launched by Dar el Orman Orphanage had positive effects on convincing several donors to make income-generating projects as *ṣadaqa jāriyya* by buying a cow for a poor family who had lost its main provider. The head of the orphanage explained, "When we did the *ṣadaqa jāriyya* project, people were responsive and contributed with lots of money, and we brought the cows and the donors attended the beneficiaries' receptions of their cows."

3.2.6 Development

Development in the context of our study encompasses primarily the aspect of alleviating the condition of the human being, i.e. enhancing living conditions and alleviating the quality of the individual through building their capacities and widening their choices. In this framework, there is a close relationship between development, human rights and social justice. Human rights encompass the rights of the individuals to develop, to participate in the development process, to contribute and enjoy the fruits of change. The right in all aspects of development also includes the right to the fair distribution of development resources, which is a corner stone of social justice.

The study revealed that there is a degree of variation in perceiving development amongst the public although most could distinguish between development and charity. For NGO board members, development is a plan and a vision for the future as it builds the capacities of beneficiaries. It was noted that those NGOs working with international donor agencies have more profound definitions of development than those who have never partnered with international donor agencies. On the other hand, the individual donors interviewed perceived development as strongly related to economic growth. "Economic development is the most important; if one invests his money in development, this will benefit the society, the country and one's self. If one puts his money in charity, this benefit goes only to himself and those who receive the money" as stated by a donor. However, donors perceive development as the responsibility of the government, not themselves. "If there is real development, nobody will stretch his hands to ask for charity", one donor indicated. However, most agreed that in present times, we do need both: part of the resources going into charity and another to development work. Most board members supported this point of view.

Religious figures heading religious institutions perceived development as a religious duty. All church priests believe that religion calls for development and that the social understanding of development coincides with the church's understanding. Arguing that religion calls for development not charity, several *shaykhs* referred to Prophet Mohamed's teachings. According to one interviewee, "The Prophet (pbuh), says, 'If the day of resurrection befalls and one of you has a seed in his hand, he should plant it'". He also forbade beggary in many sayings and called for being proactive, working, and earning money. In one of his most famous situations that calls for development as opposed to charity or *iḥsān* as a behavior is the following story: when a man came asking the Prophet (pbuh) charity (*iḥsān*), Prophet Mohamed (pbuh) asked him what he owns. The man said a cup with which he eats and drinks and a blanket to sleep on and be covered by. The Prophet (pbuh) asked him to auction his possessions, instead of giving him charity money. After selling these items, Prophet Mohamed (pbuh) asked him to take the money, buy his basic needs and buy primary tools to start a project and disappear for two weeks. The man bought food with part of the money while with the other part bought an axe to go and cut wood and sell it. After two weeks, the man showed up with enough money and a job to support himself. The Prophet told him that this is much better than asking people, accepting to help you or not. This gives a lesson on development and dignity. For the *shaykhs*, in a metaphorical description, the main "arm" of social justice, is development.

We can easily conclude that respondents reached consensus about their perception on development being more effective than charity. However, this consensus was conditional. According to respondents, development requires all forces to collaborate. "If we want development, we must allocate resources into projects; charity is only for consumption and does not solve any problem in the long run", one donor highlighted.

Finally, very few beneficiary interviewees were able to understand what development means. Few could distinguish between development and charity, and those who could, were the beneficiaries who received loans to do projects, not those receiving monetary assistance or monthly salaries.

3.2.7 Social Justice

Social justice in this research is understood and defined as the existence of opportunities granted to the most marginalized, least well-off and disadvantaged groups through establishing structural change policies and not simply top-down assistance from the rich to the poor. It should accordingly indicate equal and fair distribution of opportunities that allows for social mobility. Although social justice is not a frequently used term, respondents could relate it to equal access to resources. They also linked philanthropy to the establishment of developmental projects increasing opportunities and realizing social justice.

3.2.7.1 Social Justice and Income Distribution

The result of the study indicated that the general perception of social justice among respondents relates to the existence of equality among individuals and in the equal distribution of goods and services. The vast majority of respondents regarded the unfair distribution of resources and opportunities, the widening gaps between people, the huge gap between the city and the village, and the gaps felt by residents of cities in governorates other than Cairo, to be current manifestation of social injustice. The injustices between people in the opportunities they get, and the injustices between cities in the services they receive, are the insights reflected by the respondents, who expressed their discontent with the lack of social justice.

Among donor respondents, most agreed that social justice was a rather unattainable goal, given present circumstance. Although beneficiaries from NGO services seemed not to comprehend the term "social justice", it was still apparent that they shared similar views, but expressed them differently. For example, most beneficiaries, complained about *wasta* (personal connections) being the only way to facilitate things, such as finding a job.

3.2.7.2 Social Justice and Takāful

One female beneficiary explained, "Social justice is when everyone takes his/her right and nobody faces injustice. I did not think of this concept but I thought that people must help each other. There are many poor people who need help." This relates social justice as a concept to the idea of *takāful* as engraved in people's minds.

3.2.7.3 Social Justice and Religious Giving

In addition, social justice is also closely related to *zakāt* and the right of the poor to this money, irrespective of whether this will decrease the gap between the rich and the poor or not. As one donor respondent expressed referring to the Quran, "...and those in whose wealth is a recognized right for the needy who ask and him who is prevented (for some reason from asking)".

The belief that *zakāt* is a strong tool to achieve social justice was mentioned among some donors and religious figures. Whether Muslims or Christians, many called for going back to religious doctrines to achieve social justice. One of the donors expressed a view shared by others saying, "We must go back to the Islamic system, to apply the concept of *shura* (consultation), mubay'a (paying allegiance or election) and caliphate succession system, where no ruler remains in power for so long." He continued, "People follow the religions of their rulers, which means that people follow the principles that are adopted by the rulers. Hence a good role model is needed, such as in the time of Omar Ben Al Khattab, where his soldiers never used to steal anything when they defeated another army imitating the principles of their ruler."

3.2.7.4 Social Justice is the Basis of Islamic Religion

Respondents related social justice as a concept with Islam as a Religion. Islam is seen as a belief based on justice between people, equality of all in front of God, justice or 'adl as one of the names that God describes Himself with, overall justice as a characteristic of a good Muslim and justice as a highly recognized value. Religious figures tended to quote Quranic verses highlighting the importance of being just to others.

> "Lo! Allah enjoineth and kindness, and giving to kinsfolk, and forbiddeth lewdness and abomination and wickedness. He exorteth you in order that ye may take heed." (The Bee: Verse 90.)

> "O ye who believe! Be steadfast witnesses for Allah in equity, and let not hatred of any people seduce you that ye deal not justly. Deal justly, that is nearer to your duty. Observe your duty to Allah. Lo! Allah is informed of what ye do." (The Table Spread: Verse 8).

3.2.7.5 Social Justice and Politics

It was observed that a number of respondents connected social justice with politics, and expressed their fear to talk about it, as this will make them talk politics. One of the respondents refused tackling this subject at all, saying, "You will drag me into politics this way."

3.2.7.6 Could we Achieve Social Justice?

When we directly asked people if they think that bridging the gaps between people and providing equal opportunities could be something to be achieved through philanthropy, 83.8% of the public agreed that philanthropy could achieve social justice. The following table reflects this.

Table 11: Could Philanthropy Achieve Social Justice?

	Frequency	Percentage
Yes	1665	83.8
No	302	15.1
DN	4	0.2
NA	29	1.5
Total	2000	100

Most respondents stressed the need to provide equal opportunities, the need for everyone to get his/her rights, and that social justice must not only be put on the philanthropic agenda, but on the country's national plan.

3.2.7.7 Social Justice through Development Projects

Although the majority indicated that philanthropy could play a role in achieving social justice, the intensive interviews clarified that this was conditioned with directing philanthropy towards projects and not simply towards meeting the basic needs of people. Most respondents, especially beneficiaries and donors, believed that the rich giving to the poor is not a solution and that a collective community effort with government support is the required solution. The solution for them is in the creation of job opportunities and projects to employ youth. In spite of a perception that people are not the same; that God created people in ranks; and a certain satisfaction of God's distribution of *rizq* (fortunes given by God), all agreed that the people and the government have a role to play against injustice. "We do not need to be the same or equal, but these huge differences between people must decrease," one respondent elaborated. Many beneficiaries stressed that if this happens, envy against the rich will vanish, and the society will be healthier. Board members and members of NGOs stressed the need to strengthen the civic sector and develop it into a pressure group that is able to influence decision makers to prevent injustices against the poor. This should go hand in hand with reforming the Ministry of Social Affairs, as a number of them explained.

The majority of NGO board members view their philanthropic work mainly as being helpful to the poor, capable of achieving security, and reducing poverty. Other answers included that their assistance help achieve social justice. However, achieving equality was an answer that came least in importance in comparison to other direct effects of these organizations as perceived by the public. This is shown by Figure 10.

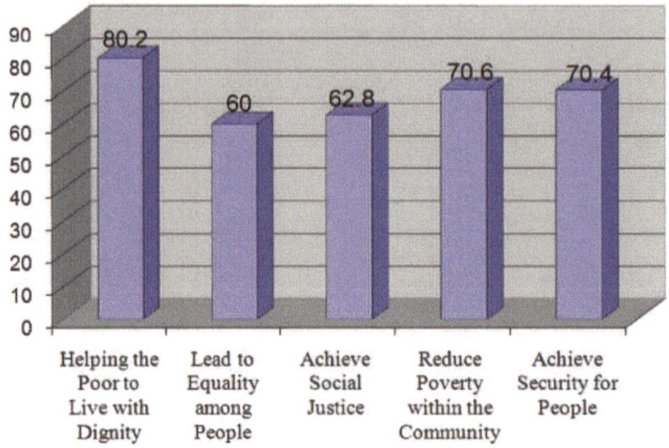

Figure 10: How Effective are Philanthropic Institutions in Dealing with Social Justice Initiatives

Nonetheless, the qualitative in-depth study revealed that from the beneficiaries' perspective, the assistance they get from philanthropic organizations would never lead to social justice or bring them even close to the rich: "The rich can help the poor but never would let him be same or better." This reflects their position on this subject through a language that shapes their thinking, "These are small things we get", "where are the rich, and where are we (*humma wayn wa iḥna wayn?*)", "we accept the minimal and everyone is not bigger than his real size (*kul wāḥid ʿala adduh*),", "*mastūra wa al ḥamdulilah*" (we are 'covered', thank God). It was observed that there is a language of acceptance to the status quo and the condition one finds him/herself into that gives easy fatalistic answers to questions of complex nature related to social justice. It is worth mentioning though that the beneficiaries who receive small loans expressed that the real change that happened to their lives was after the loans they received.

3.2.7.8 Social Justice and Religion

The application of social justice in peoples' minds was attributed to applying religious teachings and was divided into two conditions that are religiously motivated: the first is the precise payment of *zakāt*, which according to many respondents would bring the Islamic umma to the times of Omar Ben Abd Al Aziz when *zakāt* money reached an excess and all people under his reign had enough to the extent that they did not know what to do with the *zakāt* money. Second, in the existence of a just ruler who cares to achieve social justice and rules in abidance to high morals and principles.

3.2.7.9 Paying Zakāt

As highlighted earlier when we analyzed peoples' awareness to social justice as a concept, it was evident that many correlated *zakāt* and spending as a vital mechanism and a valid tool for bringing about social justice. There was a concept among respondents that social justice could be achieved through *zakāt* and through going back to religion. One of the NGO chairpersons replied when he was asked whether paying *zakāt* could decrease the gap between people, "...gaps would definitely decrease if divine justice is applied and if the rich pay what they have to pay as *zakāt*, the poor would get their rights."

3.2.7.10 The Just Ruler

Some of the respondents link social justice with the work of NGOs and with governmental efforts. One of the donors, when he was asked about how social justice could be realized, indicated, "We think a lot about how to achieve social justice. With our work with the NGO, we managed to achieve a degree of equality and justice by providing loans and retirement funds (pension,)" he said. Another NGO chief of BoD mentioned that civil society organizations must coordinate their work together in order to provide job opportunities to start with.

3.2.7.11 Achieving Social Justice: Collaborations between/among NGOs and the Government

One of the donors sees that achieving social justice is through applying religion and the existence of a just ruler, who is perceived as a role model for his people. Another NGO Chief of the Board of Directors indicates that we should go back to the rightful Islamic system where there is shura (consultation by the ruler with the people) and mubay'a (paying allegiance to a selected ruler); he refers to the old times of Islam when good rulers like Omar Ben Al Khattab demonstrated good morals and the people were shaped by his good principles. "People follow the religion of their rulers", another maintained, referring to the great influence of the principles of the rules on the morals of the people. This is to indicate primarily that a just ruler is needed for this moral system to be born, which would shape peoples' behavior and allow for the application of religious doctrines that aims to achieve social justice.

3.2.8 Human Rights

Human rights are the set of needs that must be fulfilled by each individual, irrespective of his/her society, gender, race, faith, politics, ethnic group or any other of such factors.[72] In Egypt, and because human rights is a term frequently used by the media, it came to our attention that it is more comprehendible than the concept of social justice, especially among the segment of the beneficiaries.

3.2.8.1 Basic Needs: Decent Life and Security

"We are poor, just barely sufficing ourselves (*'ala ad ḥālnā*), we drink and eat and have no interest in politics or human rights," a response given by an NGO board member reflecting the indifference noted amongst most interviewees. Most, when we raised this concept, understood its meaning. Unlike social justice, beneficiaries as well could define human rights and relate it as a concept to their daily problems, and to their right in a dignified life where they get their basic needs as human beings. The need for peace of mind and security was repetitively stressed upon as well. NGO board members added the importance of having democracy and freedom. Most donors understand human rights as the right to a dignified life and to education. The right to dignified life is for them the right to live a decent living, in food, in drinking, in having a place to live in and clothes to wear as well as in enjoying services offered by the government. Decent life is used as synonymous to a life suitable for a human being, reflecting the very basic human needs to survive. Beneficiaries indicate that the assistance they receive from NGOs helps them meet the minimal requirements to survive. As one of them put it, "Life goes on, and that is it" (*ahi māshiyya wa khalaṣ*).

3.2.8.2 The Right to Work

Among the major rights that the respondents expressed was the right to work in order to obtain a decent life. The beneficiaries interviewed complained about unemployment and its negative effects on them and their families. For them, unemployment was the main reason that compels them to go and ask people for assistance.

3.2.8.3 Equality between Man and Woman

It was observed that in the Upper Egyptian communities, the issue of women's rights and equality was raised. This might go back to the strict traditions that the Upper Egyptian woman must deal with, which make her a second citizen in her society. The NGOs that had women activists, and which concentrated on programs promoting equality between boys and girls were more conscious about gender issues and inequality between male and females as an obstacle to development. However, we must note that those types of organizations started with assistance from international donor organizations, and are not the traditional NGO types.

72 Ahmed El Rashidy. Hoquq al insan: Dirasa moqarna fi al nazareya wal tatbiq. Al Qahira: Jami'at al Qahira: Kolleyat al Iqtisad wal 'olum al siyaseya, 2003. Page, 35.

3.2.8.4 The Right to Democracy

We also noted that the higher the educational level and the higher peoples' knowledge, the more interested they become in concepts like liberty and freedom as their rights as human beings. Mostly NGO board members had opinions of democracy and freedom. Most expressed democracy and liberty as core components of human rights, but they all warned against the Government offering the people a space to talk, but offering no space to listen. Some termed this as passive democracy.

3.2.8.5 The Right of the Disabled

The issue of the disabled and their rights to have equal opportunities with others were raised in relation to the perception of human rights.

3.2.8.6 Human Rights in Islam

Many respondents affirmed that human rights as a concept is a major issue and related it as a main ingredient of Islam. According to one shaykh, human rights as a concept, comes from Islam, where people are entitled by religion to certain rights. This starts with the right to be greeted with peace (*salām*), the right of others is the *ṣadaqa* you give, whether a good word or a support, the right of those in need of your *zakāt*, the right of the ignorant in your knowledge, the right of the neighbor in good treatment, the right of the stranger in hospitality, etc. If ones deny the others their rights, and according to Prophet Mohamed's hadith on those denying the spread of knowledge to others, are those who will suffer in hell".

The religious figures affirmed that if *zakāt* money is properly given and allocated, no single needy person will exist in Egypt. One assured that "*Zakāt* is the money of the poor. If the rich do not give the poor his/her share, it would be like stealing the poor peoples' money because giving is a right and a duty in Islam. It is not a donation, but it is a right."

Human rights brought also controversial opinions and debates among respondents who constantly referred to the good old days during the time of the Prophet and that of the boom of the Islamic states, versus current times where the West preaches about human rights while violating it in different aspects. On top of the list came the United States that preaches, or as one respondent expressed "tetanten, i.e. talks a lot about human rights while kills people here and there." He continued, "Look at the vast amount of Algerians killed by the French, while the Europeans always have so much to say about human rights." Another referred to Islam where human rights is connected to people so closely that not even religion or race could interfere with these rights. Many also referred to the story of Omar Ben Al Khattab (one of the early Caliphs), who took a stand supporting a Christians who was met with injustice during the Opening of Egypt by Amr Ben Al'as. In addition to the story of Omar Ben Al Khattab refusing to pray in the Qeyama Church in Jerusalem fearing fanatics who might turn it into a mosque and denying Christians of their right to pray, claiming that their

Muslim Caliph prayed there. Such examples brought up by respondents reflected the perception of respondents to issues of human rights, that go beyond their own domain, but make them reflect on the Global human rights status to look for role models, and when these are not found, people tend to look for the past as a good guiding reference.

> "O mankind! Lo! We have created you male and female, and have made you nations and tribes that ye may know one another. Lo! The noblest of you, in the sight of Allah, is the best in conduct. Lo! Allah is knower, Aware." (The Private Apartments: Verse 13).

3.2.9 Civil Society

The study revealed that the Egyptian Public does not comprehend the translation of the Western concept: Civil Society, as it translates into *mujtamaʿal madanī*. This term seems to have been imposed by writers exposed to Western cultures and by the media. As to the concept more understood among the people was, *mujtamaʿal ahlī*, which has historical roots relating the meaning of organizations to "families" (*ahlī*) and not to "civil" (*madanī*). Apart from the different definitions of civil society or its academic or historical basis, civil society in the Egyptian environment consists of different institutions that are non-governmental in nature and that reach around 250,000 organizations.

These include Civil Society Organizations (CSOs), collaborative organizations, youth centers, commercial and industrial chambers, as well as political parties.[73] Civil Society Organizations represent the majority of the civic structure in Egypt which reached around 14,000 NGOs in 1996 and estimated to have reached around 18,000 in 2004.[74] However, although the number indicates an increase in the domain of NGOs, it could be quite misleading, as there are many of them who have gone out of business or are quite dormant.

The study highlighted that although board members and chairpersons of the BoD of NGOs are all part of the civic structure, the vast majority does not know the concept "civil society", or as it translates into *mujtamaʿal madanī* in Arabic. They cognitively mix this concept with people living in civilized areas like the cities and accordingly these will be called civil versus the uncivilized rural community. *Al mujtamaʿal ahlī*is a concept more understood, at least by the civic sector, than *mujtamaʿal madanī*. The word *ahlī* derives from *ahl* that translates into family. The connotation of *ahli* in this context relates to civil society as it is understood in the Western sense. However, the

73 Saad Iddin Ibrahim. Al mujtama' al madani wal tahawul al dimoqrati fi misr. Al Qahira: Dar Qiba', 2000

74 Amani Qandil. Al mujtama' al madani fi masr fi matla' al alfeya al jadida. Al Qahira: Al Ahram, Markaz al dirasat al siyaseya wal istrategiya, 2000.

majority of respondents do not digest the literal translation of civil society, in spite of it being the language of the intellectuals and the media. This misperception or ignorance of the term tends to alienate people especially when this is the language daily used by the media and by government officials. However, the media using a recent concept cannot obviously compete with a longer history of philanthropy led by what was known by people as "*al mujtamaʿal ahlī*". Obviously it is not strategic to adopt a different concept, just because it is a literal translation from the West, while alienating a concept like "*al mujtamaʿal ahlī*", which is deeply rooted in the traditions and mind set of the people relating more accurately to their lives.

However, donors, with no exception, could not define civil society as a term. The same applies to beneficiaries. Of course both are aware of the existence of non-governmental structures, but they are unaware of the meaning of the concept, and its relevance to them.

3.2.10 Education and Upbringing

Education and upbringing are amongst the most important variables in studying the culture of philanthropy in Egypt. The quantitative and qualitative interviews dealt with this issue thoroughly in order to comprehensively plot the factors that shape philanthropy in Egypt. Both research methodologies tackled the issue of education and its impact on philanthropy in different, yet complementary perspectives. The quantitative research's main findings focused on comparing the respondents' level of education with their awareness of philanthropic practices either religious or non-religious. The qualitative part, on the other hand, focused on education as an influential factor that affects the philanthropic behavior. The family and upbringing were major variables deeply studied in the qualitative research. The following table indicates the education level of the respondents in the quantitative survey.

Table 12: Educational Level

Education	Frequency	Percentage
Illiterate/never went to school	347	17.4
Primary Education	282	14.1
Preparatory School Certificate	139	7.0
Secondary School Certificate	656	32.8
University	537	26.9
Post Graduate Level	34	1.7
No Answer	5	3.0
Total	2000	100.0

As shown in the table above, 33% of our quantitative respondents appear to have completed their high school education. The second largest category represents those who have completed their college education, which represents 27% of the sample. About 31% of the sample did not go to schools or only finished their primary education.

As Figure 11 suggests, there is a positive relationship between the education level of the individual and his/her awareness about giving *zakāt*, *ṣadaqa* (religious philanthropy) or other types of charitable donations. The higher the educational level of an individual, the more his/her awareness about giving grows. However, in the case of awareness of zakāt and *ṣadaqa* as forms of Islamic philanthropy, the variation in educational levels does not seem to be accompanied with much variation amongst the public when compared to the relationship between educational levels and awareness about other sorts of charitable philanthropy. Since religion is the most significant basis of giving in Egypt, education does not truly interfere in the religious philanthropic behavior of people even if they are illiterate. This phenomenon was quite clear in the in-depth interviews since the desire to give was existent even among the beneficiaries who expressed their commitment to pay *zakāt al fitr* and put an effort in volunteering or giving whatever they own regardless of how little it is.

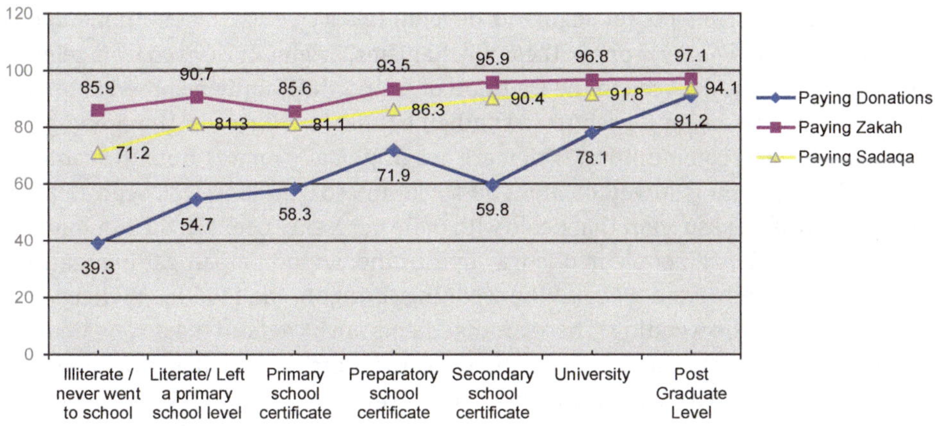

Figure 11: Educational Levels and Philanthropic Awareness Practices

On the other hand, the qualitative study revealed that the family and school teachers are significant role models and idols when it comes to philanthropic behavior. In addition, the curricula and activities of the educational institutions, including schools and universities leave significant impact on the way people give and volunteer, whether positively or negatively. The following is a detailed explanation of these factors:

3.2.10.1 The Family and Local Traditions

It was noted that the way parents practice philanthropy has a direct influence on how their children, and in return the coming generations evolve with a certain set of ethics and giving habits. This influence was reflected in the answers of both NGO board members and donors. For instance, there is a positive direct relation between having parents establishing a *waqf* before the 1950s, and finding a generation of board members coming up with ways to revive a *waqf*-inspired way of institutionalizing philanthropy. This is more the trait among NGO board members of the higher middle or upper class, who had well-off parents and a history of waqf ownership, or those who had their parents establish local NGOs in the 1950s. Others, with parents being engaged in Community Development Associations (CDAs) established by the government in the 1950s as semi-governmental philanthropic organizations, were also influenced by the idea of establishing NGOs and organizing charity, and those constitute the majority of those engaged in the social work across the Governorates.

In addition to the influence of the family, the more one goes away from Cairo, the stronger grows social interdependence (*takāful*) and traditions of giving and volunteering. These traditions are not only the result of observing the parents, but they are also the result of learning from the whole community where social responsibility and mutual support are among the most important ingredients of the society and one of the living mechanisms poorer segments develop to survive harsh conditions. Blood relations or *ṣalat al raḥim* is one of these mechanisms, originally derived from religion but over the time is diffused in the tradition of supporting family members, not only materially, but by a simple visit to strengthen bonds. In villages in Upper Egypt, or within the Nubian communities, which are geographically remote from the center of Egypt, philanthropy is a way of life. The social interdependence between families makes a web of local support that deals with daily necessary needs in the inhabitants' lives. For example, all people in one way or the other support a pair getting married, starting from offering the place of the wedding, bringing the food for invitees, and cleaning up after the wedding. These arrangements are by default the responsibilities of the neighbors, friends and families. Invitees from outside the villages are guests of the village at large. The same behavior of social support and interdependence apply to all occasions including funerals, feasts, and others. Thus, local interdependence traditions are important assets that should be nourished and strengthened; some even provide interesting concepts and models for replication.

3.2.10.2 Education and NGOs Beneficiaries

As to the beneficiaries, it was observed that due to the low economic class to which most of them belong; the majority of them either were uneducated or left school at an early age. As a result, their answers did not show a clear understanding of the voluntary activities during their upbringing period. However, many of them give and volunteer without being aware of this act. Their awareness of the duty to give is higher than their awareness of what they are doing really means. This is especially clear in rural areas where all people know each other and family bonds are stronger than those in the cities. One of the beneficiaries in Upper Egypt highlighted, "I help other people to feel that I do my duty towards my society and towards my people." The overall tradition of *takāful* and religion shapes their role as receivers, but also as givers; if not always, at least during *ʿīd al fitr* when they pay *zakāt* on behalf of each of their children.

3.2.10.3 School Activities and the Curricula

Most NGO board members who were interviewed did not engage in school social activities because their schools did not provide extracurricular activities. Those of the respondents who took part in social activities are few in number and were mostly involved in the Scout, Red Crescent or in occasional activities, such as clean-ups or plantation activities around their schools. However, it was noted that most Board Members of Christian Organizations had volunteered in Church activities when they were young; signaling a more active engagement with the activities of the church among the Christian population starting from childhood. One of the Christian chairpersons of an association used to undertake volunteer work in the village through visiting sick people, or helping the needy in some way. At first, her giving was in a simple and elementary manner, but this motivated her to study religion and to give her entire life as a nun and head an orphanage for girls in Cairo. Examples as such reflect the importance of the voluntary space institutions, whether secular or religious, create; and how this grows and extends into different fields.

As for school curricula, there is a consensus amongst Chairpersons of the BoD of NGOs, shaykhs and donors that school curricula and activities lack anything meaningful that encourages philanthropy. As a female board member from Alexandria affirmed, what plenty of respondents expressed; "There was nothing that encourages philanthropy, not in curricula, not in activities, nothing".

Most of the respondents affirmed that Religion, Arabic Language, and the National Education Curricula (*tarbiyya qawmiyya*), were the main introduction to philanthropic values in the early age. According to one of the donors, "Look now, it [Religion] became an unnecessary course in schools, which has negatively affected philanthropic concepts."

Among the few private school graduates, the case seemed not much different. A female board member pointed out, "I was in a French school, and there was nothing about voluntarism and nothing in the curricula itself."

On curricula and philanthropy, Nea ، mat Mashhour comments on these findings that in the past the curricula were stronger and involved contexts encouraging philanthropy and development. She gives the example of Prophet Mohamed's saying when a man came asking him charity (*iḥsān*) but the Prophet asked him to sell his belongings and start an income-generating project with this capital instead of relying on what people give him. This saying, she continues, enhances the students' ability to understand that self-help is crucial and that helping someone lies in strengthening his/her ability and position to get a job and not in providing charitable assistance.

3.2.10.4 The Teacher: A Missing Idol

It was evident that teachers play a significant role in influencing the philanthropic behavior of future generations. This role could be either positive or negative according to the teacher's practical behavior in front of his/her students. His/her teachings are not just through what s/he says, but through what s/he does. It is noticeable that whether NGO board members, shaykhs or donors, all expressed that philanthropic teachers who were true role models and who deeply affected their students' life became history, and do not exist anymore. Board Members and shaykhs used to indicate that their own teachers who were real models are a phenomenon that vanished in the world of today. They say phrases such as, "teachers back then were different". Many donors expressed the same opinions. According to one of them, "We missed the idol, which was supposed to be found in teachers."

However, despite the rather negative image of contemporary teachers in the minds of the Egyptian public, in the last few years, a very successful model of a locally initiated philanthropic organization that is gaining ground and reputation now in

Egypt evolved by a number of students with the encouragement of their professor. One of the young board members speaks of his organization's experience, "We started off being a small club (or family, *usra* as they describe it) in the faculty of Engineering. Our professor, who taught humanitarianism in the university talked to us about being positive and proactive and the importance of having every human ties with ones society. After the lecture, some students told him that they want to transform these words into reality and practice what he preaches. Together with their professor, they formed a club, which they called Risāla (the translation to English is mission), on the basis that they have a mission towards their society. Accordingly, they mobilized other students and started visits to hospitals and some social activities that gradually formed a students' movement. When *ahl al khayr* or philanthropists sensed their enthusiasm, they donated a piece of land, on which the NGO was built."

Generally, most of the respondents in the qualitative research agreed that the school, and the mosque, positively affected their philanthropic behavior. This concept applies to all of the interviewed segments, including the beneficiaries who despite religious benefits of doing good deeds.

Traditional religious education that follows Prophet Mohamed's sayings (*ḥadīth*) indicates that when you ease up someone's life, God or Allah will ease up your life; this is manifested in what this beneficiary and others have expressed in different ways; "When you help others, Allah will help you too."

3.2.11 Local Culture

Local upbringing in this context reflects two aspects: local traditions and popular sayings that flow from one generation to another and in this respect encourage philanthropic practices.

3.2.11.1 Traditions

Traditions are more evident in rural communities than in the urban ones. The further we go from Cairo, the stronger philanthropy appeared to be and the more the collaborations within the community at large and not simply within the family, is apparent. The spirit of *takāful*, mutual help and social responsibility was mostly a phenomenon within and amongst families and also among people living in a neighborhood or a closed community. It was most evident in Upper Egypt, and especially in Aswan Governorate where this mutual interdependence was a way of life. As one of the NGO chief of BoD indicated, our NGOs exist nowadays because our parents used to help each other and there is a strong solidarity among relatives and neighbors. We stand for each other in everything." Another NGO chief of BoD in Aswan affirmed the same idea, "Traditions here manifest in participation with other people in happiness and in sadness.

This is spontaneous participation by everyone to help others, which makes it the norm. Anyone would automatically follow the same traditions and customs".

3.2.11.2 Popular Sayings

The quantitative study revealed, as shown in Figure 12 below, that the influence of the public sayings on philanthropy is minimal 8.9%.

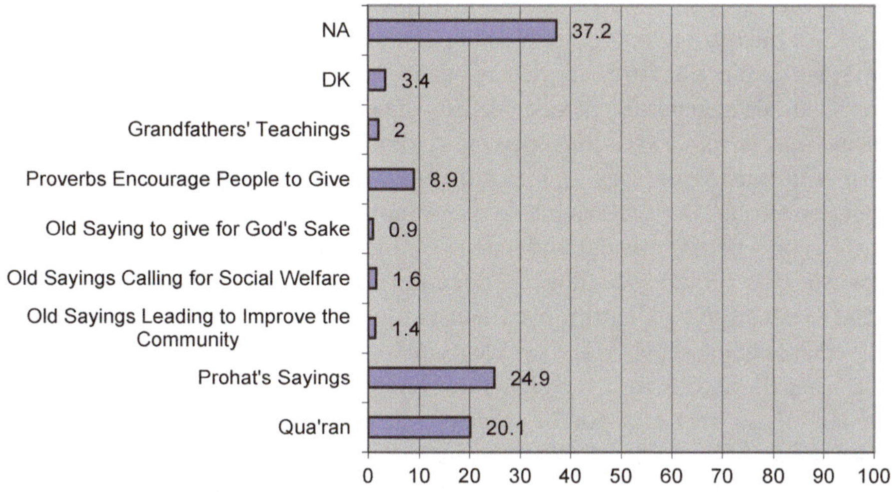

Figure 12: Culture affecting Philanthropy

The qualitative study affirmed this result; although the Egyptian culture is rich with sayings, respondents showed difficulty remembering sayings encouraging philanthropy. In particular beneficiaries could remember most of these sayings, which mainly encourage charity, such as: "Allah reward you, you who do good", "Do the good and through it in the sea", "Hand on a hand makes the far-fetched close" and others. Some donors also contributed with sayings such as, "The bag with two handles should be carried by two persons" and "Who offers Saturday receives Sunday." Finally, the Chinese saying about teach me how to fish instead of giving me a fish, was repeated by many donors and chiefs of BoD. An Egyptian version of this saying is "Give me a fish and I will love you for one day, teach me how to fish, and I will love you forever."

3.2.11.3 Transparency and Measures to Gain Trust

Transparency as a civic concept refers to the measures that aim to give credibility to the NGO sector vis-à-vis the people, the government, the private sector and international organization by announcing the NGO's mission, activities, accounts and funding sources publicly. In recent years, the concept transparency was frequently used in the media and in many instances was related to the Third Sector. Hence, it was important within the context of this study to assess how people perceive this term and the way they deal with it.

3.2.11.4 Transparency and Peoples' Awareness

Although transparency, *al shafāfiyya*, is a concept frequently used in the media, whether the TV or in newspapers and by many officials, it became evident that the majority of the respondents do only understand it in its basic meaning that describes clarity, without connotation to their relevance to the work of NGOs, government or the individuals in general. The vast majority of beneficiaries did not understand what transparency is, and a very small percentage knew that this might indicate clarity by referring to it using phrases such as "to be honest in dealing with people", "not to deceive someone" or "what is inside comes outside". However, although transparency is a concept that was not understood by all segments of the society, there was a consensus that knowing about where donation money is going and seeing results are crucial to encourage philanthropy. The lack of clarity about where donation money to *Al Azhar* is going repels many people from donating to it.

During the intensive discussions, the majority of respondents, whether board members, *shaykhs*/priests, donors or recipients believe that trust develops when people see the activities of the NGO or the mosque or church, and the services they provide. Transparency in board members' understanding is associated with letting donors and the public see results. In the *ʿīd al fitr* for instance, beneficiaries stand in rows to receive the meat or whatever the NGO is distributing. This is as far as many board members associate transparency in relation to their work.

Table 13: Public's Perception on Transparency and Accountability as Necessary Conditions for the Operation of Philanthropic Organizations

	Frequency	Percent
An Association with a freely elected Board of Directors	1526	16.2
Where all Board Members have the Right to Discuss Issues Freely	1529	16.3
When Rules are Applied in Fairness to All	1575	16.7
When the State Supervises the Operation of the Organizations	1569	16.6
When Transparency is applied in the Organization's Activity	1596	17
When Financial Accountability is Maintained	1610	17.1
Sum	9405	100

During the survey, researchers explained the concept to respondents and asked them accordingly about their perception towards the importance of transparency in the NGO's work and in which conditions it realizes. As the data in the above table suggests, different ingredients of a democratic and transparent structure seem to meet acceptance among the public, with both transparency and financial accountability coming highest in importance. This is also compatible with the qualitative analysis, and most people emphasized the importance of transparency and trust in life in general, and concerning civil social structures in particular.

3.2.11.5 Trust Building and Philanthropy

The qualitative results confirmed that due to the special sociological nature of rural areas, where people in the neighborhoods know each other well, building trust is much easier than in urban areas and in the big cities. At the same time, this creates a cooperative spirit among the people, which permits the creation of organized community actions. It is noticeable that donors in rural areas usually do not request trust procedures due to their trust in where their contributions go. On the other hand, this acquaintance does not exist for people in big cities, where donors usually ask for serious procedures to provide them with transparency guarantees. Accordingly, many of the NGO chairpersons of the BoD and shaykhs give the donors a receipt stating the amount of their donations. Among the procedures they follow as well, is keeping a list containing incoming donations. In addition, many organizations conduct case studies for each of the beneficiaries they serve, and prepare annual financial reports to show their funding sources. These reports are made available to the public. However, the credibility of people in charge of the activities is one of the most essential factors to gain donors' trust, irrespective of the annual or financial reports they see. A good portion of the interviewed donors believe that they gain trust and deal either with NGOs or mosques due to personal trust in certain people working in these places. This reflects the importance of personal connections and the existence of people of trust in attracting donations.

3.2.11.6 Trust in Religious versus Non-Religious Institutions and in Individuals

In trying to measure the level of trust to religious institutions versus the level of trust to non-religious institutions, the quantitative and qualitative research revealed different results. The quantitative findings showed that 15% of the donors, doubt that the contribution made to religious institution reach those who deserve them, while only 8% of the donors felt that the contributions made to non-religious institutions never reach those who deserve them. Thus, the quantitative results indicate that people trust non-religious organizations more. However, the qualitative analysis revealed different results. Although many donors said that they trust the NGOs they deal with mostly because they have personal relations and contacts with people working there, other donors expressed that they lack trust in organizations and only trust mosques. They mentioned that generally, men who are responsible for activities in mosques have good reputations as religious men. One donor explained, "Mosques are more transparent and clear. NGOs have many people whom we do not know. It takes them ages to make studies on the poor cases that they have. I could give to these poor families directly." From here it is evident that some donors do not value the procedures that NGOs take to allocate those in need; especially when distributing money; an activity that most donors could do by themselves, especially if NGOs are not knowledgeable about most optimal ways to channel their donations.

In addition, some donors expressed their fear of donating to NGOs because they do not exactly know where their money is allocated. Besides, donors fear that once they channel their charitable donations through institutions, they would never have the opportunity to object to the procedures as to how their donations will be distributed. Only 4.5% of the respondents who contributed their charitable donation through institutions indicated that they do not feel entitled to influence the activities of these institutions.

It became evident that donors prefer organizations with a high degree of transparency. When we asked them whether they would fund *Al Azhar* (*Mashyakhat Al Azhar*), which makes many ads on TV to attract *zakāt*, the quantitative analysis showed that donating to *Al Azhar* scored very little 6.7% among the respondents. The qualitative analysis reflected the same picture where most of the interviewed donors objected giving to *Al Azhar* because they do not know where exactly these donations go. According to one donor, "There is no way I give to *Al Azhar*; there is no clarity; why should I give them money; what will they do with it". It is, therefore, understandable that the lack of transparency and participatory nature of philanthropic institutions is the major reason behind the reluctance of donors to channel their donations to their accounts.

Despite the status of *Al Azhar* as a major religious institution and although it might be actually making serious attempts to use donations in the best possible ways, it leaves the public uninformed with where and how the donations are used. The TV advertisement that repeatedly asks people to donate leaves them with a big question mark in their minds: If I donate, where will the money go and how? Therefore, it is of great importance that *Al Azhar* seriously addresses this problem by providing the public with a transparent and comprehensive image on its philanthropic activities. If the public sees and feels this change as well as believes it, *Al Azhar* might have a better potential to be a more successful philanthropic institution.

As shown in the below figure, good reputation by board members is the most important factor for donors to gain trust; serving the community follows 18% and manifests in what people in the intensive interviews described as "seeing where the money goes"; and maintaining transparency 20.7% are among the main sources of trust to donors.

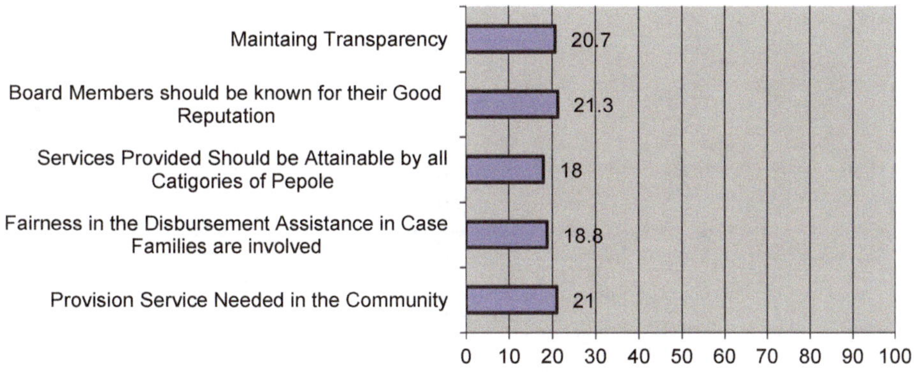

Figure 13: Perceptions on Aspects of Gaining Trust with the Local Community

3.2.12 The Role of Media in Mobilizing Philanthropic Resources

Media has a great influence on people; even on their philanthropies. However, according to the quantitative analysis, until now, philanthropy in Egypt has not sufficiently taken advantage of the power of mass media. As demonstrated by the quantitative data, very small percentages of people respond to media announcements about activities related to philanthropy; like those ads for *Al Azhar* collecting zakat for instance. However, this is a fact that could be debated on the basis of the preference to give to a specific organization; not necessarily to judge the effect of the media on their choice.

3.2.12.1 The Effect of Media on NGOs

Using TV and Media by NGOs rates rather low, and is limited to richer NGOs or those who are connected to famous public figures and have the support of the government. Most NGOs in general rely mainly on holding lectures and panel discussions, discussions in mosques or churches, and the printing of booklets to let people know about their activities.

Although TV is considered one of the strongest influences on peoples' behavior, the study revealed that its degree of effect on philanthropic behavior is minimal with only 14.3% against, for example, 24.8% going for the kind of service the NGOs provide or the transparency measures applied by the NGOs.

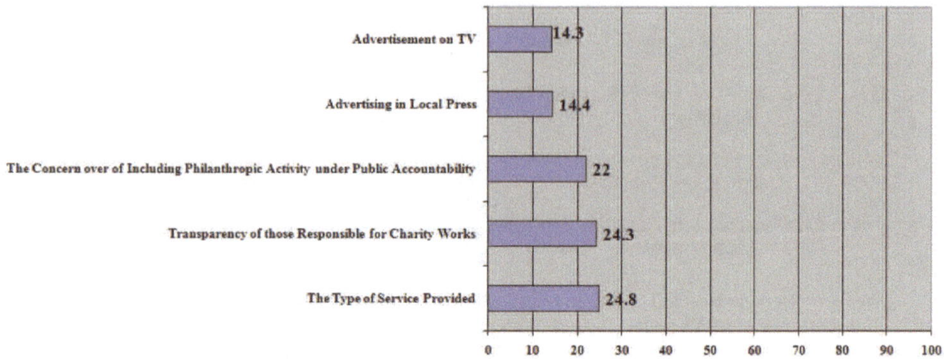

Figure 14: What Encourages Philanthropy

Thus, seeing ads of other NGOs on TV do not necessarily compel NGO chairpersons of the BoD and shaykhs to support or work with them, but might raise their awareness to some issues and relate them to their own communities. For example, seeing the TV program on the Cancer Institute in Cairo makes them generate resources for cancer patients in their local districts or governorate. "Why give to the Cancer Institute in Cairo, while we have cancer patients here?" On the other hand, TV ads might have a counter effect, because people tend to think that there are plenty of people donating. "It is unfair to compare between an elephant and an ant; the Cancer institute in Cairo has many people behind it. We do exhibitions for our products." said one board member. Most board members, especially out of Cairo, see that their regions and areas need more than "Egypt", as they refer to Cairo: "I would not donate to the Hospital in Cairo and not to *Azhar*, our people are more worthy, why should I give to people I do not know in Egypt".

3.2.12.2 The Effect of Media on Beneficiaries

As for the beneficiaries, none of the interviewed beneficiaries, except two cases, got acquainted to an organization through TV or any other source of media. In addition, almost all beneficiaries revealed negative attitude towards resorting to media as a way to solve their problems. The majority of beneficiaries expressed that they did not get any benefits from the media for several reasons. The first is that they feel that they are living in remote regions that are far from Cairo. Those who expressed this reason are mainly from Aswan, Minia and Gharbeya. One of the beneficiaries who is living in Aswan said, "Nobody answers, nobody comes here to see our problems. If I were in Cairo, I would have called Tarek Allam" (a famous TV anchor who held a program that rewards poor people). The second reason is that many beneficiaries have a pessimistic attitude that even if they try, nobody would answer them. This was explained by a beneficiary who said, "I don't think I would travel and make the effort. At the end there will be no result." A third group of beneficiaries are those who seriously thought about resorting to media, especially to the famous anchor Tarek Allam, but failed to find the contact information. They all, without exception, said that their main problem is that they don't know how to reach the media. One of the beneficiaries expressed her eagerness to find Tarek Allam to solve her problem by saying, "In Ramadan, I walk and keep on looking around myself to see Tarek Allam and explain to him my conditions." Especially in Ramadan, people expect a "Santa Claus" to fulfill their shopping list. The fourth group of beneficiaries is the ones who were actually able to reach the media. However, despite their efforts, the majority expressed that they did not get a response from the media.

3.2.12.3 The Effect of Media on Donors

As for donors, many of them said that they got affected with the commercials of the New Cancer hospital and tried to donate. However, some of them became suspicious concerning the degree of honesty of people responsible for it. This again brings us back to the issue of lack of trust and lack of transparency measures that assures people where their money goes.

However, the effect of media on people's behavior must be considered. Farida El Shobashy*, the famous anchor in Egypt, comments on the findings that the media is crucial in changing peoples' perception and that it could play a significant role in encouraging philanthropy especially through indirect creative methods as in the film industry and the various dramas.

3.3 The Economic Environment

Before assessing the effect of the economic environment on philanthropy, we will present an overview of the economic status of our representative sample and then attempt to analyze the influence of the economic variable on philanthropic behavior.

3.3.1 Brief Overview of the Economic Status of the Quantitative Research Sample

The majority of the respondents are of low income as shown by the following table. Around (26%) receive an income ranging from 500 to 999 L.E per month. In addition, around (20%) receive less than 299 L.E per month while another (20%) have an income between L.E 300 and 499.

Only (13%) of the sample receives an income of more than L.E 1000 per month.

Farida El Shobashy, Media Person. *

Table 14: Monthly Family Income

	Frequency	Percentage
Under 100	72	3.6
100–199	125	6.3
200–299	221	11.1
300–399	239	12.0
400–499	164	8.2
500–999	515	25.8
1000+	261	13.1
NA	403	20.2
Total	2000	100.0

As for the sources of the family income, the majority of our respondents are salaried employees 76%. Very few of them are landlords or owners of agricultural lands 8.1%. The second source of family income comes from operating small workshops by the chairpersons of the BoD of the households 16%.

3.3.2 The Effect of the Economic Environment on Financial Donations

The results of the study showed that there is a definite relation between the general economic status and the amount and kind of philanthropy practiced in the society. There is a major consensus between both the quantitative and qualitative results that Egypt is facing a serious economic crisis (this is in contradiction to official figures showing an improvement in the general economic environment. This may be explained by income disparities; the rich are getting richer and the poor poorer) that is negatively affecting the philanthropic environment. Most of the respondents agreed that this crisis affected the philanthropic flow reflected in the low rate of giving exerted by donors either directly towards poor individuals or towards NGOs, mosques, and churches. As shown table 11 below, when people were asked about the reasons behind not paying *ṣadaqa*, (87.9%) said they do not have enough money to make donations.

As for those who pay *ṣadaqa*, 70% of them do not pay it on a regular basis while only 12.4% pay it more than once per week, mostly by giving it to beggars in the streets. These results were confirmed by the in-depth interviews as it revealed that the bad economic conditions affected the rate of giving. As one of the chairpersons of the BoD said, "It is evident in the last period that the donations' rate decreased and this is due to the economic conditions." Another shaykh said, "The economic conditions of most people became very weak, both the rich and the poor are negatively affected.

This is natural, and it affected me too." The decreasing rate of donation was also explained by a beneficiary saying, "The one who used to give us something, now has decreased it to half." Moreover, almost half of the interviewed NGOs declared that their incomes from donations decreased, so that they do not cover their needs while at the same time the numbers of beneficiaries are constantly increasing. One of the priests explained, "Of course the bad economic conditions are increasing the burden by creating a new class where the father is educated and works, but his income is not sufficient to cover his family's expenses. We help these families secretly to protect their dignity and feelings."

Table 15: The Reasons Behind not Paying Sadaqa

	Frequency	Percentage
I cannot afford to pay Sadaqa	240	87.9
I don't know how to pay Sadaqa	12	4.3
I found no needy people in my neighborhood	6	2.1
It seems that there is nobody who deserves it	4	1.4

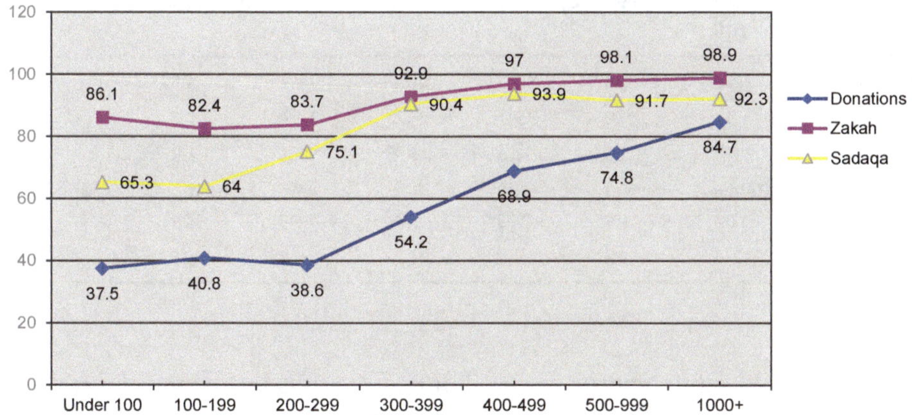

Figure 15: Income Levels and Awareness about Philanthropic Practices

The above figure shows that despite the difficult economic conditions, the existence of *zakāt* and ' *'ushūr* as a religious duty imposed on both Muslims and Christians preserves philanthropic behaviors and makes them sustainable. Although most people continue to give their *zakāt* or *'ushūr*, the amount paid is decreasing since their rates depend on the individuals' incomes.

It is noticed that the economic conditions also affected the fields of giving since it became mainly directed to fill the basic needs of the poor that take the first priority. As one of the priests said, "The preferred fields of giving are the poor families, especially filling their basic needs." Then he added, "Of course this year is not like the last two years. Even those who used to send us blankets, they sent ones with less quality while the numbers of beneficiaries are increasing."

3.3.3 The Effect of the Economic Environment on Volunteerism

The quantitative results showed no real relation between the economic conditions and the level of volunteerism. This might be due to the Egyptian culture which neglects the voluntary effort made towards helping individuals and only calculate the voluntary efforts made to organizations. The following table reflects the relations between the income levels and the kinds of philanthropy provided in the quantitative research:

Table 16: Income and Philanthropic Practices

	Below 100	**100–199**	**200–299**	**300–399**	**400–499**	**500–999**	**More than 1000**
Financial	92.6	98	88.1	96.9	94.7	95	98.6
In-Kind	37	20	35.7	25.8	27.4	38.7	47.5
Voluntary	11.1	10	3.6	8.6	10.6	12.9	14
	Below 100	100 –199	200 –299	300 –399	400 –499	500 –999	More than 1000
Financial	92.6	98	88.1	96.9	94.7	95	98.6

However, the in-depth interviews revealed different results related to volunteerism, showing that voluntary effort increases with the decrease of the economic conditions. The reason behind this is sometimes to make up the inability to provide financial donations. It is also sometimes attributed to the lack of work, which motivates many people to spend their times in useful things. That was explained by a volunteer who said, "To me, the economic conditions gave me a bigger chance to volunteer. I work as a contractor, and very often, I don't have work to do. I, therefore, prefer to spend my time in volunteering in the organization." The current bad economic status together with lack of awareness about *waqf* as a form of philanthropy are among the main reasons behind the deterioration of the *waqf* system and the avoidance by the majority to form new *awqāf*.

3.3.4 The Effect of the Economic Environment on *Waqf*

It is natural that the economic conditions also affect the practice of *waqf*. That was found when the public sample was asked why they don't establish a *waqf*, the highest answer (60.2%) as shown in Figure 16 below, was because they don't own anything to be put as endowment, followed by (30.3%) who don't even understand the meaning of *waqf*.

One of the priests said, "In Upper Egypt, there are Christian *Awqāf*, in Dayrout, Aswan and Qena. But there is no *waqf* now because of the economic conditions and the weak sense of religion. Most Christian institutions directed themselves to investment and the benefit in a commercial way." Besides, the in-depth interviews revealed that the lack of trust towards the Ministry of Awqaf is among the significant reasons for not establishing waqf. One of the donors said when asked about the reason for not making a *waqf*, "Now, nobody owns something to make it waqf, and nobody knows anything about the *waqf*, and hence nobody wants to establish a *waqf*. The government's properties are properties of unknown owners."

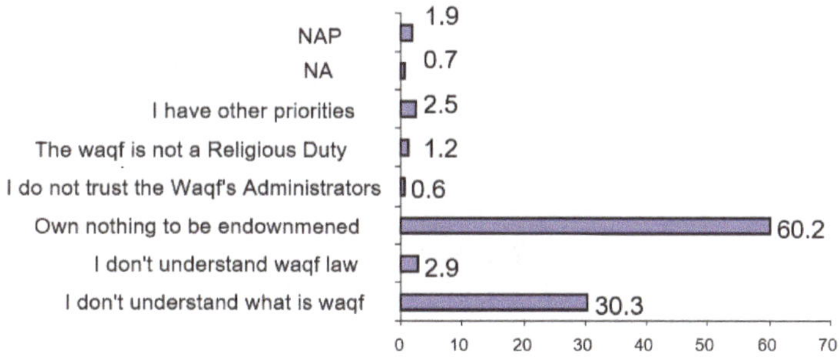

Figure 16: Reasons for Not Establishing a Waqf

3.4 The Legal Environment

3.4.1 The Effect of the Organizations' Law on NGOs' Investments

The objectives, mission, and scope of activities of all NGOs in Egypt currently follow the new law governing NGOs with the reference number: 84 for year 2002. The law permits NGOs to invest their money in banks or in saving boxes under their officially registered name. Organizations can invest their incomes in ways that guarantee a sustainable and secure income. It is therefore forbidden to invest money in stocks. As will be addressed in a later part of the report, only 30% of organizations started to invest their incomes with objectives related to secure their sustainability. However, it was noticed from the in-depth interviews that few NGOs are aware of the possibility of investing their money, thinking that it is illegal. As one of the chairpersons of the BoD expressed when asked if her NGO invests its money, “We suffer so much until we talk to donors and get assistance, but the organizations’ law forbids the investment of money.”

3.4.2 The Effect of the Organizations’ Law on the Establishment of Organizations

Figure 17 below presents the effects of law 84 for the year 2002 on the establishment of NGOs.

3.4.3 Organizations’ View towards Law 84 for Year 2002

As a result to the amendment of the organizations’ law into law 84 for year 2002, it was important to know the views of the quantitative and qualitative samples in the new law.

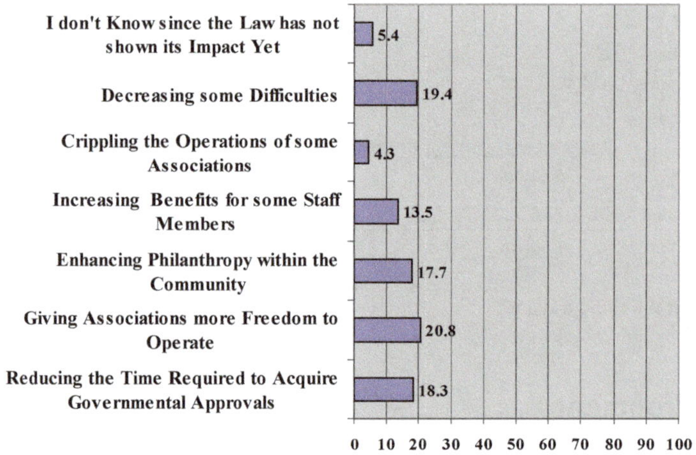

Figure 17: Perceptions of and Attitudes toward Law No 84 of 2002

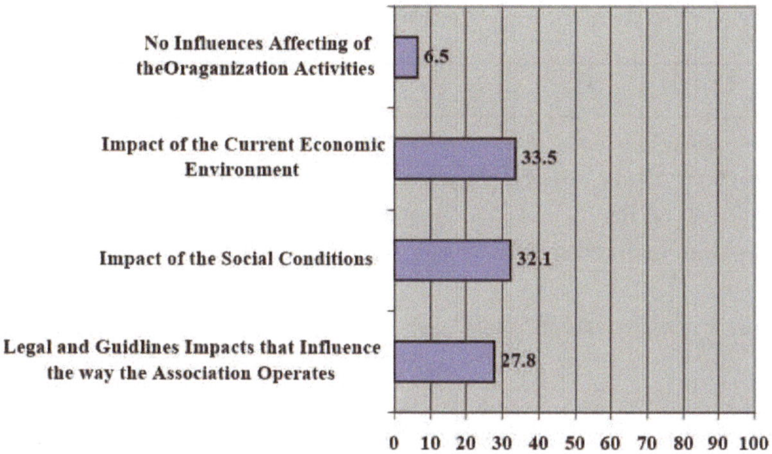

Figure 18: To what Degree are NGOs Affected by the Surrounding Environments

The above figure shows views of the quantitative sample on the new organizations' law. It seems from the results that there is a general satisfaction with the law as 76.1% stated that it provides more freedom to operate while 71.1 mentioned that it removes difficulties facing some organizations. These results comply with the qualitative sample, although the latter provided more clarifications about the pros and cons of the law. An Islamic organization head said, "Now it is easier than before. The state's security only delays our documents for almost two months. The advantage we got from the new law is that there are no geographical limits as before. We can work anywhere, and in turn, we have more than one branch in other places." Another head of an organization founded in 1980 said, "The new law made things easier. It is like the old one, but complies with the modern period. For example, in the old law, we had to take a written permission from the MoSA before getting the fund from a foreign agency, but the new thing is that the NGO can make the deal with the agency and just inform MoSA. If they don't send any disagreement during two months, it means that the permit is taken."

However, the research revealed that some NGOs have a negative stand against the new law. This was perceived when the quantitative sample tackled the legal changes that are needed by the organization in order to be able to improve their activities. Most of them referred to their needs for more flexibility and more freedom of movement in order to give them the space for more active and more effective philanthropic actions.

The formatting of this question was left as open-ended in order to solicit the required information. The following table summarizes the responses to that question:

Table 17: Reasons behind Requesting New Legal Arrangements

	Frequency	Percent
Give the Institution the Ability to Operate	101	8.4
Provide More Freedom From Governmental Routine	92	7.7
Maintain Freedom With Less Control	92	7.7
Help in Securing More Financial Assistance From Donors (Local and Foreign)	286	23.8
No Hope For the Change	189	15.8
There is No Need for such Arrangements at Present	3	.3
DN	369	30.8
NA	68	5.7
Total	1200	100

As shown in the above table, 8.4% request giving the institutions more ability to operate, 7.7% need more freedom from governmental routine, and 7.7% ask to maintain freedom with less control. It is interesting to note the helpless spirit of 15.8% of the sample who said that there is no hope for change.

The negative stand towards the new law was also expressed in the in-depth interviews by some NGO Chairpersons of the BoD. One of the Chairpersons of the BoD said, "The new law didn't bring anything new other than it increased the board to 6 years, and made the change of one third of the members every year instead of every two year, and increased the work of the general assembly to be every two years." Another NGO head founded in the sixties said, "It was easy before, but now there is so much bureaucracy. You have to take MoSA's permit in everything. This is because there are thieves now in the social work."

3.4.4 The Relationship of Philanthropic Institutions with the Government and other Institutions

The relationship between the philanthropic organizations and the government is summed up in the relationship of the MoSA, or what is now called the Ministry of Social Solidarity, representing the government and the NGOs, and between the Ministry of Endowment and the mosques.

3.4.5 The Relationship between NGOs and the Government

It is revealed from the research results that the government has a significant influence on NGOs. When asked about the factor that is most influential on the NGOs' activities, the Ministry of Social Affairs came as the second choice with a rate of 39.6% after donors, which took a rate of 40%, which is clarified in the Figure 19.

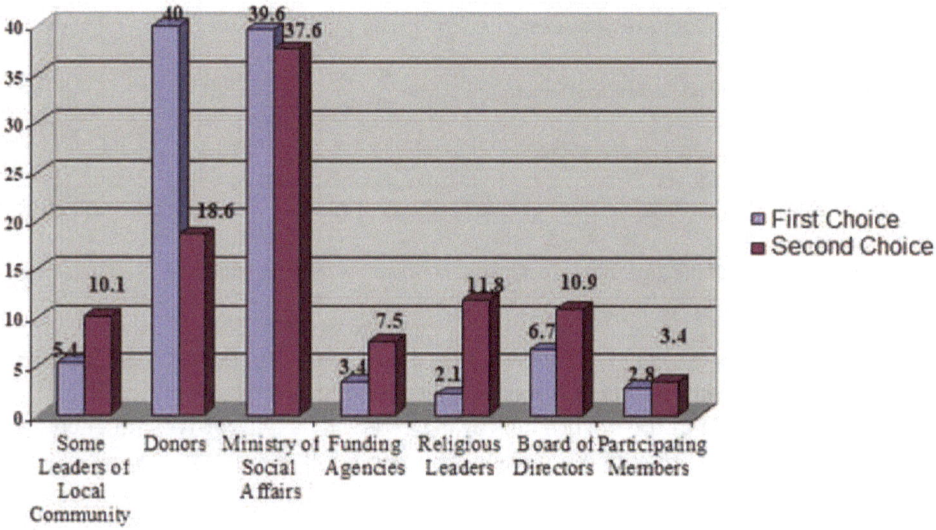

Figure 19: Relative Influence of Social Environment as Perceived by the Chairpersons of the Selected NGO

As for the nature of the relationship between NGOs and MoSA, the majority of respondents affirmed that there is a good and constructive rapport between NGOs and the employees of the Social Administration of MoSA. The majority of respondents said that MoSA provides helpful guidance during inspection and the documents' review process 95%, followed by those who said that it encourages the execution of activities 92% and others revealed that it removes difficulties facing NGOs 85%. Only 12.7% stated that it cripples the process of grant approvals while 9.1% said that it cripples NGOs when implementing their activities.

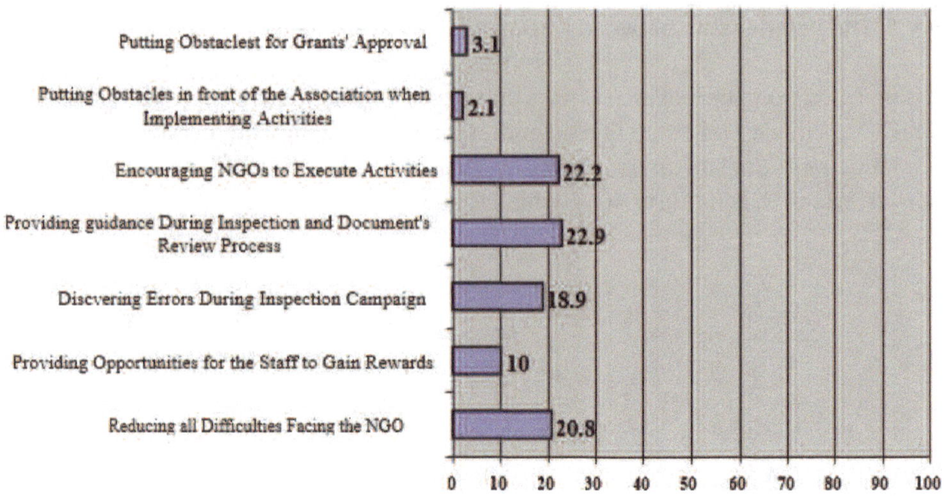

Figure 20: Perception of the Role of the Social Administration within the Ministry of Social Solidarity

The above figures were also confirmed when the NGO chairpersons of the BoD were asked about their perceptions of the state's responsibilities toward philanthropic organizations. The role of the government was perceived as supportive and encouraging in carrying out their activities as the data in Figure 21 shows.

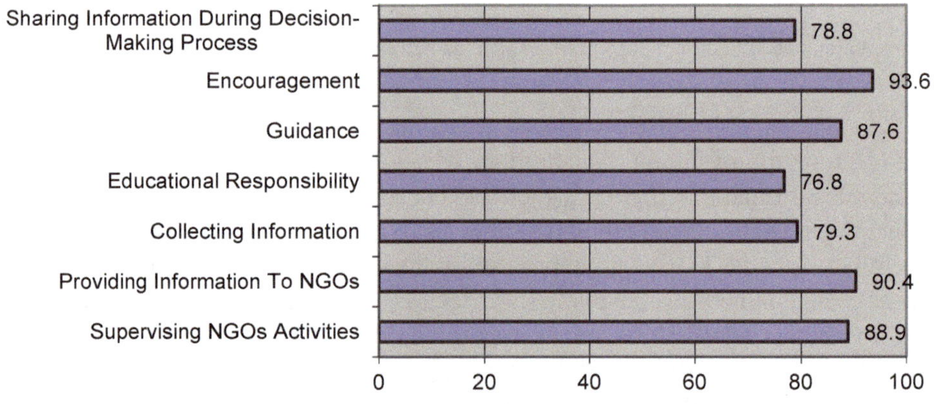

Figure 21: Perception of Aspects the State's Responsibilities toward Philanthropic Organizations

This was also supported by the qualitative study, which revealed that the majority of NGOs didn't complain about their relations with the institutions of the government. Many of the chairpersons of the BoD expressed that the procedures required for establishing a new organization have become easier and less complicated than before.

However, some of them explained that for security reasons, before registering the NGO, the government conducts an accurate investigation about the founders, which sometimes takes time.

After the registration of the NGO, there are three kinds of censorships practiced by three governmental institutions. The first one is by the Central Office for Accountancy, which inspects the financial operations of the NGOs, the second is the Ministry of Social Affairs, which is considered the formal authority supervising the associations and the third is the State's Security Department that investigates any security concerns. Many of them mentioned that as long as the NGO does not commit any act of legal deviation, these censorships are harmless.

However, few organizations showed dissatisfaction with the governmental organizations, saying that the censorship is not only annoying, but it also delays and hampers the activities and projects of the organization. As one of the chairpersons of the BoD said, "This censorship annoys us and delays our work, especially when the State's Security Department interferes."

In few cases, as will be clarified later, some organizations receive assistance from the support fund in MoSA. As one of the chairpersons said, "There is assistance in the form of staff salaries." However, most NGO chairpersons of the BoD don't know anything about the support fund. On the other hand, others stated that they wouldn't even try to get money from this fund because receiving money from it would mean more intervention from the Ministry of Social Affairs. It was also revealed from the in-depth interviews that sometimes there is a reverse relation between NGOs and MOSA as some organizations provide help to beneficiaries sent by MOSA to them. One of the chairpersons of the BoD explained, "We don't get anything from the Ministry of Social Affairs. On the contrary, they sometimes send us people to help."

To understand the relationship between the government and the religious institutions, one must consider the historical and current legal environment. Law 272 of year 1959 clause 10 declares that for mosques of specific importance, the Imam[75] is to be appointed by a presidential decree. In 1964 law 89 was issued to revise the former law giving the Minister of Awqaf the responsibility to appoint the Imams that work for the Ministry for the mosques that lie under its supervision. An amendment was added declaring that the Minister of Awqaf will do the appointments to certain criteria, which he sets to determine the Imam eligible for holding the preachers (*khuṭāb*) in the mosques. Finally law 238 of year 1996 was issued to amend the former clauses by adding a restriction to give religious classes, in addition to preaching, and sentences any Imam who does not abide by these rules of imprisonment.[76]

---

75 *Imam* is the religious figure who is responsible for holding the prayers and giving the Friday preacher.

76 Mohamed Selim El ·Awa. Azmat al Mo'assa al Dineya. Cairo: Dar El Sherouk, 2nd addition 2003, page 42–43

The study revealed that there is, to an extent, a paternalistic relation between the government and the mosques, where the government exercises a dominant role over the activities of the mosques. Relations between mosques and the government are manifested in their relations with the Ministry of Awqaf that supervises the activities of the mosques, and of Bank Nasser that supervises the activities of the *zakāt* Committee.

Concerning the Ministry of Awqaf, most of the interviewed shaykhs did not express satisfaction with the role played by the Ministry. Many of the shaykhs conveyed that the Ministry imposes many constraints, which they consider burdening. According to one of the shaykhs, "There are no problems and no facilitations from the side of the Ministry of Awqaf, but if it just lifts its hands off us, this will be much better". On the other hand, according to another shaykh coming from the North of Egypt, "The Ministry of Awqaf put its hands on our mosque and took it under its domain, appointed a government employee as an Imam (preacher) for the mosque and every Friday prayer he gets instruction from the government on what to say in his sermon. How can we advocate for anything different than what he has to say?" Another shaykh stated, "Men of religion turned into governmental employees. Before, the shaykh was highly regarded because of his education and knowledge. He used to preach for the sake of Allah and he was free of any chains. Now, a *shaykh* is a paid employee who just obeys orders that he takes from the Ministry of Awqaf. They tell him talk about the environment, he must talk about environment. He became chained."

In addition to the above quotations, many of the respondents who were engaged in building mosques expressed that they were obliged to hand over the mosques to the Ministry of Awqaf. To them, being part of the Ministry was not optional; this was a way to save themselves from the difficulties they face from the State's security, as they indicated. Beyond doubt, this relationship has direct influences on the philanthropic role of mosques; especially that this censorship imposed by the Ministry leaves no room for independent imams and civil society activists who took the initiative to build and manage the mosque, to act freely without the presence of delegated government employees. This affects the messages conveyed to people by the imams and hampers the potential of *khuṭāb* or preachers, which could have been a mobilizing source to engage and organize peoples' philanthropies. It is understandable that the Ministry (justifiably) tries to control the speeches of non-professionals or unqualified preachers, but it should also realize the problems that such paternalistic relationship might lead to. There is an important role forgone by the mosques, which were in different epochs a source of enlightenment and constructive civic actions. Needless to stay, historically, mosques were also financially independent by having their own endowments and workshops that gave them financial independence and autonomy. Containing mosques (and churches) and helping them take a proactive role in providing services and job opportunities should have a better potential for mobilizing promising actors towards development.

Another effect on the mosques' philanthropic activities is the Ministry's control over the *nudhūr* boxes, which constitute an important source of income as will be seen in a later part in the study concerned with mosques' funding. One of the *shaykhs* explained that the income of the *nudhūr* boxes is collected and distributed by the Ministry of Awqaf among its mosques for maintenance and renovations. However, he maintained that the Ministry does not provide any information about the distribution of these resources, which raises the question why many mosques are left neglected for years. This complaint was repeatedly stated by many donors and shaykhs. As one of the donors stated, "All these mosques are under the Ministry of Awqaf, but it doesn't spend properly on them, and the local people are the ones who find themselves obliged to do the spending. We just spent on the bathrooms from our own money after 50 years of abandonment by the Ministry. There are lots of things owned by the Ministry of Awqaf, but it doesn't support nor renovate them." Similar to the Azhar Institute, more transparent measures are needed by the Ministry of Awqaf to inform the public about its expenditures. If givers in nuzur boxes are considered donors, then it is their right to get a briefing on the allocation of these donations for instance. Applying transparency measures would greatly increase the credibility of the Ministry in the eyes of the individual Egyptian benefactor.

The other kind of relation between the mosques and the government is reflected in this relationship between the Zakāt Committee and Nasser Bank, which is responsible for supervising the expenditures of the Zakāt committee, starting with opening up the zakat boxes to the follow up on the receipts. None of the *shaykhs* interviewed complained about the supervisory role of the bank, however, it was obvious that the kind of social activities implemented by the Zakāt Committee are confined to certain kinds of activities, mostly charitable ones without giving chances for more creative or developmental activities like small loans to start up projects. These kinds of limitation in the work of the Zakāt Committee compel many committee members to establish NGOs where they would have more space for less restricted activities.

Nevertheless, such hindering conditions were not found in churches, which are not strictly supervised by the government. The flexibility in the churches' philanthropic activities might explain why Christians in Egypt give to philanthropic institutions with a rate of 19.9% while only 8.3% of Muslims gives to philanthropic institutions with more preference to directly donate to individuals. It might be understandable that the government takes more restrictive measures with the mosques for security reasons. However, these measures should be designed in ways that do not hamper the philanthropic role that could be played by mosques and direct it towards constructive development; especially that the religious character that distinguishes mosques and gives them a high credibility is an influential asset that enables them to boost philanthropy in Egypt if put in an enabling environment.

3.4.6 The Relationship among NGOs

As evident in Figure 22 below, most NGO Chairpersons realize the importance of having a network of organizations under an umbrella organization. The reasons behind that are to assist in organizational development, which takes a rate of 58.3%, to assist in maintaining cooperation, rating 38.4%, and finally to defend the rights of the organization with a rate of 3.3%.

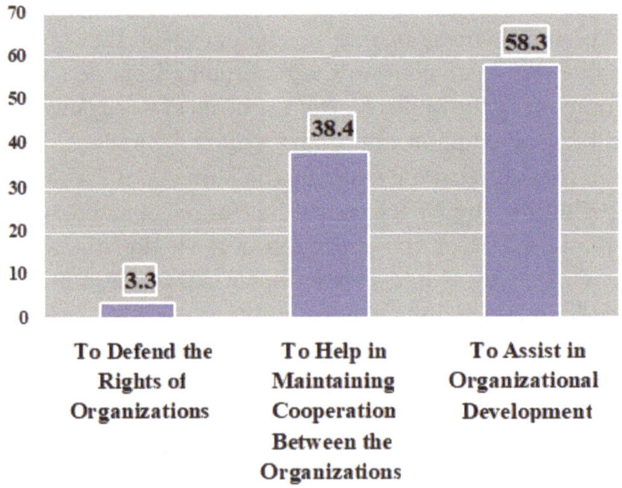

Figure 22: Reasons behind Joining a Network of Philanthropic

3.4.6.1 Organizations

In the in-depth interviews, it was revealed that there are mainly three kinds of NGOs. The first one includes those with connections with international and governmental agencies. These connections can be in the form of receiving big amounts of financial assistance or capacity building assistance. Many of these NGOs communicate and cooperate with each other through different networks.

The second type of NGOs are generally small-scaled, community based NGOs, whose interests are focused on providing charity assistance or basic services to unprivileged people. They mainly rely on local funding with little or no relation with local and international organizations. Most of these NGOs show very little cooperation and communication with other NGOs.

The third kind of NGOs are in-between the above two classes. They can give help or cooperate with each other in some activities due to some personal connections between the chairpersons of the BoD of those NGOs, but irregularly. As one of the chairpersons said, "we don't have a systematic relation with other NGOs, but we know each other personally and if we need some help from other NGOs we ask them, and they do the same."

It was noticed from the in-depth interviews that few chairpersons of the BoD refused the coordination with the other NGOs. One of the chairpersons of the BoD explained, "I don't accept coordination because it might harm the poor family. They tell you that one family should take from only one NGO, but the family takes only L.E 10 for the orphan child. Suppose there are five children, they will take L.E 50. The value of this money can do nothing now. They live all the month only with this money."

3.4.7 The Relationship between Religious Institutions and Other NGOs

A considerable portion of the philanthropic organizations that participated in our survey were secular, and it was important to inquire about their relationship with religious institutions. When the Chairpersons of the organizations were asked to report as to whether or not there is cooperation between their organization and religious institutions, almost (43%) of them answered positively to the question that was raised.

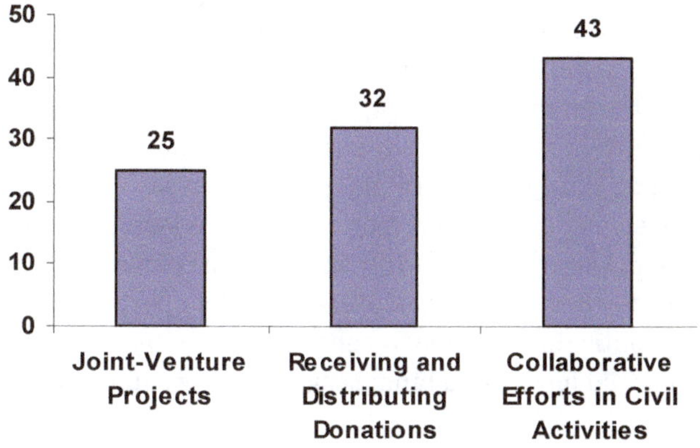

Figure 23: The Form of Cooperation with Religious Institutions

As data in Figure 23 suggests, there are three forms of cooperation that reflect a close relationship with religious organizations. This particularly concerns the collaborative efforts in civil activities with a rate of (43%), receiving and distributing donations, rating (32%). The joint-venture project, which takes a rate of (25%), could very well be the establishment of educational and health institutions.

Some NGOs are affiliated to mosques, which leads to a strong relation and partnership between them. Other NGOs target mosques for allocating beneficiaries or for publicizing for the NGO to attract donors.

3.4.8 The Relationship between Civic Organizations and Political Parties

Unlike the relation between NGOs and religious institutions, the relationship between NGOs and political parties is still to a certain degree minimal, which reveals an incomplete relation between all members of the civil society in Egypt. In the in-depth interviews, there were only two cases where cooperation between political parties and NGOs were mentioned. A donor of an NGO who is a member of a political party explained the role of the party by saying, "The party helps all people and deals with all people. It provides a helping hand through all its cadres or members. The idea is not just about collecting money; it is about participating in the good management of the society, the right allocation of resources, and the development of creative solutions that were not there before." The second case of a temporary cooperation between NGOs and political parties was described by a head of an organization who said, "We had a project before with the National Democratic Party where we distributed meals to people in Ramadan. When the party stopped, we stopped." These two cases reveal that although there is the seed of a potential relationship between organizations and political parties, this liaison is still in a very primitive form.

Abdel Hafez El Sawy *comments on the relationships between the NGOs and the political parties seeing that the current weak link is a positive sign. He justifies his position by pointing out that the political experience in Egypt is not ripe yet. Hence, the social work might be used to serve political interest, which would jeopardize the developmental goal and enforce the concept of "loyalty in return for donations". In such a case philanthropy would be directed to those loyal to a certain party and not those in need. However, when political maturity is reached, a distinction could be made between philanthropy for social justice and human rights vis-à-vis interests for political gains.

3.4.9 The Relationship between the Government and the Beneficiaries and Donors

The relation between the beneficiaries and donors and the government is manifested in their relations as individuals or donors with Al Azhar and the Ministry of Awqaf. Most of the interviewed beneficiaries were not aware of Al Azhar's role in distributing *zakāt* money. Many of the beneficiaries replied when asked if they thought of going

* Abdelhafez El Sawy, Researcher and Media Coordinator in the Economic Research Forum

to Al Azhar to assist them in solving their problems, but respondents' answerers were reflected in answers as follows, "Al Azhar? No, I didn't think of going there. What can Al Azhar do for me?" Even the few who were aware of the social role played by Al Azhar, mentioned that they refuse to go because of the difficulties they face when they go there to receive assistance. As one of the beneficiaries explained, "I know that Al Azhar gives assistance, but I can never go. When anybody tells me to go, I say no because it means that I would suffer there because of the bureaucracy."

As for donors, on the other hand, as explained before, the role of Al Azhar is quite vague and not transparent to the vast majority of respondents since there is no transparent data that would inform them where donations go and how they are distributed. Similarly, the majority of the interviewed donors held analogous feelings of ambiguity towards the Ministry of Awqaf. Besides lack of transparency, one of the problems lies in the public's unawareness of waqf as a concept in general, and the way it is associated with the Ministry of Awqaf specifically. As shown before, (30%) of the public's sample does not even know the meaning of *waqf*. As one of the donors said, "Nobody tried to make us understand what the Ministry of Awqaf really is .... I never saw any attempt by the TV to make people understand the role of this Ministry; even the Minister, we never see him talking about his role and plans."

3.5 Summary

This chapter presented the most important influences that affect philanthropy in Egypt and reached the conclusion that there are problems of misconceptions and lack of awareness among the majority of respondents with regard to concepts and forms of giving vital to institutionalized philanthropy. It became evident for instance that the majority of respondents representing the Egyptian public are not aware of the concept waqf and its implications. Most of them confused it as a term and as a function to the government and its possessions. It was evident that education and curricula do not play an effective role in promoting philanthropy among the masses, and neither does media with a negative role in encouraging giving and volunteering.

As to issues like transparency and trust, the study revealed that although many respondents were confused about their meaning, most were aware of the importance of clarity and seeing results of NGOs' work to maintain trust.

It was also evident that the economic environment plays a significant role in philanthropy, whether in the size of giving or the form (material, in-kind, volunteer effort). Tight economic conditions are one reason why many people do not consider establishing a *waqf* for instance.

Finally, the chapter discussed the nature of the relationship between NGOs and the government and the internal relationships between NGOs and their interface with other associations such as foundations, political parties, mosques and churches.

4 Individual Donors' and Receivers' Philanthropic Behavior

4.1 Introduction

This chapter deals with three main components: the first is the motives behind giving, the second is the personal preferences among Egyptian givers and receivers of philanthropy, while the third is the real practices of philanthropy and its commonly exercised forms.

4.2 Motives behind Philanthropy among the Egyptian Public

Based on the quantitative and qualitative studies, it came to our attention that there are several motives behind giving among the Egyptian public. These motives vary between religious motives and social and personal motives.

4.2.1 Faith-Based Giving

The Egyptian public, when surveyed about the primary motives behind their donations and volunteer efforts, indicated that the religious motive is their primary drive. It is either perceived as a religious duty since giving is an order in both Islam and Christianity or as a way to please Allah (God in the Arabic language) and get closer to Him. The following Figure indicates this finding, and also reveals that Muslims and Christians in Egypt are similarly religiously motivated, which reflects a faith-based culture of giving irrespective of religion.

The in-depth interviews affirmed what the survey suggested that religion is the most important motive behind philanthropy. Asked about their motives in advancing philanthropic help, donors say that it is, "Serving God, in general, as the Holy Book says", and they quote, "what you do to any of my little ones, you do to me". The majority of the interviewed donors, regardless of their age, gender, occupation, education and geographical location, shared this as their primary motive. As some of the donors said, "It is the obedience of God", "I seek God's satisfaction through obeying Him and His prophet (pbuh)". This tendency to donate for religious motives complies with the opinion of the majority of the Chairpersons of the BoD of organizations who perceived religion as a significant fundraising tool. Even among beneficiaries, who were to a large extent under the poverty line, philanthropy manifested in the *zakāt al fitr* or small *ṣadaqa* they give. Most of the beneficiaries give because of a religious motive, and their aim is to gain credit from God (*thawāb*), not because of a sense of a responsibility towards their society. "I take LE 25, if you tell me donate LE 5, I would

https://doi.org/10.1515/9783110697032-004

do so, because God bless the little. There are people who do good (*aha el khayr*), and we are people of faith, we believe Allah is One and we pray. We get patience from God and no one can be late if it comes to doing the good".

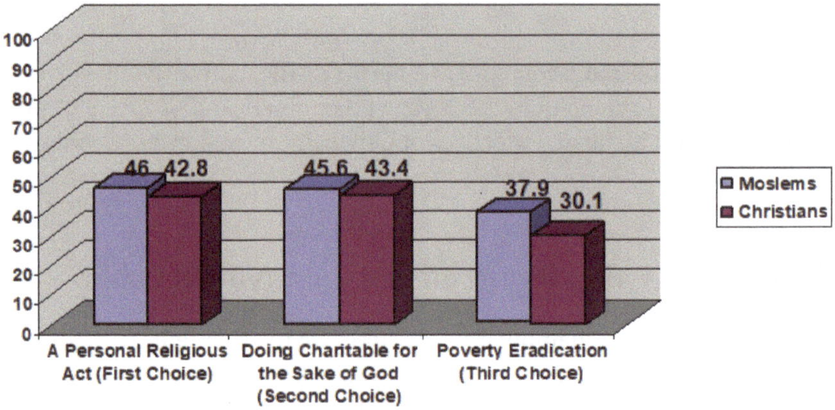

Figure 24: Motivation behind Philanthropic Practices

4.2.2 Paying *Zakāt*

The basic motive behind paying *zakāt* is the same as the motive of being philanthropic in general. As shown in the Figure below, the primary motive behind giving *zakāt* is to promote religious values. This is followed by giving back the right of the poor, which is interesting as it reflects the idea of the right of the poor to the money, rather than considering this money as a voluntary act of good or as a gift.

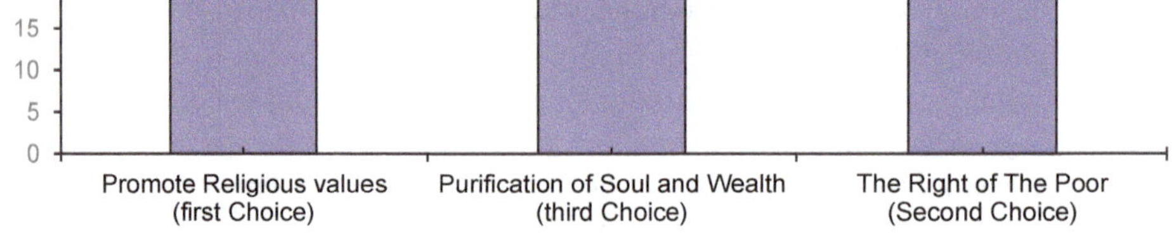

Figure 25: Why People Pay Zakāt?

4.2.3 Protecting Blessings (Religiously-Driven Motive)

Besides giving for the sake of fulfilling a religious duty or of satisfying God, the in-depth interviews revealed that some donors give with the intention to protect the blessings they are enjoying during their life time. This motive has a religious base since they feel that if they help the poor, God would protect the blessings that He provided them with. As one of the donors said, "Honestly, I save myself from diseases. When I help somebody who is sick, God protects me from illness. Also my bothers are businessmen, and they believe that if they don't pay their *zakāt*, God would prevent them from His blessings." Another donor explained the reason for sponsoring two orphans by saying, "I heard that there are children here, and I have two girls. I sponsor two children because if I die, I hope that they find somebody to help my children".

4.2.4 Compassion-Based Giving

Another important motive behind philanthropy among the Egyptian public is what we term compassion-based giving, which is related to an internal feeling of compassion than to a feeling of social responsibility or social interdependence. As revealed in the in-depth interviews and expressed by many donors, it is the naturally inborn tendency in every human being to help the others. That was expressed by one of the donors who said, "Helping is something inside the human being; it is a psychological motive; it is the instinctive love of doing good things". Like the above religious motive, it is noticed that this answer was not confined to only one category of people. Rather, it was made by both males and females with varying ages and incomes and from different governorates.

4.2.5 Affiliation to One's Own Community

A fourth motive behind the giving behavior of donors is their sense of affiliation and responsibility towards their own community. Here the idea of *takāful* or social responsibility might fit better. It is not only the psychological need to help the others; it is the feeling of attachment to one's own people and place. The quantitative research revealed that the motive to the general economic and social welfare of the community is the least motive, making a rate of 0.5 as a first choice, 0.9 as a second choice, and 9.1 as a third choice. This poses serious questions on the concept of "general benefit or public good (al manfaʿa al ʿāmma) vs. individual good (al manfaʿa al khāṣa)and how people define self-benefit vs. collective benefit and how this affects regarding themselves as responsible for the overall good of the society and not only their own good – even if it entails gaining heavenly credit by giving.

Table 18: Motive behind Philanthropy

	First Choice	Second Choice	Third Choice
Costumes and Traditions	13.3	4.7	21.0
Religious Duties	45.8	39.3	7.3
Getting Closer to God	37.2	45.5	13.3
Reducing the Number of the Poor in the Society	2,4	6.7	37.3
Cooperation with the Government to Reduce the Number of the Poor	1.0	3.0	11.5
For the General Economic and Social Benefit	0.5	0.9	9.1
No Answer	-	0.1	0.7

On the other hand, the qualitative results showed that the more we move away from the cities like Cairo, Giza and Alexandria, the higher the motive to serve the public good. In Upper Egypt in general and in Aswan Governorate in specific, a high sense of affiliation and responsibility towards ones own community was noted. As one of the donors in Aswan explained, "I serve the people of my own village, and here in the village, we are all relatives. This means that when I make any service to the village, I consider myself serving my relatives". However, despite this feeling of commitment in various Governorates, there were little efforts to organize and develop strategic long-term plans to achieve change in the community.

Mashhour Neamat comments on the willingness to serve the public good in the peripheries more than the center that in the small cities and villages there are lesser services and hence people are inclined to contribute to enhance the status of their community through focusing on the public good.

4.2.6 Allocating Leisure Time for Philanthropy

Another important reason for people's giving, especially volunteering, is spending their leisure time in a constructive way. This is mainly afforded by three main categories of people; either housewives who do not work and whose children became adults, or by elder men who are on pension and need to spend their time in useful work, or by graduate youths who still didn't find jobs. To most of these people, voluntary work is not just something in which they spend their time; it is also a valuable effort that gives a meaning and a goal to their lives. That was explained by a woman who is 53 year old and a member of an NGO, "Working as volunteer means happiness to me. I don't work and my children are grown ups now, so I have more leisure time where I could do something useful." Another volunteer said, "Someone like me on pension,

I don't have work now, so I volunteer with my time and money in a community development organization." It was also found that volunteering is a chance for girls, especially in Upper Egypt, who graduated and are kept unemployed at their homes. That was explained by one of the volunteer girls who said, "Volunteer work came by chance. We all finished our diplomas and were kept at home. We didn't know anything about volunteering and wanted to get a job. When we joined the organization and attended the meetings, we loved it and felt that we are not normal employees. People now talk about us and we have access to all the homes in the village."

4.2.7 Gaining Social Prestige

To gain a reputation that the person is a generous philanthropist is one of the motives that has been strictly denied by almost all of the donors. As one of the donors said, "If I donate for the sake of gaining a certain status, God will not give me the *thawāb* or the credit of giving. Prophet Mohamed said: if you want people to say that you are generous, and so they say, then you have already taken the credit you seek." This position is affirmed by the study results that show that most giving in the Egyptian society is secretive.

Kamal Imam comments that to gain prestige is attained by different approaches other than philanthropy. Those seeking a certain social image and prestige usually resort to elections according to Imam; "these images are rather bought", he said.

4.2.8 Taxations

It is the norm in many countries that NGOs as well as Donors (individual donors and corporations) enjoy certain tax exemptions; this is done in order to encourage their philanthropies and enhance corporate social responsibility (CSR). Thus, in the context of our study we seek to identify the effect of tax-exemption as a motive for philanthropy and corporate social responsibility. Although tax-exemptions in Egypt on individuals' donations mounted from 7% to 15%, this percentage is relatively low if compared to other countries. In the United States, tax-exemptions reach up to 50%[77]. In Egypt, donations paid to declared NGOs, charitable institutions, as well as to educational entities and hospital under the supervision of the government are subject to a deduction of around 7% of the net annual profit. The paid donations to NGOs that follow NGOs governing law 153 of year 1999, should be around 10% of the income and

77 Amani Qandil. Qawanin Al-Munazamat Al-Ahliya fi Itar Dawli Moqaran. Cairo: 1999, p.59–61.

are not subject to deduction from any other incomes that are in the domain of the unified tax imposed on the normal people[78].

In this context and as our quantitative study revealed, the current tax-exemption law does not encourage them to donate and that tax-exemption does not effect their motivation behind philanthropy. The intensive interviews showed that most of the donors explained that taking advantage of one's donations to reduce taxations would take away the credit of giving. In their point of view, philanthropy has a divine credit and in the case of profiting from tax-exemption it will lose the purity of giving for sake of God or for the welfare of others. This position was expressed by some of the donors by indicating, "this is God's right; I should pay it and even add more", "I have never demanded tax-exemption for my philanthropy, and if I do that, the meaning of giving would be lost".

Thus in Egypt, it seemed to us, that the tax exemption law as applied is not appealing to the largest number. In our point of view, this result is due to several factors:

First, in the context of this study, it is noticeable that many of the respondents are government employees whose salaries are not considerable and are routinely subjected to tax deductions. Hence, officials as such are not interested in calculating their philanthropies and revisiting the process of taxation accordingly. However, it must be noted that intensive interviews with businesspersons did not bring different results than those of the salaried employees.

Second, there is a strong cultural perception that undermines publicly declaring philanthropic contributions and also in claiming tax exemption. A belief in the importance of the secrecy of giving contradicts with the demand to deduct taxes.

Third, many people are not aware of this exemption and accordingly not familiar with the procedures they should undertake if they donate.

These factors contribute to the fact that although most of the people (83%) take a receipt upon donating to religious institutions, and although 74% see the importance of following up on the annual reports of the NGOs, only 14% approved that donors should get tax-exemption on their donations. We do not think this result should discourage policy makers to enhance tax-exemption laws on donations on the ground that they are socially not accepted, right the contrary. It is believed that advocacy for tax exemption clauses within the tax law is required and lobbying for the social benefits of philanthropy and potential financial gains from tax exemptions could increase the capital pool available for social giving. Especially in relation to Corporate Social Responsibility, there should be a serious attempt undertaken by the private sector, the legal authorities, the government and the civil society to reach a formula that responds to each sector's aspirations and expectations and one that would encourage a socially responsible business sector enjoying legislative benefits.

78 Abdel Salam Shehata. Dalil al-Dara'ib. Kitab Al-Ahram Al-Iqtisadi. No: 146, Marh 2000, page, 54

4.2.8.1 Is a More Effective Tax-Exemption Law Needed?

Hatem El Qaranshawi[79] sees that the problem lies in the formulation of the tax law itself and in the minimal amount of exemption declared. He continues that this exemption levied on philanthropic contribution was 7% and has been reduced to (5%) in the new law. In addition to the complexity of procedures required to obtain such exemptions in practice. This in his opinion constitutes a serious problem of law formulation.

Kamal Imam adds that people in Egypt in general resist paying taxes because they do not see social justice around them. He stresses that in order to change philanthropy from an individual action to a communal action practiced by the community at large, there must be a legislative change, as the current law does not encourage those philanthropists who wish to obtain tax-exemption.

From the above positions it is evident that there is dire need to put efforts in reforming the tax law in order to encourage philanthropists and put into effect a larger role to be played by CSR. It is also envisioned that such a legal reform will bring closer philanthropists and the NGO sector. This would in turn lead to a more institutionalized and intuitions-directed (against person-to-person) form of giving.

4.3 Preferences for Philanthropy among the Egyptian Public

After understanding the motives of giving among Egyptians, in this coming section it is important to identify their preferences in terms of domains and methods of giving.

4.3.1 Preferred Domains of Giving among Donors

4.3.1.1 Relatives and Neighbors

As shown in the Figure below, people in their donations would first assist their relatives (78.6%), and second come people living in the same neighborhood (36.3%). The religious concept of " al aqrabūn awlā bi al maʿrūf (the relatives should have priority for our support) from the prophets sayings and "dhu al qurba wa al aytām" (the relatives and the orphans) from Quran, manifest in the preference of the public in their philanthropies.

79 Hatem El Qaranshawy is Professor of Islamic Law, Azhar University. He was engaged in a workshop organized by the researcher to comment on the data collected.

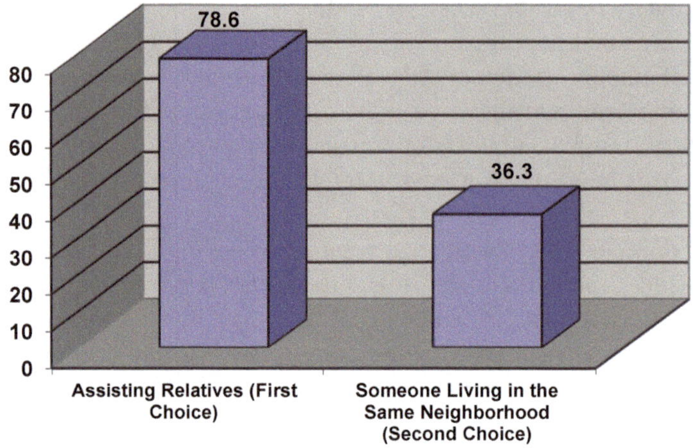

Figure 26: Traditional Form of Charity

4.3.1.2 Assistance to the Poor

Giving assistance to the poor either on an occasional, seasonal or regular basis is one of the easiest and preferred forms of philanthropy among the Egyptian public. This trend is widely practiced either by helping poor families through providing them with monthly salaries or by distributing money or in kind donations during the seasons like the fasting month of Ramadan, or occasionally by giving charity to poor people they already know or to beggars in the street.

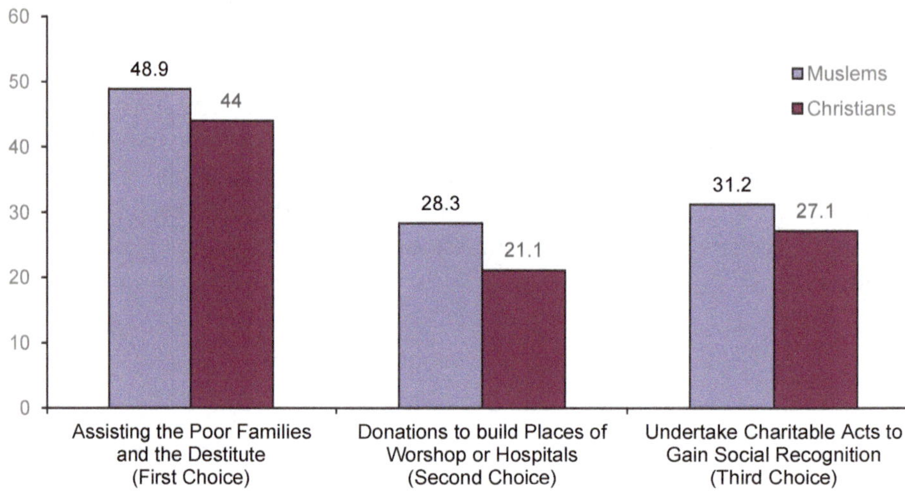

Figure 27: Forms of Charitable Giving in Egypt

4.3.1.3 Orphans

The field of orphans is one of the most attractive fields of giving among the Egyptian public. When asked about what makes people donate without thinking, 20.7% of Muslim and 22.5% of Christians of the quantitative sample revealed their preference to give to the orphans. As one can see from Figure 28 below, Muslims and Christians alike are appealed primarily to give to orphans, even before donating to Mosques and Churches (Christians (19.1 %) and Muslims (17.6%).

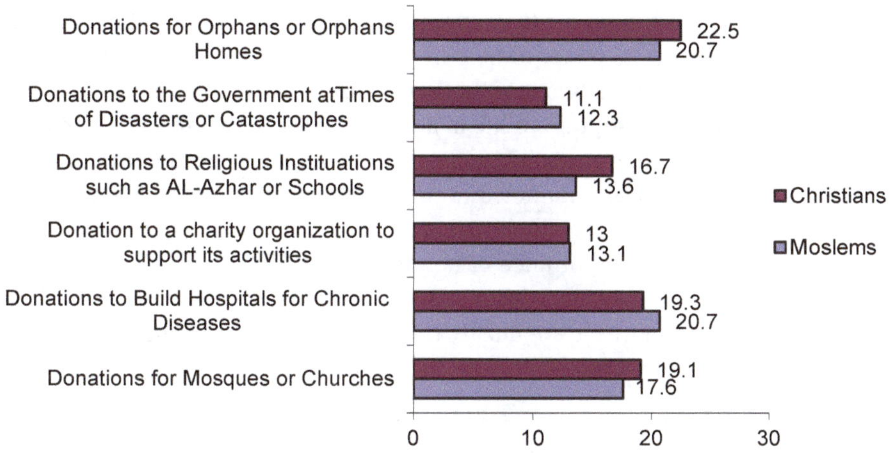

Figure 28: What Moves Egyptians to Donate?

This result has been strongly confirmed with the qualitative research as most of the respondents expressed their keenness to donate to orphans. As one of the Shaykhs explained "people feel the orphan is deprived of so many things and hence they feel compelled to help him/her. Also the Prophet recommends us to be kind to orphans and in doing so we find the road to paradise", he concluded. Apart from the strong compassion with orphans, this tendency is results from a religious belief that sponsoring orphans in Islam is one of the roads towards Paradise; a concept which is clearly presented in one of the most repeated (especially in the media) of Mohamed (pbuh). The *ḥadīth* explains that the Prophet and the sponsor of an orphan are as close as two fingers in paradise. Most of the donors repeated this saying justifying their preference to give to the orphans. The same applies for Christians who share the same compassion for orphans; as one of the Priests said, people always prefer helping the brothers of God (those in need) and the orphans". Priests highlight the importance of tithes ('Ushūr) and indicate that they should be divided on different aspects of benevolence, yet that priority should be given as follows: First, the bigger part should be allocated to the sons of martyrs, widows and orphans. Second in priority come the servants of God in the churches and to the churches in general. Third comes giving to family members and relatives then to the needy from the believers and last to non-believers[80]. These religious preferences show some differences when compared to the Islamic belief, where *zakāt* is not to be spent on mosques or people of religion and where the poor, family and relatives come first in importance. This differences reflect in giving habits of Muslims and Christians as will be shown later in this chapter.

Despite the fact that caring for the orphans is a positive philanthropic behavior, it has also a negative effect since it neglects other segments that are still in need of help and support like the elderly. That was mentioned by an old beneficiary who said, "I went to several organizations, but they all refused to help me because it helps only the orphans, and most people prefer to help the orphan not the aged." Hatem El Qaranshawy adds that it is understandable that people are more compassionate for orphans because they have no support in life in addition to the high importance placed in religion for their support, yet people donate for their food and shelter not for their education. This giving must be channeled to the development of the orphans and to their education, he stresses. However, there are various *ḥadīth* and Qur'anic versus about philanthropy and the importance of helping people help themselves through developing their skills, yet the most widely used by the media are the ones that affect peoples' thinking most, and these are mostly those that encourage giving to orphans and to charitable occasional causes.

> "Therefore the orphans oppress not, therefore the beggar drive not away, therefore of the bounty of thy Lord be thy discourse." (The Morning Hours: Verses 9–11).

4.3.1.4 Providing Medical and Educational Assistance

Due to the severe economic conditions that the majority of the population is facing and the inability of the government to meet the needs of the poor, many people directed their philanthropy by giving medical and educational assistance to fill the needs of the poor. That was explained by a head of an NGO who said, "There is always sympathy with people who have chronic diseases and severe illness like cancer. We receive lots of donations for this purpose and we send it to the Cancer Hospital." Another donor said, "Education and health are the most important fields of giving. There are lots of families who face difficulties in educating their children. Maybe it is easy in the primary and preparatory stages, but its getting difficult in the secondary stages and higher education."

---

80 See: Michael Maxi Iskandar. Owel Mawsou'a 'an Al-'Ushour wal Bukour wal Nuzur. Maktabet Al Mahabba: 2000; p.29.

4.3.1.5 Donating to Build and Renovate Mosques

The study results showed that many of the donors prefer to donate to build or renovate mosques. The popularity of this field stems from the religious belief that this act is a sustainable *ṣadaqa* or *ṣadaqa jāriyya*. It could be also due to the belief that the concept of *iʾmār al masājid* or restoring mosques is a religious duty since it is considered to be the house of Allah or God. In addition, this idea could be also enhanced due to the failure of the Ministry of Awqaf in many instances to provide adequately to maintain mosques. Besides building and renovating mosques, many people tend to donate to the *zakāt* committees. In another category of mosques including mausoleums where certain religious scholars or sacred figures are buried, there usually exist *nudhūr* boxes, where many people prefer to donate money when certain wishes of them get fulfilled. These people do not care much about where the money goes; as long as they put the *nudhūr* they committed themselves in the boxes. The income of theses boxes are mostly spent on mosque decorations, Quran Books, and other mosque needs. Lately, *nudhūr* are generating more than money. People bring to mosques, as one shaykh said "candles and fabrics for the mausoleum decorations as well as things like clocks, vacuum cleaners, and other decoration materials for the mosque."

Despite the fact that donating to build or renovate mosques is an important matter, the problem stems from the reluctance of the majority of many people to donate to other projects. As a head of one organization said, "I face a problem in the education project we have in Komombo. The village could spend L.E 70,000 on a mosque, and if you ask them L.E 10,000 to be put in a project, they refuse. There is someone who is very rich in the village, he refuses to give me L.E 100 for the education project and pays thousand of pounds for the mosques."

Mashhour Neamat explains that people tend to donate to mosques because they believe that whoever builds or assists in building a mosque will gain a palace in heaven. She doubts that people are aware that it is not possible (legitimately) to donate to mosques from one's *zakāt* money. Accordingly, Mashhour stresses on the importance of educating people about *zakāt* and philanthropy.

4.3.1.6 *Ṣadaqa Jāriyya or* Sustainable Giving

The popularity of this field has been revealed in the results of both the qualitative and quantitative research. When asked about the preferred form of philanthropy if money is available, *ṣadaqa jāriyya* was the second choice after giving to poor relatives and friends. as highlighted in Table 19.

It is also noted that the availability of lots of money is a condition in people's mind to make *ṣadaqa jāriyya*. In addition, as mentioned before, the concept of *ṣadaqa jāriyya*is related to very constrained ideas. To the majority who understands the concept, it is mostly related only to build a mosque or to make a water-fountain (a public place for drinking water or *Coldeir* as people put it referring to the current commercial brand-name of the water-fountain) or to print Quranic verses in small booklets; all these are methods done for the spirit of a dead relative. However, *ṣadaqa jāriyya* in its true meaning could be manifested in several projects that are currently needed in the society like building hospitals or schools or establishing projects to reduce unemployment. It is a form of endowment that aims at perpetuity of the good deed, financially and service-wise, i.e. practically it is synonymous to *waqf*. It is a philanthropic methods of institutionalizing philanthropy in ones life and beyond.

Table 19: The Preferred Forms of Donations if Money is Available

	1st Choice	2nd Choice	3rd Choice
Help the Closest People, Relatives and Friends	70.9	11.2	8.1
Special Help to the largest Number of People in the Society	3.2	17.1	10
Help the largest Number of Institutions and Local Organizations	3	8.9	8.7
Help Islamic or Christian Organizations Outside Egypt	6	2.4	3.9
Start a Charitable Project to Benefit the largest Number of People	6.3	.8	24
Do a *Sadaqa Jariya* or waqf	9.8	26.6	26.4
Go to Pilgrimage or *Omra* (visit to Mecca) more than once	4.6	6.5	9.2
Help Others to Go to Pilgrimage or Omra for the First Time	1.6	3.3	9.7
No Answer	0.2	0.3	0.4

4.3.1.7 Burying the Dead

Although this field is one of the least attractive forms of giving, it does exist mostly in villages. In addition, if an organization includes burying the dead among its activities, many donors get encouraged to participate in it to save the situation of a poor to be buried. People would also be tempted to participate in this act as it has a religious credit or *thawāb*.

4.3.2 Preferred Fields of Assistance among Beneficiaries

4.3.2.1 Income-Generating Projects

On the beneficiaries' side, most of the beneficiaries have expressed their preferences to receive income-generating support, which is mainly in the form of loans to start small enterprises or in the form of a job vacancy, which most of the time is provided for some at the NGOs. There are two major reasons behind the beneficiaries' preference. The first one is that income-generating activities would provide them with the opportunity to have a sustainable source of income without being obliged to continuously depend on others' support. As one of the donors said, "Loans are better because I became able to work, open a house, and feed myself". Another one explained, "A kiosk is preferable because the one who would give me today, will not give me tomorrow". Another reason for this preference is that income-generating projects preserve the beneficiaries' sense of dignity. In the cases of loans, beneficiaries would have their own independent projects that would eventually allow them to pay the received money back. One of the loan beneficiaries explained, "When people used to come and help me with money, I was embarrassed, but now I have my own work".

4.3.2.2 Educational Assistance/Vocational Training

In addition to income-generating projects, few beneficiaries mentioned their preference to vocational training, through which they learn a vocation that would enable them to work and earn their living. Moreover, few beneficiaries mentioned their preference to educational aid, which includes all kinds of aid that promote education, either literacy classes, school fees, or education of children with special needs.

4.3.2.3 Financial or In-Kind Assistance

Many beneficiaries, on the other hand, expressed their tendency to receive money and in kind donations as the best and more suitable kinds of aid. It is noticeable from the analysis of the beneficiaries' answers as well as those of the Chairpersons of the organizations, the shaykhs of mosques and the donors, that many beneficiaries got used to depend on others and perceive their reception of aid as their complete right while saving any efforts to work hard to achieve their self-independence. Many NGO Chairpersons expressed this phenomenon by "professional begging". This is especially found in cases where beneficiaries are young and jobless. However, many of those who preferred money and in kind support have conditions that seriously prevent them from work. These conditions include old age, disability or serious illness. This is also applicable to beneficiaries who have simple jobs that do not bring sufficient incomes like servants in popular districts or nurses in public hospitals.

4.3.3 Preferred Methods of Giving Among Donors

4.3.3.1 Giving Secretly Versus Giving Openly

The results of the research revealed that the vast majority of the Egyptian donors give secretly than openly. When asked if they care to be discrete in their philanthropy, the majority answered: Yes

Table 20: Do you Maintain Secrecy in Giving Charitable Donation?

	Frequency	Percent
Yes	1916	95.8
No	64	3.2
Both	13	.7
DK	6	.3
NA	1	.1

As shown in the table above, 95.8% of the sample indicates to be giving secretly, with only 3.2% not keeping their giving in secret. Although there might be several reasons for the tendency to give secretly, table (21) below shows that most of the respondents attribute this preference to Religion. While 40% considered giving secretively a religious duty, 26.7% thought that it is done for the sake of God; hence it should not be disclosed. In addition, the intensive interviews that asked donors about the way of giving that would satisfy the beneficiaries, 56.7% of them mentioned that giving should be secretive. As seen in table 21, this is the condition mostly chosen to reflect donors' perception of the importance of secrecy in giving to beneficiaries.

Table 21: Reasons for Maintaining Secrecy in Giving Charitable Donations

	Frequency	Percent
Because Secrecy is a Religious Duty	799	40.0
Not Embarrass or Offend the Recipients (the Needy)	564	28.2
To Know Who is the Beneficiary	9	5.
To Spread Benevolent Activities	36	1.8
For God's Sake	533	26.7
Just to Follow Customs and Traditions	5	.3
Because God asks us to give Sadaqa in Public and in Secrecy	32	1.6
NA	22	1.1
Total	2000	100

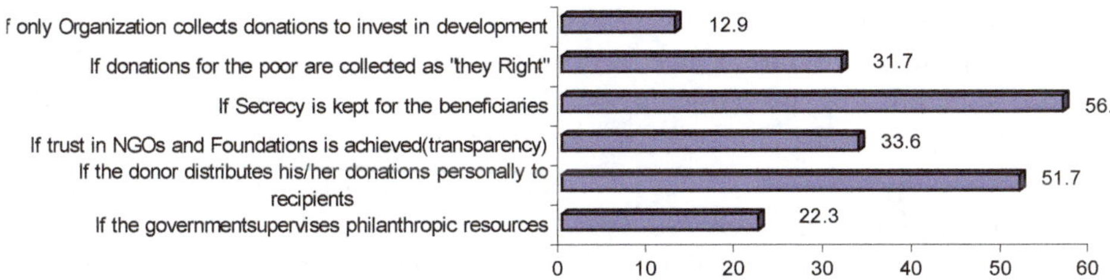

Figure 29: How Can Charitable Donations Make Beneficiaries Satisfied

However, does giving have to be in secretive? People of Religion in Islam had a different point of view. Many of the *shaykhs* affirmed that giving in Islam doesn't have to be always secretive. One *shaykh* explained, "There is nothing bad if you show your giving on the condition that it should not be for the purpose of showing off in front of people to appear as a generous person. You can make giving openly if you want to be a good example to others and encourage them to give too. In this case, giving openly is acceptable." He quoted the Quran: "If ye publish your almsgiving, it is well, but if ye hide it and give it to the poor, it will be better for you, and will atone for some of your ill-deeds. Allah is informed of what ye do." (The Cow, verse 271)

Another *shaykh* indicated, "In the day of recurrence, those who gave in order to be said by people that they are philanthropists, or that they pray to be called pious, and it was said, there is no credit to expect from God because they already got the reward they seek. However, giving in public to give an example and encourage others, this will be rewarded by God". Here it is an issue of intention (*al niyya*) and people who intent to donate, seeking God's consent, in secret or in the open have their reward from God.

The issue textually for Christians is different. As one Priest explained, giving must be in secret. It preserves the dignity of the receiver, especially among students". This is supported by relating to the Bible: Matta): "But when thou doest alms, let not thy left hand know what thy right hand doeth That thine alms may be in secret: and thy Father which seeth in secret himself shall reward thee openly."

As to secrecy in giving and whether this hampers transparency, Mashhour maintains that it does not. She highlights that anonymous givers do get a receipt and accordingly secrecy and transparency are achieved.

4.3.3.2 Donating to Individuals versus NGOs

In general, the results of the research showed that most of the Egyptian public prefer to give to individuals more than to organizations. There are three main reasons behind this preference. The first reason deals with the problem of trust as most donors feel more secure to give to individuals than to organizations. One of the donors said, "I prefer to give to individuals. I will not give to an organization unless I really trust it, and there are few organizations that work without slogans. I like to give to the needy by myself and guarantee that the donation reaches him/her." The issue of trust was also mentioned by one of the donors who expressed his complete refusal to donate to any organization that has any relation with the government. According to him, "I give organizations and individuals whom I trust. I totally refuse to give any organization that is related to the government". Second donors prefer to give to their relatives. As one of the donors explained, "The relatives have the priority to get our help. If I know that my brother needs help, should I leave him and go to help a stranger?" The third reason behind this preference is the slow procedures taken by the organizations until they send the donations to the beneficiaries.

However, in the in-depth interviews, we focused on donors of NGOs and religious bodies to assess why they tend to give to institutions. The majority expressed their preference to give to organizations as they are more able to coordinate work and supervise beneficiaries. That was explained by one of the donors by saying, "I like to give to an organization that I trust, but at the same time I give to individuals. I prefer the organization because it has supervision and coordination."

The quantitative results complied with the above results. When the respondents were asked about the way they channeled their donations the last year, the majority asserted that they donate their money to individuals as shown in the following figure:

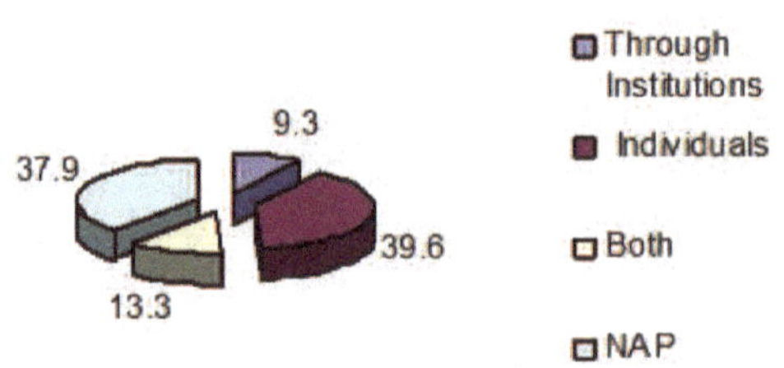

Figure 30: How did you Channel your Donations?

As showed in Figure 30 above, 39.6 % of the respondents channel their charitable donation directly to individuals of their choice, while 9.3% prefer giving to philanthropic institutions known to them, and 13.3% give their donations to both. Based on these results, it is deductible that philanthropy in Egypt is scattered and individually based (personal), which hinders attempts of organized philanthropy.

4.3.3.3 Religious Giving to Individuals versus Institutions

We also tried to measure the methods people use to transfer their *zakāt* and *ṣadaqa*. The results we reached were not much different from their preferred means in channeling donations.

As shown in the following table 23, a total of 81.1% of the payers of *zakāt* and *sadaqa* direct it to individuals while only 6.4% channel their religious giving through institutions.

Table 22: The Way of Channeling Zakāt and Ṣadaqa

	Frequency	Percentage
Through Institutions	128	6.4
Through individuals	1621	81.1
Both	165	8.3
NA	2	.1
Not Applicable	84	4.2
Sum	2000	100

The main reasons given were because of the small amount of faith base philanthropy that they pay, which does not constitute a worth being value that deserves to be sent to an organization (26.5%), and second that most of *the zakāt* is paid to relatives and hence they do not need an intermediary to channel them (26.7%). In addition, around a considerable 15% do not channel their religious giving through organizations either because they do not know anything about their existence and role (7.5%) or because they do not trust in them (8.2%).

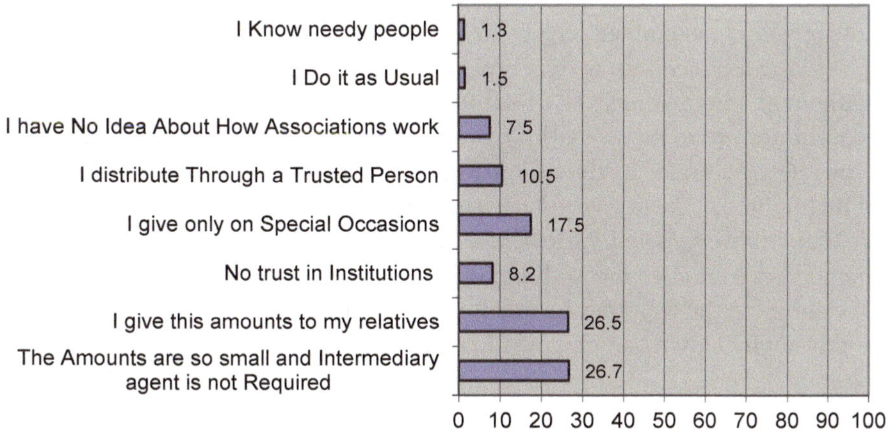

Figure 31: Why Zakāt/ʿUshūr and Ṣadaqa are distributed To/through Individuals (person to person giving)?

As to those who channel their religious philanthropies to institutions and not to individuals, table (23) shows that the largest number among the respondents (13.2%) expressed that institutions are more capable of channeling donations, while around (23%) were divided between the fact that donors trust distributors of resources in the institutions (11.2%) and that organizations distribute resources according to *sharīʿa* (Islamic Law) (11.7%). Among the least in importance was the interest to channel religious philanthropy to institutions because they are more involved in doing development projects (8.2%) which affirms the lack of interest or awareness to channel philanthropy toward development projects.

Table 23: Reasons for the Disbursement of Zakat/Ushour and Sadaqa through Institution

	Frequency	Percent
Because They are More Capable	263	13.2
Because I Trust Those Responsible for Distribution	226	11.3
Because They do the Distribution According to Religious Law or Shari'a (Islamic Law)	233	11.7
Because They direct The Money towards Developmental Projects	163	8.2
Because I am Busy	65	3.3
I Don't Know Any Body Else	12	0.6

In the intensive interviews respondents explained that philanthropy boils down to trust that this money reaches those who are in most need and prefer to give to relatives. As one donor explained, "I give to individuals; will only give to an institution I trust, .. as long as I feel I can deliver my giving directly to those in need, I prefer to do that without an intermediary. Also relatives deserve more than other; if my brother is in need, should I go to the streets and look for the needy while he needs help?" As to those people who prefer to give to institutions, this depends on their trust. As one donor highlighted, I like to give to a trust worthy NGO, at the same time I give to needy people that I know personally. However, I like to give through an NGO because they have supervision and better coordination".

In examining the Egyptian social fabric, we concluded that there is variation between this habit of giving among the Christians and the Muslims.

Table 24: How did you Channel your Donations?

Ways of Channeling Charitable Donations	Moslem %	Christians %
Through Institutions	8.3	19.9
Directly to Individuals	41.2	21.7
Both	12.1	26.5

As shown in the data presented in the above table, 41.2% of the Muslims give directly to individuals, and only 8.2% give to organizations, signaling a noticeable tendency to give individuals. As to what concerns the Christian respondents, there are no major differences discovered between their tendency to give individuals or institutions. (19.9%) tend to channel their philanthropy through institutions, while 21.7% give directly to individuals. There are a number of reasons for this variation between the Muslims and the Christians. Among these are the fact that Christians tend to give to Churches as part of their religious duties and domain for the spending of their tithes. Part of the giving, as earlier indicated, should be directed to support churches and servants in the church. In contrast, *zakāt* is not to be spent on mosques, nor are people of religion entitled to receive donations. Voluntary giving of *ṣadaqāt* and *nudhūr* are giving that Muslims could allocate for mosques, yet it is not compulsory.

Another reason is the significance to support people of kin and neighbors among Muslims, which compels them to give individually and not through organizations. This coincides with the deterioration of the role of the Azhar Institute and the Ministry of Awqaf, which results in the lack of institutionalization of philanthropy.

On the preference to give to institutions among the Christian respondents, Hatem El Qaranshawy refers this to the higher degree of freedom that churches and Christian philanthropic organizations and institutions enjoy in comparison to the Muslims'. He adds that there is a much higher freedom of action granted by the security authorities to NGOs related to the church than those NGOs associated to mosques. He believes that this freedom of action given to the Christian bodies is bigger than the freedom permitted to the Azhar itself. This freedom directly affects the level of trust, because there is more room to act and more space to apply transparency measure; hence more potential to gain trust and attract donations. In return, this encourages the Christians to give to religious and philanthropic institutions because they can see more and accordingly trust more. In the case of Islamic organization or even the Azhar Institute, the donor does not know where his/her money is going, and in addition he/she has no authority to question the accountability or participate in the decision making, El Qaranshawy concludes. Mashhour Neamat on the other hand, relates the Christian's giving to institutions to the fact that the church provides religious lessons, but also computer classes to children, organizes trips and recreational activities, and manages many developmental activities. This encourages people to give to the organizations related to the church, she concludes.

El Qaranshawy takes further Mashhour's point to affirm that historically the mosque took a similar position. It was the nuclei of the city, the place where people go to look for a job, ask for resources, discuss issues, attend seminars, and other developmental activities. He draws attention to the old mosques in old Cairo and Gamaleya area where all mosques had workshops and commercial stores as part of their buildings. Business activities as such were the source of income to sustain mosques and support their activities and the neighboring environment. El Qaranshawy adds that mosques were accordingly the driving force for mobility and social change and from its dynamics more infrastructures were built and jobs were created in the surrounding streets and alleys. He maintains that the proverb that says, What is the purpose of building a mosque that does not provide bread for people? (*jamīʿ bilā ʿīsh laysh?*), shows that a mosque without vocational workshops, industries, etc, will collapse because there are no resources to provide for its maintenance. This saying is one of the closest examples that promotes the idea of social enterprises and the importance to have a business model for social projects.

4.3.3.4 Geographical Affiliation of Philanthropy

As mentioned before, giving to people living in the same neighborhood was the donors' second choice (36.3%) coming right after their choice to give to their relatives (78.6%). These two choices boil down to giving to those close to us, or *al aqrabūn.*

The in-depth interviews confirmed the above results. The majority of the interviewed donors preferred giving within their own villages or districts. The most common reason behind this preference was religious since Islam encouraged Muslims to give those who are closer to them as the first priority. One of the donors expressed this concept by saying, "Our religion says that those who are close to us have the priority to receive our assistance".

A second reason behind this preference is people's sense of affiliation towards their community. In the intensive interviews we sensed anger in the statements of donors living in remote Governorates other than Cairo, Giza and Alexandria because they feel that their own money in the form of taxes are taken to be spent on Cairo while their governorates lack many services. As one of the donors explained, "The taxes of Tanta go to Cairo and Alexandria. Where are the rights of poor people living in Tanta?" The qualitative study revealed the wish of the respondents to refer to Religion in organizing philanthropy and especially in making use of the local resources within the Governorates to develop them, not to flow into bigger Governorates like Cairo.

A third reason for preferring one's nearest place is the donor's knowledge of the poorest of the poor and the most disadvantaged in the community. One of the donors clarified, "I like to give my village, and if I meet a poor person outside my village I wouldn't like to give him because within my village, we know each other, but I don't guarantee if the outsider is truly in need or not".

However, there are donors who have different points of view. A number of the intensively interviewed donors in the qualitative sample affirmed that their selection is not based on the nearest place. but Rather on the needs of the needy. Wherever the beneficiaries are, the most important criterion is that they truly need support. As one of the donors expressed, "Egyptians are Egyptians wherever they are". It is noticed however that all donors who hold this position are located in urban cities, mostly in Alexandria, and Giza. The sense of affiliation to one's community is mostly spread in rural areas.

Mashhour gives the example of a religious NGO (al jamʿiyya al shariʿiyya) where branch organizations fundraise locally and spend the money in the same geographical area. This permits people to commit to enhancing the status of their own surrounding and create a sense of belonging and collective work during projects' design and implementation.

This geographical affiliation in philanthropic practices is promising for models such as community foundations. It promises sound fundraising techniques that adhere to traditional *waqf* structures and religious heritage that prioritizes philanthropy to those close by kin or by geography. In addition, it is a model that secures efficient monitoring and evaluation procedures to assess the effect of the foundations' work in their target locations. A recently emerging model as such is presented in the coming Chapter on the establishment of the Maadi Community Foundation (*Waqfeyat al Maadi Al Ahleya*)), the first community foundation to be established in Egypt and one pioneering model that aims at reviving the waqf system, challenging the government dominated system of *awqāf*.

4.3.3.5 Giving to other Countries

Most of the donors expressed their refusal to give outside Egypt, insisting that poor people in Egypt should have the first priority to receive help. As one of the donors expressed, "There are people in Egypt who are under the poverty line, why would I leave these people and think of outsiders?" Another donor added, "What is needed at home is forbidden to the mosque" (an Egyptian proverb).

While most of the donors preferring to give inside of Egypt, some donors expressed their sympathy with Muslims who suffer from poverty and misery allover the world and especially in Palestine. The reason behind this could be the sense of a religious duty to help distressed Muslims especially those who were forced to leave their homes, wherever they are. In Islamic faith, the issue of helping out those Muslims who are displaced and forced to leave their houses is as a compulsory call for assistance.

4.3.3.6 Preferred Methods of Receiving Assistance among Beneficiaries

4.3.3.6.1 Receiving Assistance from Organizations not Individuals

Contrary to donors who mostly prefer to give to individuals, most beneficiaries expressed their preference to receive donations from organizations rather than individuals. This preference is due to two reasons: keeping the sense of dignity of the beneficiary and the sustainability of aid. As one beneficiary said, "The organization is better because nobody in the organization would offend me by saying I give you money. Another one explained, "When an individual gives me in the morning, he would disgrace me in the mid of the day. I mean if he gives me L.E 100 at 10 am, at around 10:30 am, I will find 100 persons know that he gave me." This reflects embarrassment that many poor people have to put up with because they are desperate to receive assistance.

The second reason is that the organizations' help is sustainable and does not rely on the individuals' financial conditions. As one of the beneficiaries said, "The organization is better because it is continuous. But if I take from you once, next time, I will not take from you."

4.3.3.6.2 Receiving Assistance Secretly not Openly

Complying with the donors' preferences, most of the beneficiaries expressed their preference to receive assistance secretly since it preserves their dignities. That was explained by one of the beneficiaries who said, "I like to receive help secretly in order not to hurt my kids. For example, they asked my home number, but I refused to give them the number of my neighbor in order not to know that I receive help from the organization."

However, this secretive assistance is constrained only to those beneficiaries who receive financial or in-kind aid. But this feeling of shame doesn't face the loan beneficiaries as they consider it as a temporary loan to start a project, then they will return it back. On the contrary, sometimes the success of the project and the change that happens due to this success is a source of pride to the beneficiary. As one of the loan beneficiaries said, "I like to say that I received a loan."

4.4 The Practice of Philanthropy in Egypt Today

After being oriented with motives behind philanthropy and the preferences of both donors and recipients to the methods of giving and receiving, this coming section attempts to reveal and discuss the current practices of philanthropy, its magnitude, trends, patterns and forms as practiced by Egyptians today.

4.4.1 Estimates of Philanthropic Resources in Egypt

Estimating philanthropic resources is vital to the development process in Egypt. These resources constitute the local contributions and philanthropic assets that support the disadvantaged and marginalized in Egypt. Not only was there no official or non-official estimate of these resources before this study, but also these indigenous efforts and resources were never highlighted within the work of development practitioners throughout many years of work in Egypt. From here, and from a belief in the importance of local assets in development, we carried out a primary estimate of this local assets.

4.4.1.1 Estimates of Egyptian Philanthropists

The study revealed that 62.1% of the Egyptian public donate annually.

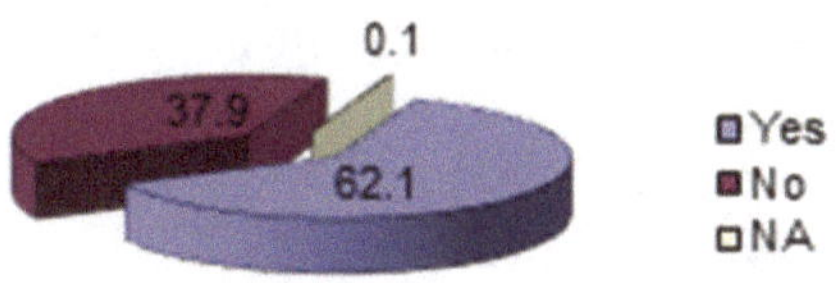

Figure 32: Did you give any Donation this Year?

4.4.1.2 Kinds of Donations

It came to our attention that the monetary giving is the form most prevailing in Egypt, followed by in-kind donations and finally by volunteer effort.

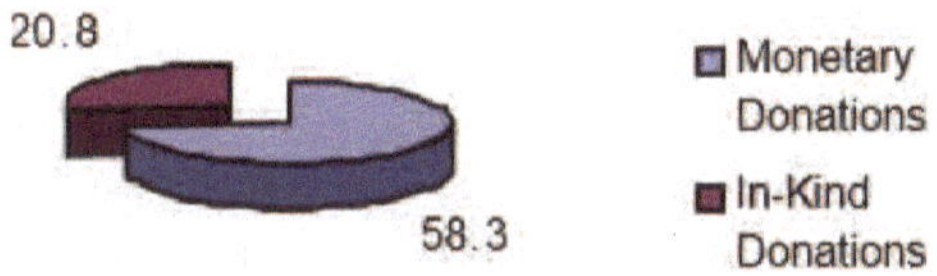

Figure 33: Monetary and In-Kind Donations

The above figure shows that the monetary donations constitute (58.3%), which is more than double the in-kind donations that make up (20.8%) of the Egyptian philanthropy.

4.4.1.3 Types of Religious Giving: *Zakāt al Māl*, *Zakāt al Fiṭr*, and *Ṣadaqa*

As shown in the Figure below, religious giving is distributed among *zakāt al māl*, which constitutes (43.2%) *zakāt al fiṭr* (85.4%) and *the ṣadaqa* (85.9%).

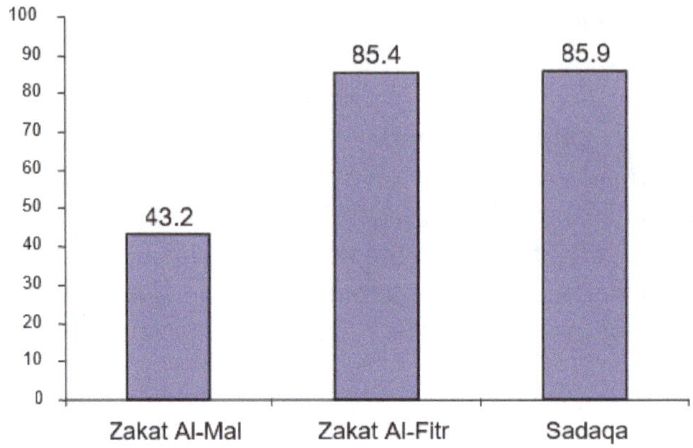

Figure 34: Types of Religious Giving: Zakāt al Māl, Zakāt al Fiṭr, and Ṣadaqa

Out of the 7 types of *zakāt*, we focused on *zakat* al-mal and *zakat al-fitr*, as the two most commonly known and paid *zakāt* in Egypt.

4.4.1.4 Zakāt al Māl (Zakāt on Monetary Possessions)

43.2% of the respondents reported that they pay *zakāt al māl*, while 45.8% indicated that they do not for following reason. They do not meet the conditions of paying *zakāt al māl*, which is to own what corresponds to the minimum value of 85 grams of gold for a whole year. The 97.4% of those who pay their *zakāt al māl* said that they paid it in cash, while 11.9% paid their *zakāt* in the form of food, cloth, or other necessities of the needy.

4.4.1.5 Zakāt al Fiṭr (Breaking-the Fast Zakāt)

Paying *zakāt* al-fitr is a common practice among the Egyptian public even the very poor ones as 85.4% of the respondents reported to be paying it. The reason why most of the respondents reported to be paying it goes to the fact that it is a small amount (around L.E 5 to L.E 8), and as mentioned before, it is an obligatory religious duty on every person who owns enough to feed himself/herself and his/her family for one day. Thus, it is obligatory for those who are considered very poor as well. The majority of those who pay *zakāt al fiṭr,* (96%) said they pay in cash, while the remaining 4% pay their *zakāt al fiṭr* in food, cloth and other necessities for the needy.

4.4.1.6 Ṣadaqa

As for *ṣadaqa*, around 70% of those who pay it reported that it is paid on an irregular basis. Only (12.4%) of the public seem to have the habits of paying *ṣadaqa*more than once a week, most likely to beggars in the street. It became obvious that the majority pays cash *ṣadaqa* (84% of respondents), while 35% give their *ṣadaqa*in the form of food and clothes, and only 10% volunteer their time and consider it among their *ṣadaqa*share. The table below illustrates this finding:

Table 25: How Do You Pay your Sadaqa?

	Frequency	Percent
In cash	1690	84.3
Offering Food	340	19.7
Buy clothes for needy	274	15.9
Volunteering effort	177	10.3

4.4.1.7 Other Kinds of Zakāt

Besides *zakāt al māl* and *zakāt al fiṭr*, there are other kinds of *zakāt,* which could be categorized as *zakāt al māl*, yet are classified differently to specify payment responding to certain domains like *zakāt* on agricultural production, *zakāt* on animal stock and others. Results show that some of the respondents pay these kinds of *zakāt*, but at lesser degrees, depending on the profession of the respondent and what he/she owns. Table (26) shows the different kinds of *zakāt* and ، *'Ushūr*as paid by the publics.

Table 26: Types of Zakāt and 'Ushūr Most Prevalent by the Public (excluding zakāt al māl)

Type of Zakat/ushour	Frequency	Percent
Agricultural Products	197	10.5
Livestock	110	5.9
Animal Products (Honey or Milk)	67	3.5
Gold & Silver	293	15.7
Trading & Industries	262	14.0
Bank Savings & Deposits	340	18.2
Extracted Treasures	10	0.5
Prizes	6	0.3

4.4.1.8 Accuracy of Estimating Zakāt

The research results revealed that 62% of those who pay *zakāt* calculate it by themselves while 20.3% go to religious persons to help in the calculations. It appears that most of the respondents do not calculate their *zakāt* accurately, as they should if they abide by the Quran. Sometimes this is not due to lack of faith but a conviction that they pay more. As one of the donors said, "There is nothing called to calculate it with a paper and a pen; if you give God more, He will be saving this for you." On the other hand, sometimes wealthy people haphazardly decide to pay a big amount of money without accurate calculation, which could still be much less that what is due as *zakat*.

4.4.2 Estimates of Annual Charitable Giving in Egypt

In order to understand the potential of philanthropy in Egypt and gear it towards development, it is essential to assess this potential. As mentioned earlier, no figures on the size of philanthropy in Egypt are given in any official or academic source up to this point. Hence, this attempt here is the first to provide an estimate based on the representative sample of the population.

Many respondents refrained from telling the amounts they donated in cash on the assumption that charitable giving should be given discreetly following the Islamic tradition and also the Christian according to the Egyptian faith-based culture of giving. Therefore, we based our estimates on those who provided information on the amounts of their philanthropy and made an average estimate accordingly.

Local philanthropic contributions (excluding volunteer effort) according to my study, reached a yearly figure of LE 5, 454, 022, 706 [81] (Five Billion and Four Hundred Fifty Four Million and Twenty Two Thousand Seven Hundred and Six Egyptian Pounds) in 2005. This makes an equivalence of USD$ 950 Million; i.e. close to 1 Billion USD Dollars annually.

This estimate is reached by multiplying the total number of Households in Egypt which according to the Central Agency for Public Mobilization and Statistics (CAPMAS) in 2004 is estimated to be 14,507,000 households (by *) the percentage of those who declared paying donation (by*) the average each of these households pay annually.

81 The total philanthropic contribution calculated here does not include the subsidies provided by the Egyptian Public (non-governmental subsidies) that are granted to the poorest of the poor through the provision of health and educational services in mosques and churches and associated organizations.

Table 27: Estimation of the Yearly Contribution of Egyptian toward Charitable Donations *(Zakāt, Ṣadaqa)*

	Kinds of Infaq (donation) Charitable Donations	% Having paid Donations/ Zakat	Average paid per household	Estimated Amount Paid Yearly Per Household	
1	cash Donation	58..3	180	*14.507.000*.583*180	1.522.364.580
2	In-kind donation	20.8	169	14.507.000*.208*169	509.950.064
Zakat					
1	Zakat	43.2	264	14.507.000*.432*264	1.654.494.336
2	Zakat El- Fitr	85.5	40	14.507.000*.855*40	496.139.400
3	Sadaqa	85.9	102	14.507.000*.859*102	1.271.074.326
Total in LE (Egyptian Pounds)					5.454.022.706

* The total number of households of 14.507.000 has been provided by the Central Agency of Public Mobilization and Statistics, Egyptian population Data on 1/1/2004

However, one must note here that we could not get estimates of the *nudhūr* for instance, which is a huge sum of money that goes into *nudhūr* boxes and people give it on occasions related to aspiring to fulfill a certain wish. These are subjects to the management of the Ministry of Awqaf.

4.4.3 Estimates of Annual Volunteer Efforts in Monetary Terms

Volunteerism and social solidarity (*takāful*) are what come to peoples' minds next after helping the needy either through monetary or in-kind types of giving. Volunteering was described to the respondents as a working commitment for the benefit of the community, or the environment or the individuals outside the family, with no explicit financial interest. Only a proportion of (6.4%) of the adult population reported to have volunteered their time. This proportion represents a number of 928,448 households in 2004.

Thus, according to our calculations volunteer effort was estimated to reach LE 314,743, 872 Million annually (in 2018). This number was reached through the following calculation:

Approximately 928,448 individuals volunteered an average of 2.5 hours per month offering their services free of charge (in 2004–2005). This makes about 2,321,120 hours of volunteering-time per month, which translates into 27,853,440 hours per year. Should we consider the value of a voluntary hour with a minimal cost of L.E 11,3[82], the overall value of voluntary work in Egypt is estimated to reach L.E 314,743, 872 Million or around USD$ 20 Million annually (in 2020).

4.4.4 Per Capita Philanthropy and Volunteer Effort

In 2018, according to the World Bank, Egypt received US Billion 2.06 of economic foreign aid to Egypt. Thus the per capita share of economic foreign aid in 2018 reached USD $21.5.

My study revealed that the per capita share of philanthropy and volunteer effort (calculated in 2005) reached LE 80 or equivalent to USD$ 14 yearly, which was higher than the per capita share of economic aid at that time.. According to the World Bank Report of 2003, the per capita share from foreign economic assistance is USD$ 13 (noting that the population then was 67,555,000). If we compare this per capita with the per capita share of philanthropy, as shown above, we realize that it has a considerable importance, especially in a large aid-recipient country like Egypt.

Considering that the philanthropy effort is still the same in 2018 we can approximate that philanthropic contributions would reach LE 9 398 950 000 or almost 9.5 Billion Egyptian Pounds. The volunteer effort value in 2018 is estimated to be equivalent to LE 314,743, 872. Thus, the total philanthropic contribution in 2018 can be estimated to be LE 9 713 693 872 or almost LE 10 Billion. Dividing the philanthropic contributions on the population of Egypt (around 100,000,000 in 2018), the capita share will be LE 97 or equivalent to 6 USD. It is noteworthy that the per capita share of philanthropy decreased from 2005 to 2018 and this is attributed to the devaluation of the Egyptian Pound.

4.4.5 Form and Pattern of Philanthropy in Egypt

4.4.5.1 Charity-Oriented Philanthropy

Our study revealed that philanthropy as practiced in Egypt today is charity-oriented and at its best, service oriented. People not only give their philanthropies to individuals, but those who give to institutions tend to donate to charitable organizations or those who provide services, and not to development association. When the respondents were asked to indicate the institutions they tend to donate or volunteer in, the result showed that Charity Association comes as first choice (11.8%) while development organizations rating very small (1.2%).

82 This calculation is based on 2020 minimum salary which is LE 2000 for 176 hours of work per month

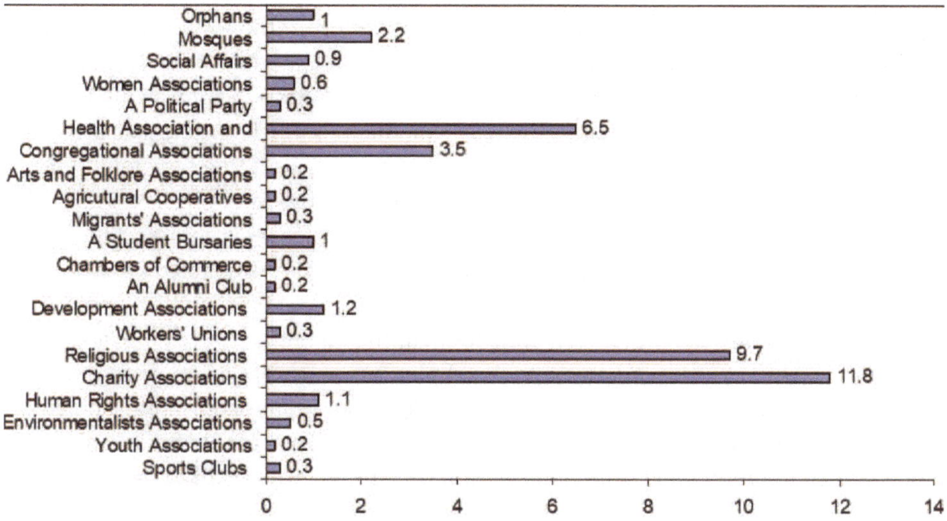

Figure 35: Beneficiary of Donation and Volunteer-efforts by Types of Organization

It is obvious from our data that people tend to donate and volunteer first in charity associations, followed by religious organizations and third to health organizations where they can assist people with diseases, especially chronic ones. As Figure 35 illustrates, contribution to development associations is minimal, rating as low as contribution to human rights, which might be considered a luxury that cannot be afforded when surrounded by severe cases found in the charitable organizations, religious institutions or in clinics.

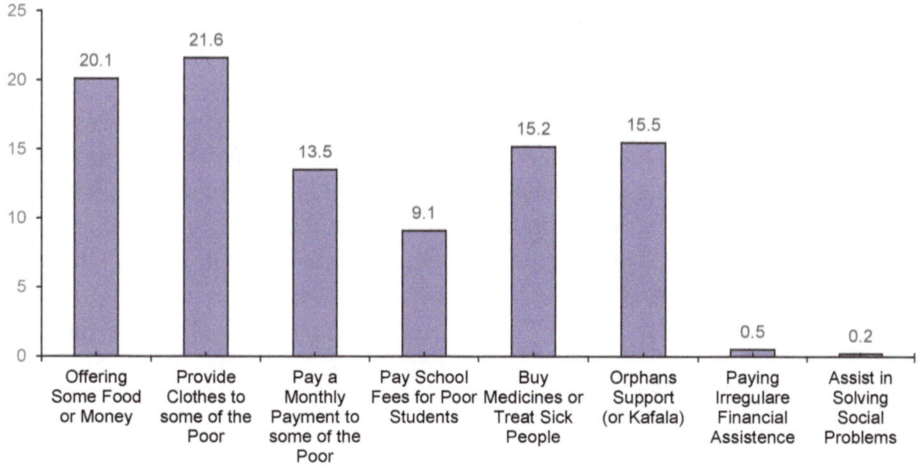

Figure 36: Type of Donations Most Prevalent among the Egyptian Public

As shown in the above Figure, it was evident that philanthropic contributions mostly go in the form of charity as clothes (216%), food (20.1%), medicine and orphans' food and shelter, while least given to solving social problems through sponsoring income-generating projects as explained to the respondents It is worth noting that investing in paying tuitions is also low. However, in a country claiming free education for all, maybe people feel less compelled to contribute. During the in-depth interviews, the tuition problem and the money that NGOs try to raise for that signals a phenomena, which reflects that philanthropy is drained in meeting the basic needs that are expected to be provided by the governmental system.

However, in the in-depth interviews, "Depending on the case" was the most common donors' response when it came to the choice between charity-oriented or development-oriented assistance. However, several donors complained that they faced serious problems when they tried to go for development oriented assistance by sponsoring certain projects. Problems included failure of projects or cases where dishonest beneficiaries took the donors' money and disappeared. Moreover, many donors resented philanthropy for development for several other reasons. One, being the concept of giving for development is not legitimate culturally. One of the donors who are also a board member of an NGO prefers to develop his NGO's activities towards development by giving small portions of capital for beneficiaries to start small projects. Yet, he has a partner who is not convinced with the idea. Several donors said the concept of starting projects is not realistic since it needs significant capital. That was explained by a donor who said, "No, unfortunately these things need big sums of money in order to make someone stand on his feet".

As donors are accustomed to person-to-person giving, donating for development is far-fetched. Development-oriented philanthropy is associated with allocating big bulks of money to start projects or invest in education. It is hence attributed to be the responsibility of the government and not to philanthropists in their eyes.

4.4.5.2 Community-Members Oriented Giving

We showed earlier peoples' tendency to give to their neighbors and relatives. It was noted in the in-depth interviews that the Diaspora Community have the same concept in directing philanthropies towards people of their villages and communities, either through building mosques or supporting family members. As to migrants within Egypt, who settle in Cairo or Alexandria and are originally coming from villages in Upper Egypt for instance, they also have affiliations to their communities and their philanthropy is directed to support members of their community living in the Cities or newcomers. The primary focal activity when they settle in the cities is to create a cultural club or an NGO. The most active initiatives and gatherings as such, as per our in-depth study, was the Nubians who hold remarkable support mechanisms for their communities in the big cities.

4.4.5.3 Rural-Urban Difference in Giving Practice

Table 28: Sample Ural/Urban Distribution

Area	Frequency	Percent
Rural	564	28.2
Urban	1436	71.8
Total	2000	100

This table highlights that 72% of the respondents live in urban areas while 28% live in rural ares. This, to a great extent, reflects the actual distribution of the Egyptian population, where the urban areas are inhabited by around 60% of the population.

In our attempt to assess whether there are differences in giving practices based on the geographic variation, it was evident that respondents who live in urban areas differ from those living in rural areas in the percentages of their giving of *zakāt* and *ṣadaqa*. As one can see from table (28) and (29) below in light of the percentages of those who contribute to charitable donations, rural-urban residence appeared to have a much more significant effect on the percentage of the people who donate either in cash or in-kind. The percentage point difference is +8.9 in favor of urban residents as it is clear from the data presented in Table 29. This might be explained by the fact that the inter-personal charities in urban areas that go to beggars and poor people in the city is much higher and consumes much of peoples' donations irrespective how much they pay their religious duties of *zakāt* and *ṣadaqa*. In rural areas, social and economic differences between people are minimal with a higher degree of social justice realized, while in bigger cities the gaps between people are huge. Hence *takāful* support mechanisms in the village rely mainly on the religious duty that each person gives, while their economic condition does not permit more contribution. However, the emotional *takāful* and support in the villages, especially in Aswan governorate, appeared to be much higher than the urban areas, as it turned to be an integral aspect of their daily lives. As one of the Chairpersons of the BoD in Aswan said, "The tradition we have is to cooperate with all the people both in their happiness and in their sadness." Another one said, "We are here like one family. The society and the family are interrelated, and if we hear that somebody has a clash with another, in the same night we gather together to talk to them and solve their problems."

Table 29: Rural–Urban Variation in the Practice of Islamic Philanthropy

	% Urban	% Rural	% Point Difference
Paying Zakat	93.9	91.0	+ 2.9
Paying Sadaqa	86.6	84.0	+ 2.6
Paying Donations	64.6	55.7	+ 8.9

Table 30: Rural-Urban Variation in the Practice of the Forms of Philanthropy

	% Urban	% Rural	% Point Difference
Monetary	95.0	94.3	0.7
In-Kind	36.9	24.9	12
Voluntary	10.7	9.6	1.1

4.4.5.4 Gender-Sensitive

It became evident, as one can see from table 31 that gender differences in religious philanthropy suggests that females adhere to Islamic teachings of paying *zakāt* and *ṣadaqa* more than men. As to donations in general men tend to donate more than females. These differences could be attributed to the fact that females are more connected and concerned with family members, relatives and neighbors. Hence, they are keener to pay their *zakāt* and *ṣadaqa* to causes they touch and feel for. Males on the other hand, due to the nature of the oriental way of life, are more often in cafés and on the road in general. This makes them interact with the needy and beggars on the streets and compels them to donate to such causes.

Table 31: Gender Differences in the Practice of Islamic Philanthropy

	% Male	% Female	% Point Difference
Paying Zakat	89.6	95.9	-6.3
Paying Sadaqa	85.5	86.2	-.7
Paying Donations	64.6	60.1	+4.5

Table 32: Gender Differences in the Practice of the Forms of Philanthropy

	% Male	% Female	% Point Difference
Monetary	94.9	94.7	0.2
In-Kind	28.9	38.1	-9.2
Voluntary	12.3	8.8	3.5

From the above table, it is noticed that there is no significant differences in the monetary donations between males and females while there is a difference in the in-kind donations. The reason behind that might be attributed to the fact that women are the ones who are aware and responsible for the in-kind properties of the family like clothes, blankets, etc. On the other hand, the table shows that the voluntary efforts made by males are more than females. The reason of this phenomenon is not clear, but could be due to the fact that men enjoy more freedom of movement than women in the Egyptian society.

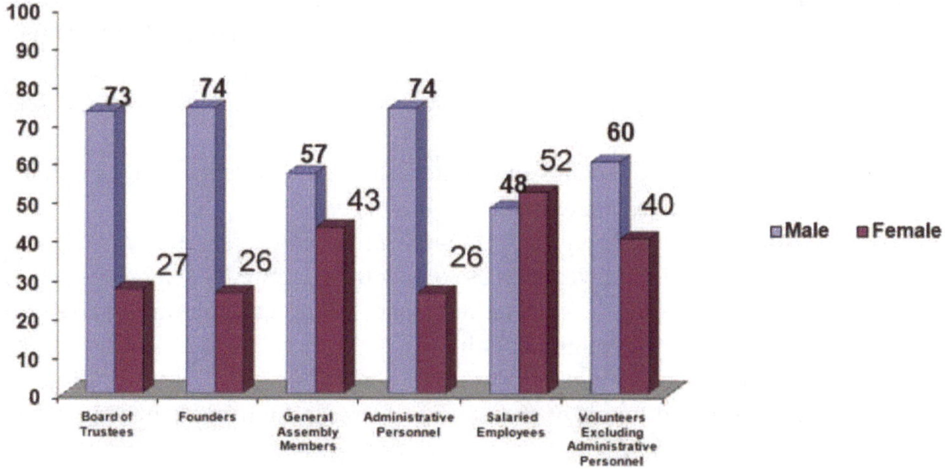

Figure 37: Organizational Membership by Gender

As it is evident in Figure 37, female representation is lower than males in most of the structure of the organizations, especially as founders, Board Members and the General Assembly. However, females outnumber males only in the category of salaried workers. This might be due to the low cost jobs at the NGOs that are delegated to women; also due to the fact that females have easier access to houses than males within the culture, therefore they are depended on more as extension workers.

4.4.5.5 Age Difference and Philanthropy

The study undertaken revealed that the age segment that mostly provides monetary donations is more concentrated on ages that are above 75, followed by 36–45, then 56–75. As for the segments of 36–45 and 46–55, they are the most segments that provide in-kind donations. Voluntary giving is more concentrated on the segments between 46–55, 56–75 and those below 25. As mentioned before, voluntarism becomes more attractive to mothers whose children became adults, men who are on pension and newly graduated unemployed youths.

4.5 Summary

The quantitative and qualitative interviews revealed that the religious motive is the strongest driving force behind philanthropic behavior for Muslims and Christians alike. This in return affects the fields and forms of giving, which translates into acts like giving to relatives and neighbors in response to different Quranic verses and Prophetic sayings promoting philanthropy to those who are close either through kin or geographically. Giving orphans is also among the highest preferences due to its religious importance, together with supporting mosques and churches. Contributions to build, renovate or maintain mosques is considered a form of *ṣadaqa jāriyya* or sustainable giving.

Secrecy in giving is a phenomenon spotted among the Muslims and Christians alike who believe in its high divine reward.

We also came across differences in philanthropic behaviors between rural and urban areas manifesting in motives such as serving the community at large, devotion and other motives that seemed to exist more among the rural communities and small Governorates than bigger cities such as Cairo.

Finally the chapter presented current philanthropic practices in Egypt through describing the nature and trends of giving and volunteering. It became evident that philanthropy in Egypt is mainly scattered, charity-oriented and mostly person-to-person based. On the other hand, it was revealed that the magnitude of local philanthropic contributions is considerably high and would yield big promises to the development process if properly mobilized and allocated.

5 Philanthropy between Theory, Present and the Future of Organized Philanthropy and the Rise of Community Endowed Foundations: Waqfeyat al Maadi Community Foundation (WMCF)

5.1 Introduction

This chapter deals with philanthropy at three levels: a) the theories on which philanthropy is based, highlighting peoples' hypothetical ideas and understandings of philanthropy from a theoretical abstract point of view and relating it to some practices. b) The actual practices of and the features distinguishing institutionalized philanthropy in Egypt; demonstrating the characteristics of a sample of existing philanthropic institutions, their establishment, mission, activities, etc.) Finally this chapter elaborates on the outcomes of this study as a whole, compiles the vision of interviewees for philanthropy in Egypt as well as articulates some recommendations to be taken into account.

Last but not least, the chapter presents a practical aspect to this field work symbolized by the actual establishment of a civic-led foundation that was founded by the researcher and now comprises a Board of Trustees of most prominent community members of the community of Maadi with the mission to revive and modernize the model of community *Waqf*.

5.2 Philanthropy at the Theoretical Level

The theoretical base of philanthropy is derived from two main sources;
1. The religious and faith-based heritages
2. Perceptions related to social justice.

The influence of Religion in its abstract form manifests in ideas such as the right-based approach to philanthropy; according to this approach, giving is believed to be the right of the receiver and not a benevolent act towards him/her. Theoretically people cognitively connect philanthropy to Qur'anic verses indicating the entitlement of the needy to a "recognized" or a set amount of one's income; hence in theory their giving is right-based. There are other theoretical backdrops that shape philanthropy stemming from religious teachings, yet there are also conjectural basis rooted in theories of social justice. The coming section discusses these theories in more details:

https://doi.org/10.1515/9783110697032-005

5.2.1 The Religious Basis of Philanthropy (Concepts and Related Practices)

As mentioned earlier, religion is the driving force behind philanthropy in Egypt. Faith-based giving is the most dominant characteristic and hence religious teachings and beliefs tend to shape the ideas that motivate giving. They give substance and provide a theoretical framework to the religious basis of philanthropy.

5.2.2 The Right Based Approach

Most Egyptians believe that giving is not a charitable donation for which they should be thanked. Rather, for them, it is a religious duty that should be cordially practiced, and what is called "the right of God" (*ḥaqqAllah*) and "the right of the poor" (*ḥaqqal faqīr*) must be given to those in need, out of one's income. Those who are entitled by virtue of right (due to their status) to receive *zakāt* and *ṣadaqāt*are listed in detail in the Qur'an. As one Chairman expressed it said reciting a verse in Qur'an that indicate that virtue and justice do not realize in praying but they are fulfilled in the belief in God, His messengers, angels and texts and in giving the needy out of his love, he cites the following verse from the Qur'an: "It is not righteousness that ye turn your faces towards East or West; But it is righteousness to believe in God, and the last day, and the Angels and the Book and the Messengers; to spend of your substance Out of love for Him, For your kin, For orphans, for the needy, for the wayfarer, for those who ask, and for the ransom of slaves, to be steadfast in prayer, and practice regular charity, to fulfill the contracts the contracts which ye have made and to be firm and patient in pain (or suffering) and adversity and throughout all periods of panic, such are the people of the truth, the God fearing." (Chapter 2 The Cow, verse 177).

In many aspects of the study it was confirmed that the respondents pay *Zakāt* because it is a religious compulsory order dictated by God (*farḍ*) and that is the right of the needy, not a volunteered benevolent act of giving. This right in people's perception is the right of God; as one respondent indicates, "the right of God given through people". Another indicated, "Giving the needy is not charity, it is a religious duty; as God says these acts of benevolence (*ṣadaqāt*) purify us, which means that by giving we serve ourselves more than anything. Here he recited the Qur'anic Verse that says: "take alms of their wealth, wherewith thou mayst purify them and mayst make them grow, and pray for them. Thy prayer is an assuagement for them. Allah is Hearer, Knower." (Chapter 9 Repentance, verse 103)

The Sufi groups go beyond material giving, and follow Prophet Mohamed's Saying that says, "Whoever has a gift should give back to he who has not". This means as a Sufi head of board explains that, "This gift is not only material, not only food or drink, but it is anything that Allah granted us like our senses. We should not use our senses only for us, we should give *zakāt* on our ability to see and our ability to hear by helping others who are deprived of these senses, he conducted". Finally, he recited some Sufi poetry that stipulates that even some nice words from someone who has nothing else to give, may keep him away from troubles and evil.

For Religious leaders, their engagement in channeling philanthropy to the poor is part of their mission in realizing human rights to the poor, especially *zakāt* is perceived by them as the "human right of the poor". One of them said, "*Zakāt* is the money of the poor. If the rich do not give the poor, this means that he stole money from the poor because giving is a right and a duty in Islam. It is not a donation, but it is a right." As for donors, most of them agreed that helping the poor and paying *zakāt* and *ṣadaqāt* is a duty. One of the donors explained, "This is what God asked me to do. It is the right of God that I owe Him through giving the poor." Even illiterate people who did not join schools, were able to recite verses from the Qur'an and sayings of the Prophet that encourage giving. As one of the beneficiaries stated, "He who alleviates the suffering of a brother out of the sufferings of the world, Allah would alleviate his suffering from the sufferings of the Day of Resurrection." However, although this right based approach is deeply rooted in the Egyptian philanthropic culture, most of the beneficiaries feel that the assistance they receive from individuals or from organizations is not their right, but an extra charity for which they should show gratitude. That was explained by one of the beneficiaries who said, "The assistance I get is small thing that helps, but after all, I should be grateful to the one who give to me." This feeling of gratitude exists more among the Christian recipients and as one of them explains, "the assistance that I get is not my right, but it is love that we receive from the church because it knows well our conditions". Another beneficiary states, "What I receive is not my right, it is help that I receive from the church and to which I should be thankful".

5.2.3 Prevention of Catastrophes Beliefs

It became evident that the culture of giving in Egypt is also connected with a sense of fear. This fear is manifested in the fear of envy and hatred from the poor and the fear of losing blessings as a kind of punishment from God if one does not abide to the duty of giving. This fear has been expressed by many donors, explaining that giving is important to save the society from envy and also to protect the blessings that they enjoy especially health, children and money. As one donor stated: "If I buy one Kilogram (kg) of fruits for myself, and another kg for a poor man, then he will not envy me and if his son dresses like my son, his son will not hate my son." It is remarkable that this concept of prevention of hatred and of losing blessings through giving has both a social and psychological base. However, it also has a religious base since one of the aims of philanthropy in Islam is to spread peace among members of the society and avoid the envious feelings that results when there are large gaps between the rich and the poor.

5.2.4 Giving for Development Beliefs

The research revealed that there is a close relation between philanthropy as construed by religion and development. Many respondents have referred to Prophet Mohamed when he refused to give donation to a man despite his poverty since he was young, healthy and capable of work. Instead of encouraging him to beg by giving him charity, he encouraged him to work and be a financially independent person. The Prophet asked him to sell his simple belongings to raise a capital that enables him to start a small project, which in his case was cutting and selling wood. The literate and to a certain extent cultured respondents who told this story considered this example given by the Prophet more than 1400 years ago a lesson of the importance of mobilizing local resources and ones' skills to develop and flourish.

However, and despite the significance of the referred to Prophet's Saying, very few respondents were aware of it. Some of those who were cultured attributed this general ignorance of the Saying to its deletion from the school curricula despite its existence in the school books in the past. In addition, there are several Sayings that have been mentioned by the prophet Mohamed that encourage work and development, but again, very few respondents were able to mention them. An example of these is, "The best earning is the one that a man gets from his work." In addition, several respondents, especially mosques' shaykhs affirmed that *Zakāt* is an economic tool to prevent the stagnation of resources. However, despite the fact that Islam has a wealth of resources that encourages growth and the allocation of philanthropy in ways that would boost development, this idea is generally absent in peoples' mind, which makes them perceive philanthropy only in the form of charity without envisioning it as an opportunity to make a real change. It remains a problem of theory versus practice, where generally Muslims in Egypt follow the path of prophet Mohamed (*Sunna*) in various aspects, yet to what concerns philanthropy this is not the case. This sheds the light on the importance of the exposure to sayings and stories as such and the gap created due to their absence from the education.

Hatem El Qaranshawy comments that in principal *Zakāt* money could be invested in the construction of factories, as well as invested in farms and other developmental income-generating projects. However, as the case in any investment, these projects should be carefully studied in advance. The main condition for the usage of *Zakāt* money in investment according to the Islamic *sharīʿa*; is the *Zakāt* receivers' ownership in the capital. This means, as El Qaranshawy explains, that in the case of industrial, commercial or agricultural projects the receivers should be share-holders and partners. This would compel them to work with more enthusiasm and hence a feeling of trust prevails and at the same time the ownership base expands. He continues that *Zakāt* mainly aims at enriching the poor and not simply meeting their basic needs; investing *Zakāt* in projects where transparency measures are applied would allow donors to follow up on their expenditures and share-holders to review the financial statement, expand their business and increase profit.

5.2.5 Promotion of Public Interests Belief

Islam is a religion that gives priority to public over private benefit. When asked from a religious view point about whether it is preferred for a Muslim to perform multiple pilgrimages (*Ḥajj*) and visit Makkah (*'Umra)* or to donate for the needy, all the *shaykhs* affirmed that donating money is much more preferred if one has already done pilgrimage once in her/his lifetime. As one of the *shaykhs* explained, "The first pilgrimage is a duty and must be done, but the second one is an extra effort (*nāfila*). Helping the poor in the community should have the priority over a second pilgrimage. The prophet (pbuh) was asked who is the person who is the best companion, he said the one who is most useful to people, and the best thing is to enter joy on a Muslim." Some *shaykhs* gave an example by mentioning with a story about Abdullah Ibn Mubarak who gave away all the money had saved to do pilgrimage in order to help a woman whose husband died without leaving her and her children anything to eat. When he came across this poor family on his way to Makkah, he gave them his camel and the savings he had sacrificing his personal benefit to perform *Ḥajj* for the interest of this needy family. However, after the end of the pilgrimage, some people came to congratulate him for seeing him in Mecca doing the pilgrimage. He was confused and then had a dream of someone telling him: "You rewarded a woman, and God rewarded you and sent an angel to do the pilgrimage on your part."

On the other hand, many of the interviewed beneficiaries expressed discontent when the issue of pilgrimage was discussed. They conveyed that they are provoked to see some of their well-off relatives go to the pilgrimage more than once while neglecting their severe conditions without help. They also criticized the companies that announce pilgrimage and *'Umra* prizes and expressed their desire to channel these prizes to philanthropy. These views were also evident in the results of the quantitative research since 82% of the respondents agreed that philanthropic activities should have the priority over the additional pilgrimage or *'Umra*. Despite the theory, at the practical level, it is evident that the private benefit, which is going to pilgrimage or *'Umra* more than once from a belief that this adds to one's heavenly credits, has the first priority among the majority of people. This reflects the preference to serve one's private interest even in seeking God's consent, over the public one, although it is religiously not correct.

5.2.6 Islam, Social Justice and Social Cohesion

Kamal Imam clarifies that the idea of social justice in the Western sense, whether the capitalistic or the socialist ideologies, is different that social justice in the Islamic perspective. In Islam, social justice is based on three aspects:

The first is an aspect of conviction, where people believe that they are the caliphs of God on earth. This conviction makes them share a sense of ownership in the earth, where they are also entitled to acknowledge others' rights in this ownership and the right of others in parts of their incomes (*Zakāt*). Thus, this brings the issue and the responsibility further than fulfilling a religious duty, and closer to a social responsibility and mission. The second aspect is the legislative part, which acknowledges private ownerships and sees that development is achieved through individual ownerships. Through inheritance laws, one knows that his/her possessions would go to their offspring and accordingly people are compelled to work more, from a belief that this effort will not be lost but would eventually go to ones' beloved. The third aspect is the role of the government in collecting philanthropy money and distributing it on the needy. Thus, the government has the right to intervene and employ these resources. Some religious analysts went to the extreme by demanding enforcement measures on the rich people to pay the due money to the needy as it is their acknowledged right. Kamal Imam continues that accordingly, the theory of social justice in Islam seems to be accomplished: as the rich people are Caliphs to God on earth, so are the poor people. There is no difference between rich and poor as they have exactly the same legal position. This is utmost justice. As to justice in the legislation, this lies in the fact that whatever one owns is not absolute. Hence, it is not ones duty to distribute possessions and transfer them from big ownerships to small ownerships but rather through the rich giving to the poor what enables him/her to be productive.

Imam continues that the different ranks between the rich and the poor do not contradict justice. He argues that the status does not necessitate that the rich remains rich or that the poor maintains his/her poverty. Religion teaches us that the earth created by God is vast and people should be proactive and work their best to wonder around looking for possibilities and move the development wheel. As to those who imagine that being poor is part of fate, they adopt a retarded philosophical position. The idea of fate originates in whatever is written in the divine knowledge and is not known for human beings; thus, how would one knows it if it is destined for him/her to remain poor or sustain being rich. Therefore *Zakāt* is prescribed to be given to adjectives and not to specific people because poverty characterizes people now who might be rich tomorrow.

On this point, Abd el Hafez Al-Sawy comments that people do not need to be all on the same level to reflect social justice. For him, social justice does not mean equal division of resources. In agreement Mashhour Neamat maintains that social justice in Islam is not meant to reflect quantitative justice where people are entitled to receive exactly the same resources. Social justice philanthropy in Islam, she emphasizes is manifested in the idea of *ḥadd al kifāya* (the limit for sufficiency) where philanthropy meets the level of sufficiency of the recipients.

Some of the *Shāfiʿī* and *Ḥanbalī*groups, El Qaranshawy adds, put the condition that philanthropy should be directed to bring those in need and the poor out of their poverty and not simply to meet some of their needs. The main aim is to enable them to reach their subsistence level in order to empower them to start helping themselves forward. If, for instance, there is a merchant or a businessperson who is in need for equipments to undertake a project or rescue his/her business, philanthropy should aim to provide him/her with whatever equipments that enable him/her to work and make a living out of the profit. Philanthropy could take the form of providing an agrarian land to somebody, which would be a sustainable source of work and income to him/her and their families.

However, the challenge still stems from the absence of a strategic plan for the future where all the local resources are constructively used to face the problem of social justice and to move on from just fulfilling the basic needs towards opening the door for a sound and sustainable development.

5.2.7 Social Justice Theory Basis (Concepts and Related Practices)

Social justice refers to an ideal society where justice refers not to the administration of law, but to an economic status. Different ideological, political and social economic systems have presented different views on social justice and methods to reaching it. Below the study attempts to, present a number of concepts and practices from an Egyptian point of view and according to respondents of study surveys.

5.2.7.1 Social Justice and the Divine Will

A limited view of the theory of Social justice as a concept and as related to religion can be a major challenge to development work. Theology in such cases may be interpreted in ways becoming a hindrance rather than a catalyst for positive change. Hence, social justice is one of the most crucial concepts that this study addresses, and it became evident, that some respondents relate it to religion and understand this relation in a misguided way. To many of them, achieving social justice among people is not the responsibility of human beings; it is rather God's role to distribute His wealth and to enrich or impoverish whom He wishes this position was reflected in the answers of many respondents, as one of them said, "It is God who distributed His wealth on people. This is something related to God. Justice is God's role and we can't as human beings achieve it."

The threat that underlines the position that relates social justice to God's duty lies in the fatalistic approach that emerge among many people and makes philanthropy for social justice impossible.

In this case, the poor surrender to poverty without trying to affect change since poverty is God's will; and on the other hand the rich views the condition of the poor as God's will and accordingly does not relate their status to issues of social justice. Therefore, to some donors, their philanthropic contributions are merely ways to fulfill religious and social duties and/or to satisfy their human psychological needs with no real attempt to achieve social justice.

5.2.7.2 Social Justice through Job Opportunities

The majority of respondents believed that reducing the gap between the rich and the poor is a difficult matter. Most donors were skeptic about the possibility to achieve social justice through philanthropy. Donors in general held the view, at least in theory, that philanthropy should help create job opportunities and income-generating projects and, in turn pave the way for productivity and self-dependency. One donor explained, "There is nothing called the rich donating to the poor, this is not the correct way to enhance his social and economic status. The rich must provide job opportunities to the poor that will enable him to enhance himself. There might be variations in incomes between people, but most importantly is to have all earn enough to provide them with a decent life", he concluded. Another believes that "investing in projects that employs people is social justice philanthropy." Finally, another donor affirmed that, "The society that lives just on receiving charity is a society based on slavery. But if there is a redistribution of wealth and resources where every person gets an opportunity to work and to live decently, things will change to the better." However, these points of view remain in theory. Most donors, Muslims and Christians alike, indicated that they are satisfied with their philanthropies mostly because they fulfilled their religious obligations (96.8% Muslims and 92.2% Christians) and accomplished self-satisfaction and peace of mind (96.8% Muslims and 96.4% Christians).

As for recipients, they generally find the assistance they get marginal and definitely not satisfying their needs. Social justice for them is an impossibility. The respondents symbolizing the needy sector are desperate for a decent life; however, for them issues such as closing the gaps between the rich and the poor are not attainable or even imaginable. "The eye will always remain under the eye-brow" (*al ʾayn mā tiʾlash ʾan al ḥā*jib) which is an Egyptian saying meaning that the lower levels of society will never be able to reach higher standards, one respondents expressed; "all what we need is just a decent life", she concluded.

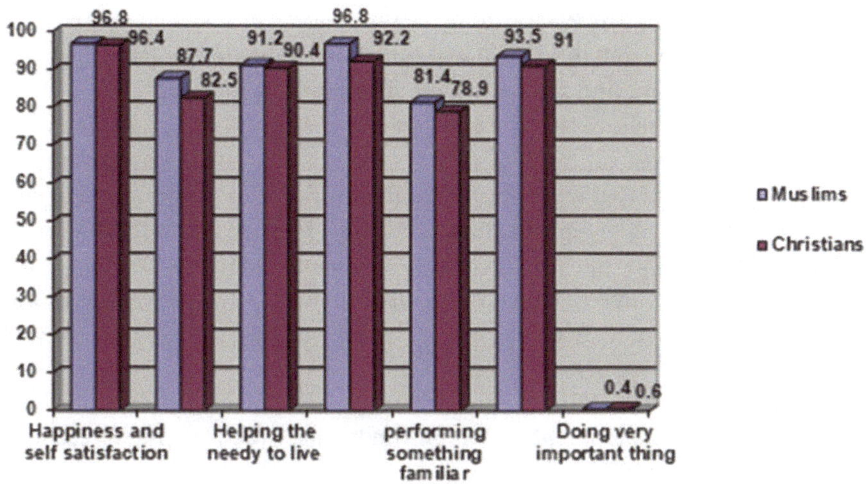

Figure 38: What Does a Philanthropist Feel When He/She Engages in Charitable Giving?

5.2.7.3 Social Justice and the Role of the Government

Another problem lies in peoples' expectations from the government and limiting issues of social justice to this governmental role. Social justice philanthropy is accordingly a restricted concept, because people do not see civil society capable of responding to issues of significance on the macro-level. However, the intensive interviews with respondents reveal that people share ideas on how to decrease widening gap between people and on restoring principles of social justice philanthropy. As one respondent expressed, in order to achieve social justice, we need to generally understand what this concept implies. We need a public vision and a national mission that we seek to achieve, he concluded. Another affirmed that the solution lies in strengthening civil society and in enabling this sector to be of pressure on the policy makers to protect the poor and the marginalized and to lift injustices. He continued that strengthening civil society should be connected to a change policy within the Ministry of Social Affairs (MoSA).

5.2.7.4 Social Justice and Religious Institutions

As for the religious institutions, achieving the concept of social justice in terms of strengthening the poor by assisting them in establishing sustainable sources of income or creating job opportunities for them is absent. However, like most of the civil society institutions in Egypt, the majority of religious philanthropic organizations interviewed in this study adopted the mission to serve the poor by responding to their severe poverty, and meeting their basic needs. Some of them have perceived their activities as an effort to achieve social justice by describing it as an attempt to redistribute wealth. As one of the Sheiks said, "I take from those who have and give to those who have not."

Another *shaykh* said, "The objective is saving peoples' lives. The one who doesn't find food, we provide him with food, the one who doesn't find clothes, we provide him with clothes, the one who doesn't find shelter, we provide him with shelter".

Some of the *shaykhs* believe that the concept of taking *zakāt* and *ṣadaqāt* to distribute them on the poorest of the poor contributes to social justice philanthropy, while others are convinced that investing *ṣadaqāt* in projects for the poor and in creating job opportunities is indispensable to achieve social justice philanthropy. However, the challenge remains that the civic sector is overwhelmed with emergency needs without having developed a collective strategic plan for alleviating poverty and dealing with issues of social justice.

5.2.8 Moving Towards Development: Between Theory and Practical Challenges

As mentioned above, although most of the respondents are aware of the difference between the concept of development and that of charity, the dominant trend that is exercised in Egypt is ad-hoc charity. Below the study explores the prevalent forms of giving in Egypt and recommends ways to move towards a developmental giving approach

5.2.9 Prevalent Forms of Giving in Egypt

As seen in Figure 39, which explores the types of assistances that is provided to beneficiaries, charity is the most prevalent form of giving.

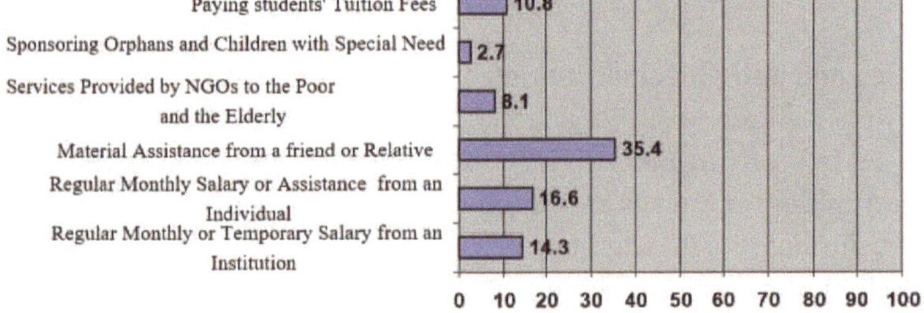

Figure 39: Types of Services Provided to Recipients

As we can see from the above figure, 35.4% of the poor respondents, representing the poor in Egypt, rely on assistance from friends or relatives which is a restively high percentage that signals the practice of kinship-philanthropy. Another significant result is the dismal percentage of 1.3% poor respondents receiving assistance in the form of a capital to start up a project. It became evident that this small percentage of poor people receives this kind of assistance only from some institutions and almost none receive capital to start up projects from individual philanthropists. In the qualitative interviews we did come across some cases where donors mentioned to have given assistance in the form of capital or equipments to help the recipients help themselves. However, this is an insignificant percentage as confirmed by the quantitative results.

It was accordingly important for us to find out what people think about these phenomena and whether they find it possible, from a future perspective, to eventually channel giving and direct it to serve development. Thus we asked respondents about whether they think it's possible to redirect local philanthropic resources to development projects, as shown in the Figure (40) below, and a vast majority of (74.2%) of the Egyptians public believed that it was possible while (21.5%) found it difficult. This segment attributes their position to the fact that giving to charity is much easier and does not consume much thinking, especially when direct charitable assistance to meet immediate basic needs requires their contributions.

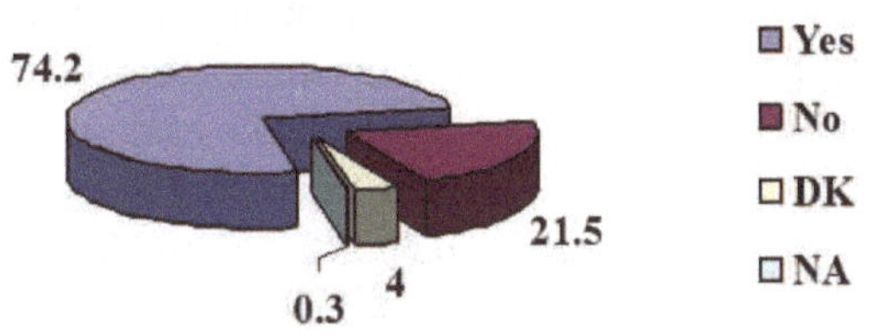

Figure 40: Possibility to Direct of Philanthropic Activities to a set of Development Projects instead of Charity

5.2.10 Challenges facing Philanthropy for Development

Looking in more details at the reasons that were given by the 21.5% who believe that channeling philanthropy towards development is not possible, Figure 41 highlights that 64% believe that *ṣadaqāt* (in this context indicating charity) is faster in meeting the immediate needs of the poor.

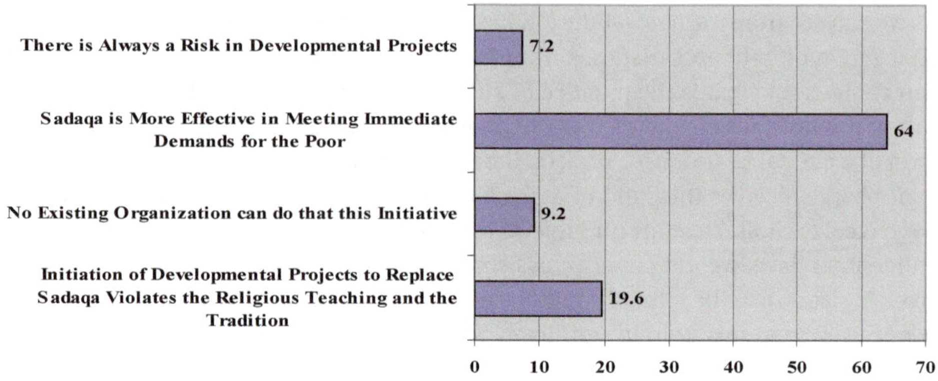

Figure 41: Reasons behind the Reluctance to Initiate Developmental Projects

For many, poverty is so much spread and a vast amount of people are deprived of their basic needs, to an extent that necessitates the priority to respond to them rapidly by charitable means. It is also indicated that 19.6% believe that their giving should go to charity because putting it into development projects contradicts with the teaching of Religion; a point of view that should be seriously investigated and put into consideration when thinking about the religious messages given by *shaykhs*. Another interesting number given is the 9.2% who attribute their position to the nonexistence of organizations in charge of development work. Although this is not the majority, yet it is a considerable percentage that should not be neglected and which reflects a considerable portion of people who are not aware of the existence and role of development organizations. On the other hand, 7.2% feel that there is always a risk in developmental projects and accordingly prefer charity. This problem does not only face individual donors, but also Chairpersons of the NGOs who do not prefer to undertake development-related programs like small loans projects for instance, fearing that this would bring more trouble than good. Especially in Aswan Governorate we came across many, so called development practitioners working in NGOs who did not accept the idea of small-loans projects because they prefer grants and donations that respond to direct needs. This is a culture that prefers easy meeting the needs money than investments in people that is more long term and difficult to assess. Hence, changing such a culture is in return not an easy task and requires education, awareness, the display of successful local models that initiated change and the introduction of strategies on the application of development techniques.

The intensive interviews carried out with respondents enabled us to gather more practical reasons that hamper philanthropy for development. The coming section reveals the outcomes of our intensive discusses with respondents indicating the reasons behind the tendency to donate to charitable causes and not development-oriented activities from the point of view of donors and receivers.

5.2.10.1 The Small Amounts of Donations

Most donors, even those who believe in development, are among the middle-class donors who either donate small amounts of money or volunteer that can not be effectively used for development or with their efforts by being members in an NGO or a mosque. As one of these donors explained, "If I could build a factory to absorb unemployment, I would have done that. But in reality, I could only afford to donate for charity" As a result of the limited amount of donations by each, most people haphazardly channel their donations directly to the poor and the needy. As for those donors who channel their donations to organizations to be distributed on beneficiaries, the great majority of beneficiaries find it impossible to use the tiny amount they get to establish an income-generating project. As one beneficiary stated, "The L.E 20 that I receive monthly can never start up a project. The start up fund should be at least L.E 1500." Therefore it is the norm that only institutions working with international grant-making associations provide capital to start-up projects; individual philanthropists and small philanthropic organizations tend to limit their activities to charity.

5.2.10.2 The Priority to Meet Basic Needs

Poverty and the miserable economic conditions of a large segment of the population in Egypt compel philanthropists and philanthropic organizations to direct available resources to meet basic needs like food and medication. Even philanthropists and associations who believe in the importance of philanthropy for development lack the proper agenda and follow the vicious circle of donating to meet basic needs. One of the donors explained, "When I first feed him, second I could provide him with education. There is a segment that is really under the line of poverty and accordingly need direct charitable assistance." Aid-recipients in NGOs could not agree more. Whether sick, being unable to work, or supporting orphans, all agree that they need the charity they receive, yet wish to be enabled to work to sustain their living. A grandmother who takes care of her grandchild indicated that the grant from the mosque is an orphan-sponsorship for her grandchild, yet it would be much better if she finds the means to own a small project to support their living and secure the future of the child.

This charity or development investment is not an easy decision to make; however in light of the absence of a development agenda by civil society practitioners and by visionary philanthropists, philanthropy resources are directed to respond to charitable needs. In this process most resources are not effectively used or do not reach the most disadvantaged. In orphanages, especially in occasions, plenty of resources are spent to buy food for the orphans and in most cases not necessarily basic food, but chocolates and junk food in abundance. This mismanagement of resources is one consequence of the tendency to give for charity, especially in the absence of a strategic plan for poverty eradication.

5.2.10.3 Lack of Experience among the Beneficiaries to Run a Development Project

Most beneficiaries do not have the expertise to start up a small project and run it successfully. As the intensive interviews clarified, a number of beneficiaries did attempt to start new projects, but lacking skills and experience led their initiatives to fail. According to one of the beneficiaries, "I tried starting up a small project before; I used to make cheese and sell it, but I lost. If I had succeeded, I would have been able to buy a room to live in." The problem that often confronts beneficiaries is marketing; especially that most of the projects that they start are similar to each other's, due to their simplicity to comply with their abilities and skills. In addition, most of the philanthropic organizations are not able to make successful feasibility studies to ensure the elements of success in the project carried out by beneficiaries.This scheme needs to be developed by development practitioners and the private sector has a space to excel in demonstrating its social responsibility in the form of consultancies to small initiatives as such.

5.2.10.4 Lack of Trust among the Donors

Another problem that hinders funding to small income-generating projects is the lack of trust among donors visa vie the needy and the philanthropic organizations alike. Some donors mentioned that they had a negative experiences with beneficiaries when they tried to help them establish a project by providing the seed capital. Most of theses donors expressed their disappointment because in many cases the beneficiaries took the capital claiming the project failed or in some instances even sold the equipments they have received from the private philanthropists.

5.2.10.5 The Beneficiaries' Health and Age Conditions

To some beneficiaries, the concept of development can not be applicable due to their current circumstances, especially bad health or old age. That was mentioned by a beneficiary by saying, "It is over for someone like me. Being 75 or 80 years old, shall we still think of a project? All what I could think about is to eat and drink in the remaining days I shall live."

5.2.10.6 The Organizations' Focus on Charitable Activities more than Development

It was evident that most organizations concentrate their activities on giving charitable aid to poor families or on providing services to the needy more than on creating job opportunities or initiating developmental projects that invest in empowering their target communities. This trend has affected beneficiaries who had wished to start projects to support themselves and their families. As one daily worker in an NGO indicated: "NGOs give only to the people in need; they do not provide loans and grants to people start up projects". This reflects the mental division between people in need, who are associated with receiving regular or non-regular assistances and those who wish to receive funds to start up small projects.

5.2.10.7 The Culture of Dependency among the Beneficiaries

The intensive interviews revealed that many beneficiaries got used to take advantage of peoples' giving and to easily rely on asking the help of others. This developed carelessness and dependency limiting their own ability to seek their inner strength to improve the quality of their lives. One of the *shaykhs* termed this "prevailing attitude" as the "professional begging", which "became a widespread phenomenon among many Egyptians", he said. That was also explained by one donor who mentioned, "There is someone I know who wanted money to buy vegetables and sell them. After two months, she came back to ask for money again. When I asked her if the project was not working, she said yes it is, but I need more money from you."

5.2.10.8 The Government's Bureaucratic Obstacles

Bureaucracy and governmental red tape facing development of new projects discourages NGOs and private philanthropists from taking this route. Many are reluctant ant to help when it comes to facing bureaucratic headaches. As one NGO's Chairperson described, "There are a lot of problems that we face in order to obtain the Governmental approval to establish a small kiosk for example. The problem in the cities is more serious than in villages. In villages, they are all relatives, or they know each other and the rules are softer, but in big cities, the procedures are long and decisions are firm."

5.3 Philanthropy at the Institutional Level

5.3.1 Description of the Sample

A sample of 1200 philanthropic organization was selected from the Ministry of Social Affair's directory issued in 1997/98, where quantitative interviews were conducted with Chairpersons and board members of these institutions. The qualitative study selected a 3% sample, which constitutes 58 institutions of those included in the sample frame, with a total of 120 in-depth interviews with Directors, donors and beneficiaries taking place. In addition in-depth interviews have been conducted in 19 mosques and 6 churches that are socially active.

5.3.2 Location of the Organizations & Religious Institutions

Approximately 60% of the quantitative sample organizations are operating in Cairo, Giza and Alexandria. Organizations in the Nile Delta and Upper Egypt represent 30%

and 9% respectively. These organizations were distributed over 10 Governorates, namely: Cairo, Giza, Alexandria, Sharkeya, Menofeya, Gharbeya, Aswan, Menia, Qena and South-Sinai.

As for the qualitative research, 57 organizations were interviewed in six governorates, namely Cairo, Giza, Alexandria, Gharbeya, Menia ad Aswan. This is in addition to 19 mosque and 6 churches.

Table 33: The Location of the Sampled Organizations

Governorates	Frequency	Percent
Cairo (Metropolitan Areas)	392	32.7
Giza	138	11.5
Alexandria	197	16.4
Sharkeya	156	13.0
Menofeya	129	10.8
Gharbeya	73	6.1
Aswan	19	1.6
Menia	64	5.3
Qena	23	1.9
South-Sinai	9	.8
Total	1200	100.0

As to urban-rural distribution of NGOs in the quantitative study, as highlighted by Figure 42, the majority o NGOs (84.2%) are located in urban areas. In the qualitative interviews, 83% were located in urban areas (18.6%) of them were located in shanty places and (23.25%) in rural areas. The mosques and churches intensively interviewed were distributed as follows: 15 mosque in urban areas and 4 in rural ones; and 5 churches in urban areas and only one in a rural area.

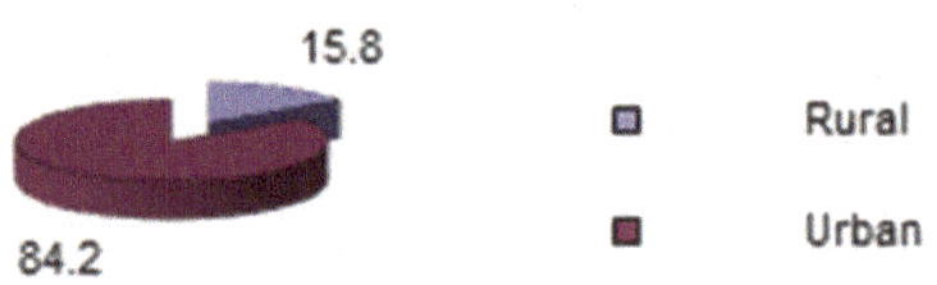

Figure 42: Rural-Urban Distribution of the Quantitative Sample Organizations

5.3.3 Who Was Interviewed?

Table 34: Interviewers' Positions in the Organizations

Po Position Held	Frequency	Percent
Chairperson of the Board	28	23.8
Vice-Chairman	33	2.8
Executive Director	304	25.3
Deputy Executive Directors	3	.3
Financial Manages	189	15.8
Administrative Clerks	105	8.8
Volunteers	11	.9
Members	21	1.8
NA	249	20.7
Total	1200	100.0

Most of the interviews were conducted with the Chairpersons of the NGOs, and the above table (40) presents the occupations of the interviewed persons within the organizations:

As shown in Figure 42 above, (84.2%) of the organizations in the quantitative research are located in urban areas, while only (15.8%) are located in rural areas. As for the qualitative research, (83.2%) are located in urban areas, (18.6%) of which are in slum areas while (23.25%) are located in rural areas. As for the 19 mosques, 15 of them are in urban areas and the remaining 4 are in rural areas. Only 1 interviewed church is located in rural area and the rest are in urban areas.

5.4 Volunteerism in the Civic Sector

According to our sample, more than 66.4% of those who occupy positions in the organizations are volunteers who do not receive any financial benefit for their time, while only 33.4% take salaries for their work in the organizations. When we tried to investigate their occupations outside the organization, it became clear that about 70% of them are professionals and businesspersons. The following table shows the occupation characteristics of the respondents in details:

Table 35: Occupation Characteristics of Respondents

Occupation	Frequency	Percent
Professionals (Doctor, Lawyers, Teachers...)	217	42.6
Owners of Private Projects	137	26.9
Administrative Occupations	98	19.3
Salesmen	1	0.2
Service Workers	10	2.0
Social Development Workers	25	4.9
Working in Agriculture	1	0.2
Skilled Workers	9	1.8
Army or Police Officer	4	0.8
Total	502	100

Within mosques, the size of employees and volunteers is an indicator of the size of the mosques and the activities that are carried out. The majority of the studied mosques have a combination between volunteers and employees. The employees vary in number depending on the size of the mosque. In small mosques, the number of employees varies between two to three, who are mostly government employees appointed by the Ministry of Awqaf. *Awqāf* employees are mainly workers, the imam and the mu'dhin. In big mosques, employees may reach more than 250 workers. It is noticed that the mosques that have the biggest number of service oriented and to an extent development-related activities, are those who employ the biggest numbers of workers.

In churches, there are people who offer their services in the church as volunteers. These are called " Khaddām" or servants; these are the social workers in the churches. Some of them donate their money, effort and time to the activity which they are in charge of serving, which reflects their utter conviction and commitment to such work. Volunteers in the churches included in our intensive interviews, ranged between 85 and 350. However some pastors said that all the members of the community volunteer in different activities.

It was also observed that the more recent the organization, the heavier it depends on volunteers. Our survey indicated that 23.4% of those doing work for local NGOs receive a salary while 66.3% are volunteers. The following table shows the average number of their weekly volunteered hours within philanthropic organizations.

Table 36: Average Number of Weekly Hours Spent within the Organizations

Number of Hours	Frequency	Percent
Less than 25 Hours per Week	460	38.3
25–49 Hours	424	35.3
50–74 Hours	219	18.3
75–99 Hours	23	1.9
100 Hours and More	15	1.3
Total	1141	95.1
NA	59	4.9
Total	1200	100

Our intensive interviews with respondents also revealed that even those salaried workers contribute by volunteering extra working hours to the organizations they work for. For instance, one of the employees in an NGO said, Any person works according to the working hours and to the salary he/she gets, but here I do not strictly follow the working hours indicated. As long as work needs me, I stay. So at times I am an employee and at others I am a volunteer. I am an employee during my working hours and volunteer when I exceed my working hours."

5.4.1 Reasons behind Volunteering

The motivation chart that contains the reasons for joining the organizations is diversified. The respondents were asked to choose multi-answers variants. From the answers received, it was found that there are points of similarities and differences between the motives behind giving in general and those behind volunteering. The similarity is manifested in the religious motive, which is common in all kinds of giving either material or voluntary. On the other hand, the care for the general welfare of the society did not have the same weight among donors in general as much as it did among volunteers. In addition, unlike volunteering in NGOs, gaining a social status and respect in the community was not considered as a motive among individuals who provide material donations. The following figure shows in details the reasons behind volunteering in certain NGOs:

Figure 43: Motives behind Volunteering in Philanthropic Organizations

As evident from the above Figure 43, volunteering to abide to a religious duty is the first motive (17.7%), followed by almost the same rate of (17.5%) of the respondents volunteering to fulfill a feeling of satisfaction for doing social volunteer work. The sense of responsibility towards the whole society exists among 17.1% of the volunteers, while developmental motive is shared by 16.9% of the volunteers. In addition, and in spite of the religious motive also behind volunteering, there is no direct relationship between volunteering and pleasing Allah/God. Only 0.4% related their volunteering to pleasing God. This might relate to a different interpretation of the right of God (*ḥaqq Allah*) in this volunteer work; a concept seen in material giving but not in volunteering time and effort, which is regarded a religious duty but not as the right of God. This is an interesting finding, especially that *ṣadaqāt* in its theoretical sense significantly include non-material giving such as a kind word, hospitality to strangers and all forms of assistance to the general public by lifting harm off the road for example (*izālat al adhā ʾan al ṭarīq*). Also different from the motives behind material giving, (14.5%) of the volunteers indicated that they volunteer their time and effort to gain status and respect among members of their society; a motive that was denied to be a driving force behind material giving which was characterized to be secretive and discrete.

5.5 The Establishment of NGOs, Mosques and Churches:

In this section we attempt to highlight the reasons behind and environment surrounding the establishment of NGOs, mosques and churches in the light of our sample.

5.5.1 The Establishment of NGOs

The survey revealed that 79% of the NGOs were established by simple ordinary individuals. Between 5% and 13 % of the NGOs were established by community leaders and government officials. This indicates that most NGOs in our representative sample are born by local initiatives and ordinary individuals.

Table 37: Who Initiated the Establishment of the Organization?

	Frequency	Percent
A Group of Natural Community Leaders	101	8.4
A Group of Ordinary Individuals	949	79.1
A Number of Government Officials	58	4.8
An Influential Individual	70	5.8
Don't Know	17	1.4
Total	1195	99.6
NA	5	.4
Total	1200	100

That it is a legal obligation as shown by 32% of the responses. It is a legal requirement stipulated by Law 84 of 2002 which demands that at least 10 persons should sign a petition to form an NGO, and this group of persons should serve as board members.

Our intensive interviews revealed different phases in the evolution of NGOs. In some areas they started as tents (*khayma*) where people met to discuss their problems and carry out social activities until they were eventually declared as NGOs and acquired a fixed location. As one NGO manager in Aswan Governorate indicated, "Our NGO did not evolve from vanity; it is a natural development of our original tent, then to what we called a hospitality place or hostel (*maḍāfa*).

5.5.2 The Establishment of Mosques and Churches

Most of the mosques in our ample were built by community efforts or by wealthy individuals. People who are after the great credit of *ṣadaqāt jāriyya* are those who contribute in building and supporting mosques. In our sample, most mosques were built by donations collected by NGOs for that purpose or by individuals. There are also a number of mosques built by collective efforts in collaboration with the Diaspora communities who prefer to donate to their villages; their contributions go mainly to the construction of mosques from their belief in the importance of this form of donation as a *ṣadaqāt jāriyya*. Finally, some mosques are historical monuments, some of which were built by rulers in earlier centuries, including the 7th and 9th centuries.

In general and although most of the mosques were built by community efforts and resources, the Ministry of Awqaf put them under its direct management and supervision to become what is termed as the "*Awqāf Mosques*".

As to churches, their establishment does not differ much from mosques. They were mainly built by groups of Christian communities living in the same geographical area who felt the need for the existence of a church in their neighborhoods. Churches are built under the supervision of the Bishopric and upon the approval of the security authorities. They are constructed and maintained by community donations, and are mostly maintained by the priests, volunteers, and the efforts of the Christian community in the area.

5.5.3 The Size of NGOs

Table 38: The General Assembly of NGOs

Members	Frequency	Percent
Less than 10*	172	14.3
11–20	389	32.4
21–30	217	18.1
31–40	84	7.0
41–50	63	5.3
51–60	26	2.2
61–70	17	1.4
71–80	9	.8
81–90	5	.4
91–100	11	.9
101–200	26	2.2
201–300	10	.8
401–500	5	.4
500+	62	5.2
Total	1096	91.3
DK	104	8.7
Total	1200	100.0

* These organizations may have been established under Law number 32 of year 1964 or Law number 153 of year 1999 since the new Law 84 of year 2002 requires that the members should not be less than 7.

The table shown above indicates that (65%) of the NGOs have a general assembly that is less than 30 members reflecting the small size of NGOs in general.

5.6 History of NGOs

Civic work and an active social society is not the creation of the 20th century in Egypt. The establishment of *waqf* foundations and different social service structures in Egypt dates hundreds of centuries back in history. In the 8th century, during the Omayad era and after with the Abbasids, the *waqf* endowment-structures flourished and became very popular among the masses. A lot of people established endowments not only to provide services for the poor and needy, but the role of these endowments extended to establish education centers and support students, teachers, research and development. In line with this, structures to control and supervise theses overwhelmingly wealthy non-governmental social structures developed as well; from the 8th century Omayad *Dīwān Al Awqāf* [83] controlled the what used to be autonomous civic structures to the Ministry of Awqaf today, endowment-foundations in Egypt lived long phases of ups and downs. In the 19th century Egypt, there was a legislative movement that aimed primarily at introducing western legislation to these traditional social civic structures[84]. In this century the form of NGOs as a western structure was introduced and from here the establishment of modern forms of civic structures took shape.

5.6.1 Brief Overview on the History of NGOs in the 20th Century Egypt

Thus, the form of NGOs as exist today is a phenomenon that started to emerge and spread in the 19th century. Yet until the 20th century, and exactly in 1918, the number of private voluntary NGOs in Egypt did not exceed 260 organizations. These organizations were mostly concerned with enhancing political and cultural awareness as well as responding to social needs such as health and education.

Ever since the beginning of the creation of NGOs in their modern structure, the history of NGOs has passed through several phases starting from the beginning of the 20th century[85]. In brief, these phases can be summed up as follows:

83 The Diwan Al Ahbas was established during the reign of Hisham Ben Abdel Malak in the Omayad Period in Wgypt.

84 See Mohamed Kamal Imam. Al Wasaya wa Alawqf fil Shari'a Al-Islamiya. Alexandria: Mansha'at Al Ma'aref, 2002.

85 Samak, Nagwa Abdallah. Al Keta· Al Ahli wal Tanmeya Al Iktesadiya fy Misr. Center for the Study of Developing Countries, Cairo, 1999.

5.6.1.1 Phase I (1900–1937)

The first phase started after the 1919 revolution, which had an ideological effect on the creation of civic structures that are able to respond to the community's social, economic and political needs. During around the same time, the first social service schools were founded firstly in Alexandria in 1936, then in Cairo in 1937.

5.6.1.2 Phase II: (1939–1952)

In 1939, the Ministry of Social Affairs (MoSA) was founded to supervise the work of NGOs. At that time, voluntary organizations started to flourish and increase in number and activities. They enjoyed the freedom to collect donations from diverse segments of the society without any restrictions. However, with the introduction of law number 49 of year 1945, this freedom to collect donations was conditioned with a special permission granted by the Ministry.

5.6.1.3 Phase III (1952–1973)

The 1952 revolution was accompanied with a significant increase in the government's bureaucracy and control over almost all aspects of the society. In 1956, law number 384 concerned with civil society organizations was issued to modify the constitutions of these organizations and the establishment of new unions to coordinate and supervise the social services provided by NGOs. This law was a turning point in the relation between the government, civil society organizations, and the society. At that time, NGOs were put under strict supervision from the part of the government. It was the beginning of a phase of mistrust between the two parties, which was a stage of decline for civil society organizations.

In 1964 the socialist government in Egypt introduced the five-year plan and law number 32 was issued confining the role of civil society organizations to social services and totally prohibiting their interference in of the work of syndicates. Figures show that the development of civil society organizations in the sixties was quite low. There were around 3,198 organizations in 1960 and they reached only 4000 NGOs in 1964 with an average annual increase of only 200 NGOs. At that time, community development associations (CDAs) were developed by the government as semi-governmental semi-communal structures engaged in social work. As they are initiated and established by the government, they were considered and function as governmental tools for social development replacing locally and individually initiated civil-society organizations.

5.6.1.4 The Phase from the 1970s to the Present

In the 70s, with the shift in the government's regime and the introduction of more liberal economic policies and especially the open door policy, the government began to withdraw and reduce its responsibilities as the sole provider of services in the country. Philanthropy was no exception. In addition, in the 1980s, the Egyptian economic crisis started to swell, which led to the application of a comprehensive program for economic reform based on the dependence on the market, the switch from the public to private sector, and the reduction of the government's role in all aspects of life. As a result to this strategy, a partner that assists the government in carrying out its social agenda was welcomed. Accordingly, voluntary efforts backed up by civil society organizations were perceived as substantially important. Thus, this space was filled by an emerging non-governmental sector, which was not yet capable of participating in the development process as full partners. The government remained its supervisory status and control over the civic structures that slowly started to expand. In the 90s, the government's support and encouragement to civil society organizations has augmented, but still under the direct supervision of the Ministry of Social Affairs. Law number 84 for the year 2000, which provided NGOs with more freedom, but at the same time kept a noticed degree of control over their activities.

After the "Arab Spring" many governments in the Arab region felt obliged to change the law governing civil society structures and Egypt was on top of these countries seeking reform. This period from 2011 until 2019 witnessd fluctuations in the legal environment and resulted after many trials in Law 149 for year 2019 that was ratified by the President Abdel Fattah Al Sisi. The law is relatively encouraging to civic work, although restrictive when it comes to research work by civic organizations.

5.7 History of Organizations Participating in the Research Sample

Our sample organizations surveyed were all well established and some have existed since 1821. Before 1900, there were only five philanthropic organizations in Egypt. A modest growth continued until 1950's, however after the 1952 revolution, the growth rate of philanthropic NGOs sprang from (3.1%) in 1950 to (30%) increase in the mid seventieth.

Almost (50%) of our sampled organization started their activities in the mid-seventieths. Since year 2000 around (11.8%) of the NGOs (as revealed by our sample) were established. This might indicate the effect of the new NGO law on encouraging the establishment of civil society organizations.

On the other hand, the NGOs in our qualitative sample were randomly chosen and two of which dated back to the late 19th century, while (17%) of the organizations selected had been established between 1927 and 1950. With the socialist regime, the so called Community Development Association – CDA began as a movement where the local community takes part in development in a government-initiated effort.

We came across one of these CDAs in Tanta (in Gharbeya Governorate) established by the Government in the 1950s. Although the land was bought in 1942 by a group of philanthropists in the community to start a "charity organization", things have gradually changed and this piece of land was the location for what later became a "Community Development Association". As this CDA grew, and during the 1980s, it carried out a variety of development work ranging from a Women's Vocational Training Center, training programs for youth in the village on income generating projects like carpentry, computer and bee-hives, and a Rehabilitation Center for the disabled. This CDA, apart from the symbolic fees it receives from the training sessions, it rents spaces and carries out income-generating projects that support the CDA's social projects. However, most of the CDAs have typical activities that are characteristic like a nursery, and a reproductive health clinic where family planning is encouraged.

Table 39: The History of the Sampled Organizations

Date of Establishment	Frequency	Percent
Before 1900	5	.4
1900–1924	10	.8
1925–1949	37	3.1
1950–1974	364	30.3
1975–1999	609	50.8
2000–2001	100	8.3
2002+	42	3.5
Total	1167	97.3
DK	20	1.7
NA	13	1.1
Total	1200	100.0

This table above demonstrates the increase in the number of NGOs established starting from the 1950s. The form of CDAs introduced by the socialist regime might have been the driving force that led to this jump in the number of NGOs. However, it is worth investigating what simultaneously happened to the Waqf foundations, especially that also in the 50s the *ahlī waqf* was legally banned by the government resulting in further deterioration in this traditional civic institution.

As for mosques in the qualitative sample, it was observed that in most cases the religious NGOs are the creation of mosques or churches, and not vice versa. Thus, volunteering to serve in the mosque or in the church encouraged many to establish religious NGOs to expand the domain of social activities performed. As one Manager of an Islamic NGOs indicated, "long ago *shaykh* Gamal Qutb and some philanthropists gathered and decided to create an NGO and each member paid 3 Piaster; I was a student then and have became a member ever since". Another Head of the BoD said,

"The mosque gave birth to the NGO, it started with a nursery and gradually expanded".

5.8 NGOs' Activities

NGOs in Egypt are legally allowed to specialize in seventeen domains of activities. These include child care and motherhood, family care, social help, care for the elderly, care for people with special needs, cultural, scientific and religious services, family planning, social protection, care for prisoners and their families, friendship between nations, administrative activities, organization and management, development of local communities and the founding of universities and scientific institutions.

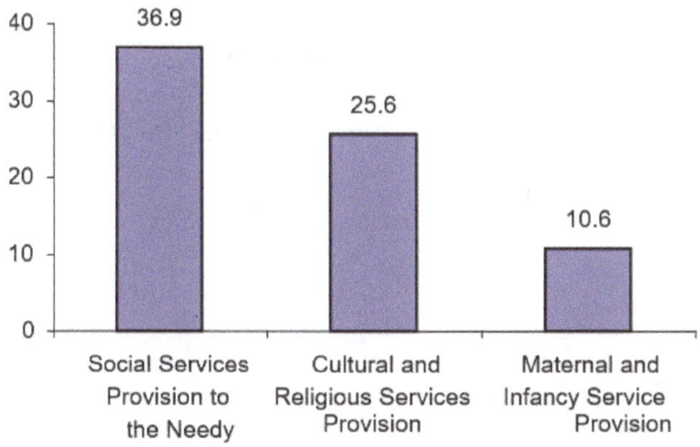

Figure 44: The Main Objectives of the NGO (As Perceived by the Chairpersons and Board Members of NGOs)

As shown in the above figure, due to the severe economic conditions that confronts a large segment of the society, most organizations work on providing necessary social assistance. They consider their primary mission is to save the poor families and their children; those mostly who do not have an outreach to the services offered by the Government. This was explained by a head of a Sufi organization, "Our aim is to alleviate the suffering of the needy around us .... So we try to fulfill the basic needs for anyone who comes and ask for help without looking at his/her religion or identity." This concept of equality in giving is confirmed by another NGO head of the Board of Directors who said, "The beneficiary does not have to be a Muslim. We deal with all religions with tolerance. The prophet (pbuh) was the best example demonstrating good treatment for all. We have Christian beneficiaries and we never say no. So our mission is to fill the needs as much as we can."

Despite the fact that many organizations have developmental objectives, it is noticed that the spread of poverty and the lack of basic services are two factors that shift their activities from development to charity-oriented or at best service-oriented activities. As mentioned by a head of the BoD, “Our objective is to develop the society. Maybe the presence of organizations like ours makes a balance in the society. A poor person can not go to a private doctor; this will be too expensive to him/her. But through the organization, he/she just pays L.E 5 to see a good physician and receive the adequate treatment.”

As for the second objective mentioned above, which is providing cultural and religious services, this is mainly related to religious organizations which aim to spread religious awareness, the understanding and memorizing of Qur’an , especially among children and youths.

5.8.1 The Techniques implemented by NGOs to achieve their Goals

Most NGOs follow some techniques to enable them achieve their missions; these are clarified in the figure below:

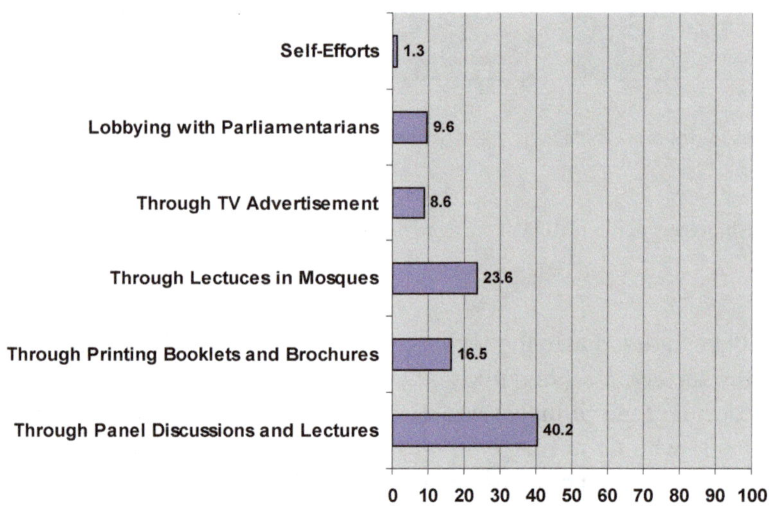

Figure 45: Techniques to achieve Missions

Most of the efforts exerted by NGOs to achieve their missions depend on their interactions with people in order to convince them with the organization and its activities. The figure above shows that discussions and lectures are the techniques mostly followed with a rate of (40.2%), followed by lectures in mosques, rating (23.6%). It is interesting to note here the significance of mosques in publicizing for NGOs. Printing booklets and brochures for fundraising is also among the significant techniques used, with a rate of (16.5%). However, it is noticeable that the rate for resorting to parliamentarians is low (9.6%) which reflects the weak lobbying tendency of the civil society and in return the lack of coordination between NGOs and the legislative authority.

5.8.1.1 The Scope of NGOs Activities

The study demonstrated that charitable activities are the most common activities in most NGOs. As mentioned before, there are several reasons behind this trend, the most important of which is the prevalence of poverty in the Egyptian population and the dire need to fulfill the basic human needs. The following Figure shows the distribution of NGOs' activities between charity and development.

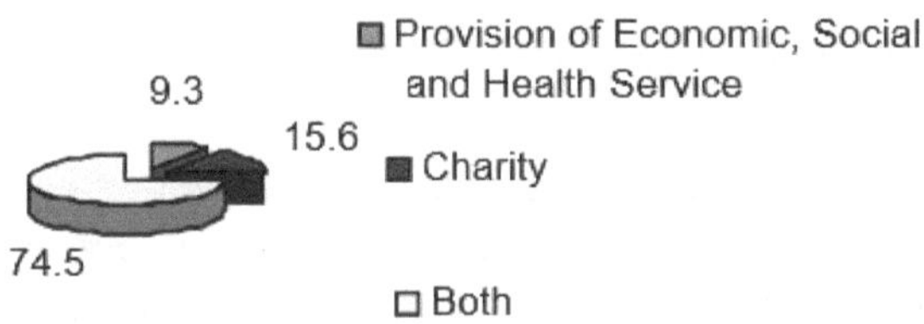

Figure 46: Main Sectors of Organizations Activities

As shown in the figure above, 74.5% of the organizations provide both charitable and developmental activities while 15.6% of NGOs provide only charitable activities. Only 9.3% of organizations are purely developmental. This combination of charitable and developmental activities was confirmed by the Chairpersons of NGOs who listed both kinds of activities when asked about the work of their organizations. For instance, board members of an NGO stated, "Out priority is to qualify families to be productive, and this we do as part of our income-generating program. We also provide educational classes at low costs, with really symbolic prices. We also provide seasonal assistance for over 350 poor families and widows who get their shares of clothes before the feast."

5.8.1.2 Charitable Activities

The following figure presents the kinds of charitable activities that are mostly common among NGOs. These activities vary between providing free services to beneficiaries, to financial and in-kind donations on regular or irregular basis from *Zakāt* money, *ṣadaqāt* or general donations received by the NGOs.

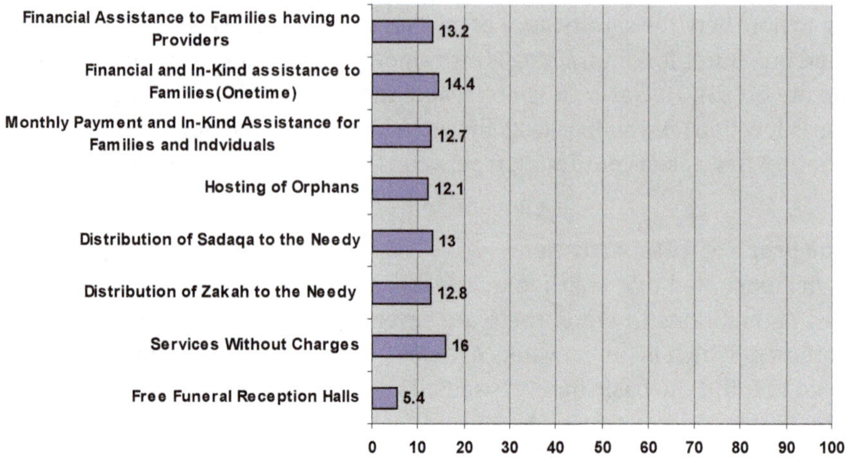

Figure 47: Scope of Charitable Activities as Declared by the Chairpersons of NGOs

The scopes of charitable activities are diversified and directed to those who are in need. However, there are priorities and among the top of these priorities are services without charges (16%), the distribution of irregular financial or in-kind assistance (14.4%), and the distribution of financial assistance to families with no male supporter (13.2%), which again reflects the significance of giving to orphans.

5.8.1.3 Development Activities

The coming figure demonstrates the varieties of developmental activities among NGOs. It is worth clarifying that the activities that are classified as developmental are most of the times service-oriented activities provided with symbolic costs to ensure their sustainability. However, developmental activities are confined to human development manifested in family planning and education as well as economic development interventions manifested in income-generating projects like providing loans to start new businesses.

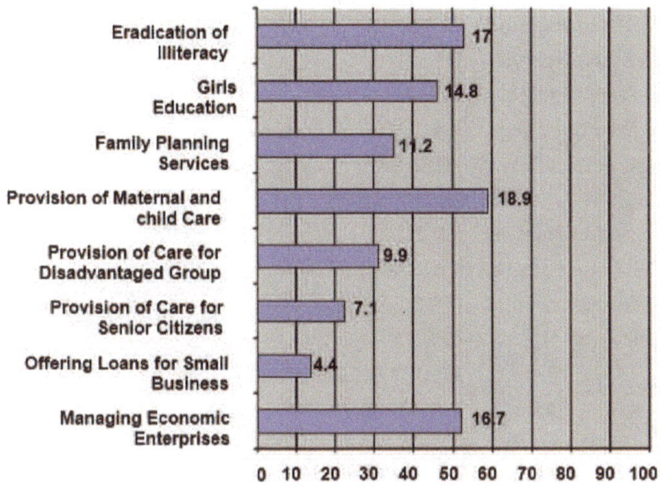

Figure 48: Involvement of Philanthropic Organization in Development

As evident from the above figure, maternal and child care is the most prevalent, eradication of illiteracy (17%). Providing health services and education at low costs (16.7%) is also an important part of the NGOs' developmental interventions. It is also noticed that many NGOs' activities are directed towards girls' education; especially in a country where more than (50%) of their female population is illiterate, this is a proactive role undertaken by some NGOs concerned with development. The care for the aged and the handicapped is also among the prominent services of philanthropic organizations, and is considered by them as development-oriented.

Despite the combination of both charitable and developmental activities in (74.5%) of the NGOs, the research results affirmed that the kinds of activities that are mostly repeated and that take the biggest part of the organizations' budgets are the charitable interventions. This is clarified in the following figure:

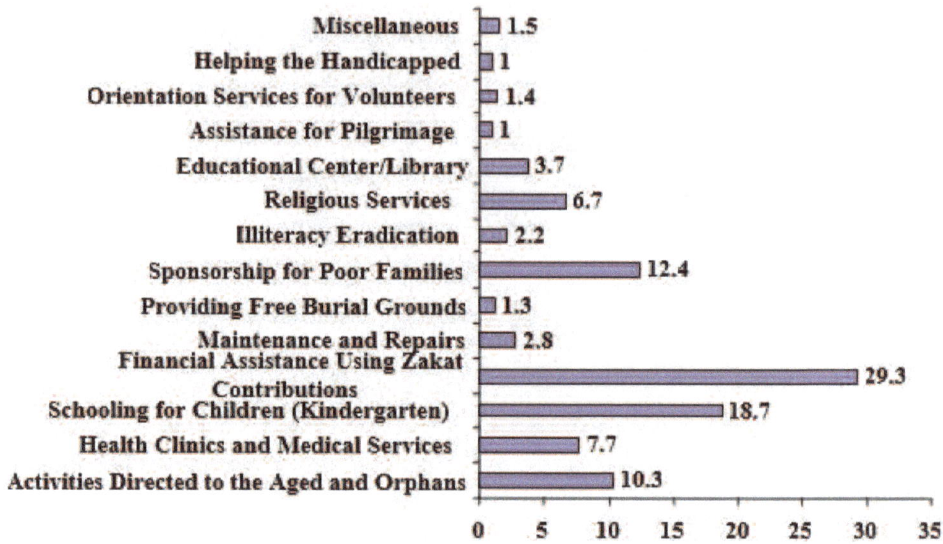

Figure 49: Yearly Budget Allocations by Type of Services Provided

The above figure shows that the allocation of NGOs' budgets mostly go to charitable or service-oriented activities, much more than developmental projects. As noticed, the distribution of *zakāt* took the highest rate, making (29.3%) and *zakāt* money goes to support the needy through financial assistances to meet basic needs.

5.8.2 The Activities of Religious Institutions

As mentioned before, religious institutions engaged in social work, whether mosques or churches, generally have two main objectives: alleviating poverty and spreading religious teachings. These objectives are clearly reflected in most of their interventions. As for mosques, most of their activities concentrate on giving financial or in-kind assistances either on a monthly or a seasonal basis for the poor. Besides the financial assistance, most of the mosques, especially the big ones, provide services free of charge or with symbolic charges like those offered by medical centers. In addition, the factor of human development does exist in many mosques, which is manifested in illiteracy classes, private classes for students, or through the provision of school fees for poor students. Although human development is part of many mosques' agendas, economic development that enables disadvantaged families to help themselves and be self-sustainable is absent. Income generating activities including the provision of loans is almost non-existence, and poor families or single mothers receive minimal contributions to help them eat and drink. Inseparable to service provision is building religious awareness, which is considered as an important part of most of the mosques' activities. These activities include religious lessons and classes for the memorization of Qur'an and the sayings of Prophet Mohamed.

Churches' activities are mostly similar to those of mosques'. Our study has demonstrated that the 'brothers of God', which is a name that refers to those who can not work, including orphans or poor students who can not pay for their education fees have the first priority to receive the help of the church. This is followed by emergency or special cases that confront some families like the disability or the serious disease of the family supporter. The care for the elderly, the refugees (especially the Sudanese Christians), and people with special needs are also of importance. Moreover, churches are very active in the provision of cultural and health services. It is very common to see recreational activities for the youth as a significant ingredient of the churches' interventions. These are closely linked to developmental activities where computer and illiteracy classes are offered to children and youth. Religious classes and seminars are part and parcel of all churches' activities.

Retreats, conferences and meetings are constantly organized by most churches aiming at helping youths discover their potentials and develop their capacities to excel. They also work on developing what they refer to as "life-skills" in order to enable youth and youngsters to cope with problems, acquire self confidence and develop a healthy personality.

5.8.3 Objectives of Religious NGOs

The research results revealed that religious associations, whether mosques or churches, have two main objectives: the first is helping the poor around their districts or villages, which is generally achieved through giving charitable aid. The second objective is to spread religious teachings and awareness through providing religious classes.

5.8.4 Sources of Funding to Religious Organizations

5.8.4.1 Funding to Mosques

Mosques mainly rely on local individual funding to carry out their social activities. They mostly receive donations in the form of *zakāt* (*Zakāt al Māl* and *al fiṭr*), *ṣadaqāt* and *nudhūr*. Some mosques get support from the Ministry of Endowment (*Wizārat al Awqāf*), especially in the form of salaries to the preacher (khaṭīb) and the mosque's workers. One *shaykh* explained, "The *Zakāt* committee collects donations from people or from Nasser Social Bank. The bank takes the donations put by people in the *Zakāt* boxes and distributes their resources on the *Zakāt* committee of each mosque. For example, if one donates money to the *Zakāt* committee in a mosque in Menia, this would be distributed by the bank on all the committees across Menia".

As to mosques where there are *nudhūr* boxes, all funding comes from individual donors. It could be in the form of cash or in-kind. There are people who give their *nudhūr* in the form of animals, like a cow for example that he/she made an oath to give to the mosque if their wishes came true. In such cases the mosques sells the in-kind donations and the money goes to the *nudhūr* boxes. In some of the big mosques, and as its *shaykh* reported, "An average of L.E. 150,000 is collected monthly sometimes...In the birthdays (*mawlad*) and death celebrations of a certain religious figure (*mawla*) who is buried inside of the mosque, around 3 million people gather from all over, bringing plenty of sheep to feed the people who camp around the mosque. In the one week of the *mawlad* celebrations, the six *nudhūr* boxes within the mosque bring around L.E. 200,000. The resources collected in one month originally, are collected in the *nudhūr* boxes in one week during the *mawlad*".

In the light of these facts, Mashhour affirmed that religious organizations could play a better role in development through the vast *nudhūr* resources that they collect. In agreement, Kamal Imam explained that nuzur are individual commitment to give and classified *nudhūr* as ṣadaqāt (not *Zakāt*) and sees great potential to direct their resources to development projects.

Compared to NGOs, mosques follow similar funding patterns when it comes to fundraising from local philanthropists, the private sector and the Diasporas. The more the social class is modest in one area, the more people volunteers. Young people (in many cases unemployed) and older people on pension are among the groups mostly attracted to volunteer. The younger ones volunteer by their physical effort and the older ones offer their time to organize events and give opinions and advices. Unlike NGOs and mostly in urban mosques, in very few cases, income-generating activities were a source of funding to the mosques as well.

5.8.4.2 Funding to Churches

As for churches, the Bishopric itself is seen as a significant funding and supervision source for the churches. Other sources of income come from donations, Ushour (or tithes; i.e. one tenth of any income), property donations and the church membership fees. For the execution of each social activity, there are communities responsible for the implementation and supervision.

The Christians Orthodox Church, in particular has no external donors. All its funding comes from the locals only.

As for government's support, most churches we encountered in our study relied on their own funding for their activities. In one church, there was some support from MoSA (The Ministry of Social Affairs) for the project of women-headed households.

As for individuals, in general they offer their tithes for the church's philanthropic work. Usually, the whole community offers their tithes. However, it does not always take place in a regular or fixed manner.

5.8.5 Local Philanthropic Organizations and Beneficiaries

In our Institutions' sample, we calculated an average number of beneficiaries of around 320 individuals per organization. Table (46) below presents a frequency distribution of these organizations by categories containing the range beneficiaries as indicated. The data shows that almost 52% of the organizations serve less than 500 beneficiaries.

There are 216 organization or 18% of the total that serve from 1000 to less than 5000 beneficiaries. During the intensive interviews, it was evident that some of the selected organizations serve more than 15000 beneficiaries, particularly those that are in charge of orphans' and senior citizens' homes. However, as one can see from the table below, from our sample it appeared that those NGOs that serve more than 15000 beneficiaries are less than 5% of the total NGOs.

Table 40: Number of Beneficiaries

	Frequency	Percent
Less than 250	472	39.3
250–499	149	12.4
500–749	114	9.5
750–999	46	3.8
1000–4999	216	18.0
5000–9999	48	.4
10000–14999	27	2.3
15000–19999	17	1.4
20000+	41	3.4
Total	1130	94.2
DK	44	3.7
NA	26	2.2
Total	1200	100.0

5.8.5.1 Outreach to Beneficiaries

Outreach to beneficiaries and means of informing beneficiaries about the services of the philanthropic organizations are clarified in Figure 50 below. As one can see from this figure, the primary outreach is attributed to the beneficiaries' awareness of the services provided (35.4%), which is mostly due to the spread of the word of mouth among poor people who inhibit the same neighborhood. In addition, NGOs' advertisements about their services are the second major source of knowledge, rating 39.7%. This is interesting because it highlights the importance of good local community-based advertisement methods, especially that media advertisements rates lowest (4%) reflecting the passive role played by media in this domain. Referral from other social organizations, either governmental like the Ministry of Social Affairs (30.1%) or other NGOs (19.7%) is also common, which reflects the importance of cooperation and coordination amongst them. Finally, the role of religious institutions is considerably important (11.8%), through their recommendation of needy cases to NGOs and their publicity to the work of NGOs. If their role is consolidated by proper planning, networks and local media coverage, better outreach and more effective distribution of resources could be achieved.

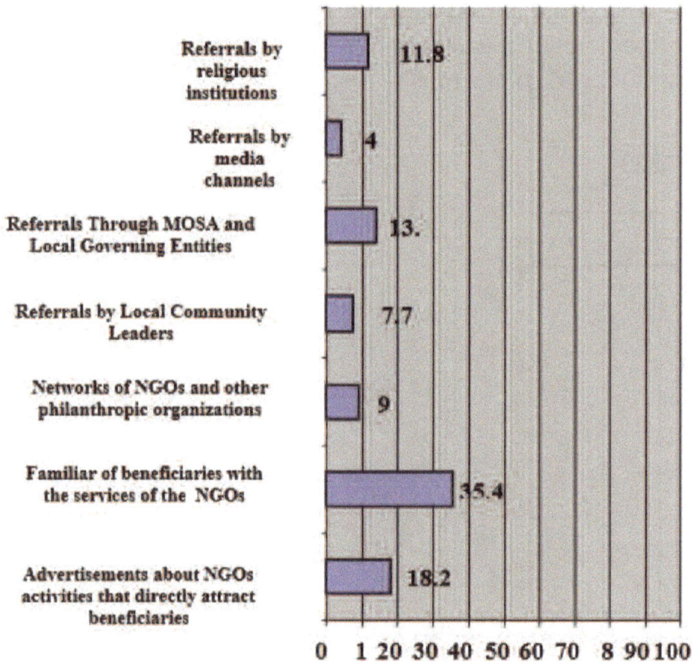

Figure 50: Outreach Programs Adopted by the Philanthropic Organizations

5.8.5.2 Guidelines for the Disbursement of Services

Philanthropic organizations tend to manage the disbursement of their funds according to individual case studies of the beneficiaries' conditions.

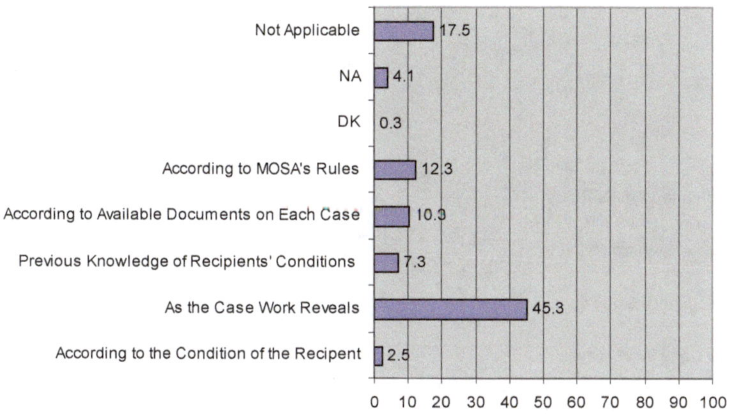

Figure 51: Guidelines for the Disbursement of Services

From the figure above, it is evident that case studies are the primary determinant factor in funds allocation for beneficiaries (45.3%).

Religious places, in urban as well as rural areas alike, and especially in areas where poverty is strikingly high, mosques and churches are confronted with a dire need to priorities giving. Most of the *shaykhs* interviewed said that they make extensive researches and case studies on the beneficiaries to make sure that they reach the most marginalized and most disadvantaged. However, this is the case for urban areas more than rural areas and slums where people know each other better and where the poor is known to everybody. The *shaykhs* repeatedly referred to their beneficiaries as the "people of the district or village"

5.8.5.3 The Impact of the Services provided by the Philanthropic Organizations on Beneficiaries:

After understanding the NGOs' objectives and activities, it was important to understand the impact of these activities on the beneficiaries' lives; especially by recognizing the points of views of both the organizations' and beneficiaries'.

When the chairpersons of the BoDs were surveyed about their perception towards the success of their organization in meeting their objectives, the following percentages were attained: Most of the chairpersons of the BoDs (49.8%) believed that their NGOs have achieved most of their objectives, while 19.9% affirmed that they almost achieved them all. A considerable 27% believed that their NGOs managed to achieve only some of their objectives and a minimal percentage of 2.8% thought that their NGOs did not achieve most of their objectives. This is a rather positive evaluation of their social interventions, which merely reflect the NGOs board person's opinion.

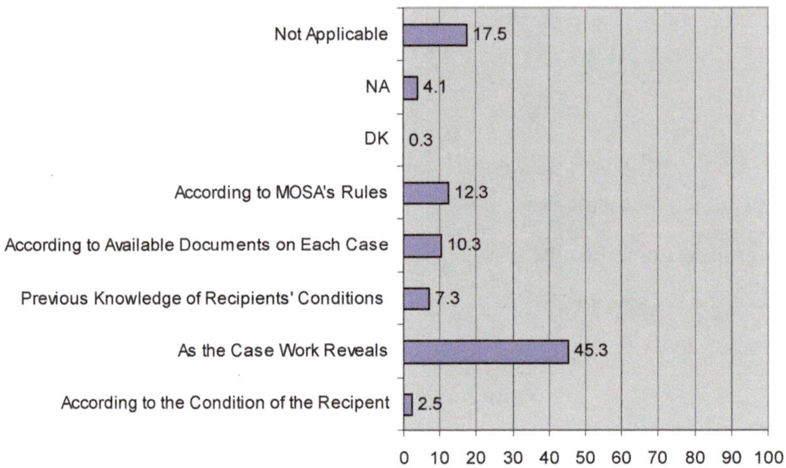

Figure 52: The Degree of NGOs Responsiveness in Dealing with Major Issues

Figure 52 presents the views of NGO' Chairpersons of the BoD toward the receptiveness and responsiveness of the NGOs' interventions with regard to dealing with issues that concern the disadvantaged. A similar result to the question that followed, the majority of the NGOs Chairpersons perceived their organizations as successful in the contribution of social development, with a rate of 75.4%. This viewpoint should be highly questioned since most of the interviewed beneficiaries are not socially developed and their basic needs are barely met by the NGOs. This is not reflected by the high illiteracy rate that characterize them, but also by the severe social and economic condition and the vicious circle of poverty and dependence on charity that shape their lives. On the other hand, and as mentioned above, a major part of NGOs social role in Egypt is to fulfill the basic needs of the poor. This social role is an achievement that was referred to by the Chairpersons of the BoD who defined their role in providing essential services to people by 71.6 % and helping families face the demands of life with a rate of 61.7%. In addition, enhancing love and mercy among people is also one of the achievements perceived by the Chairpersons rating 66.4 %. The reason behind this point of view is defended by believing that fulfilling the beneficiaries' basic needs alleviates the psychological pain that results from severe poverty and decreases envy and hatred.

It is interesting though to see that the issue of decreasing the gap between the rich and the poor came least among others.

In this previous figure, we aimed at knowing the degree of effectiveness (in the point of view of the interviewed NGO chairpersons) accomplished by NGOs' activities when dealing with different issues as stated in the graph. We put a matrix from 1–5 (Activities do not help at all; they do not help much; they help somehow; they help;

they help a great deal) and we added the percentage of "they help" with "they help a great deal" in order to reach the issues most resolved by the activities of the NGOs.

5.8.5.4 Self Evaluation of the NGO Work

The coming two figures demonstrate the evaluation of the NGOs Chairpersons and Board Members of their own NGOs in achieving stated objectives.

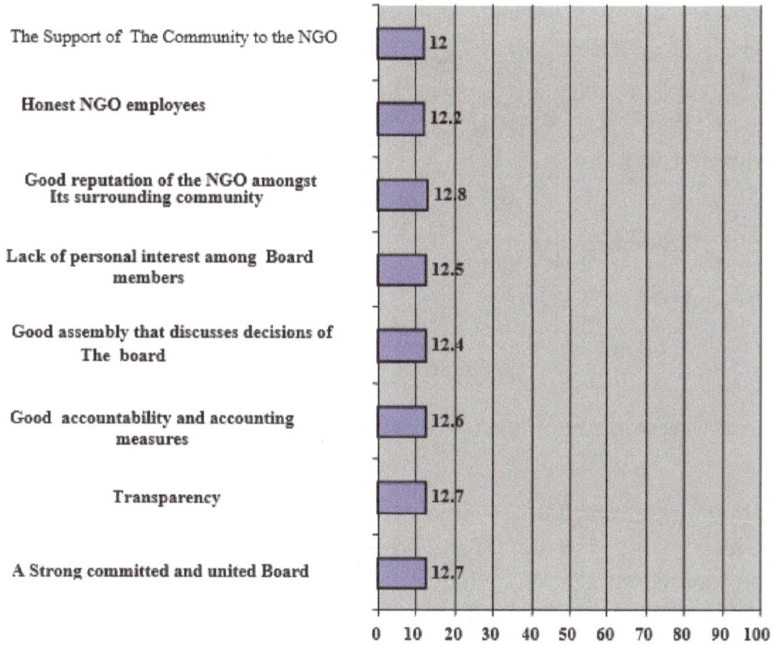

Figure 53: Perceptions towards Aspects of Strengths in NGOs Activities

It is evident that most Chairpersons and Board Members attribute the strengths of their organizations to factors that boost the trust of the community in their work starting from the NGOs' good reputation (12.8%), to transparency in decision making (12.8%) and good accountability measures and accounting system (12.6%).

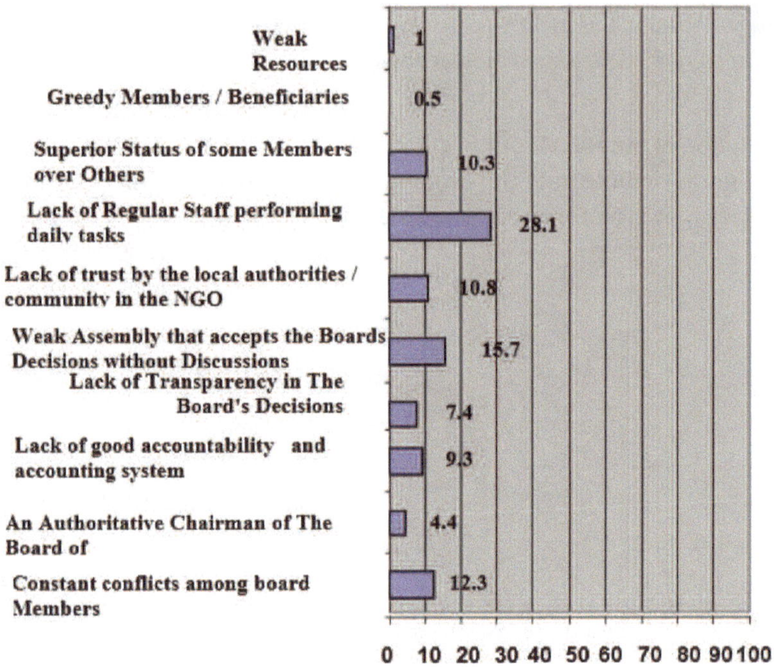

Figure 54: Perception of Aspects of Points of Weakness

This figure, other than presenting data, stimulates several questions that need further studies. First, the main point of weakness shared is the lack of staff that carries out the daily operations of the NGO (28.1%), which reflects the lack of volunteers in organized social work and the potential of more efficient use of volunteer efforts in operations as such. Second, it is evident that further major weakness is due to people responsible for the organizations, whether the General Assembly that do not take an active role in decision making (15.7%) or the constant conflicts among the Board Members (12.3%) that naturally hampers constructive work. Third, it is remarkable to find out that the funding issue, which could be thought of as the major problem, comes least in importance (1%) among all other issues that hamper the work of NGOs in the point of views of the chairperson and members of the board. This does not deny that weak funding is a major challenge (as we will see later); however in the context of this point, it proves that the board members prioritize aspects of management over funding when assessing the potentials of the organization.

5.9 Challenges Affecting the Operation of Philanthropic Institutions

The general weak economic status of the people is among the major challenges highlighted. As mentioned before, the average income of 88% of NGOs that accepted to reveal their income is less than L.E 100,000, which is considered a small amount compared to the costs of the projects and the increasing number of beneficiaries. As shown in the following figure, and in an attempt to assess the challenges that affect the organizations' operations, the major problems that were mentioned are the shortage of financial resources 63.3% and the insufficient donations 56.2%.

The above results were confirmed in the qualitative results. As mentioned before, almost half of organizations in the in-depth interviews declared that their incomes are not sufficiently covering their needs and their activities. This situation has been repeatedly stated by many of the Chairpersons of the BoD, especially in small organizations. Many of them explained that they have projects that they seek to start or that they have already started, but ceased due to the lack of funding. A board member of one NGO stated, "The first problem we have is money. If this problem is solved, we will start a project for widow mothers." In addition, many of them face a double-faced problem; one is the limited budget and two is the constant increase in the number of beneficiaries. As one of the *shaykhs* said, "Prices are burning, and those who were of low-income (*maḥdūdī al dākhil*) became of no-income (*ma'dūmī al dākhil)*". According the Priest of one church, "the number of needy families raised from 100 to 550 families in one year." It is noticed that those organizations that are able to cover their activities have one of the following three criteria; either they depend on funding from donor agencies, or enjoy highly social or religious credibility, or concentrate on income-generating activities.

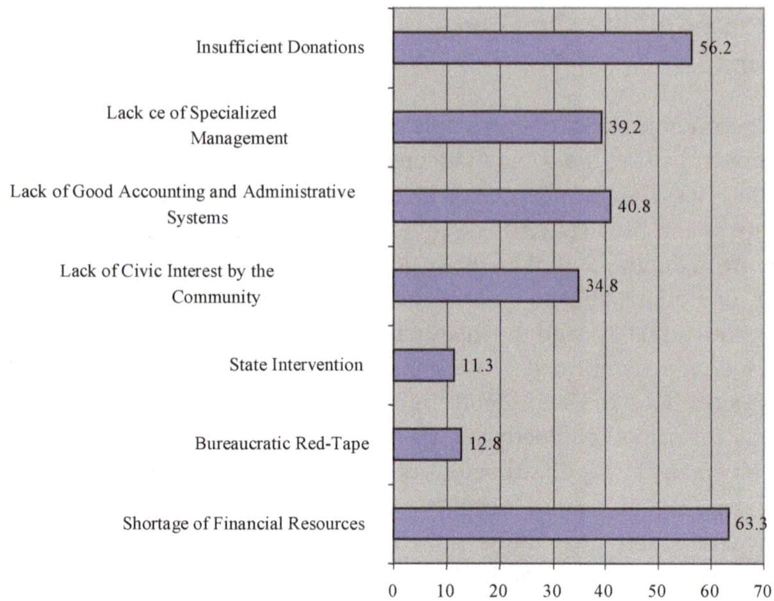

Figure 55: Assessment of the Problems Facing the Organizations

However, one should not neglect that administrative inefficiency and lack of good management come highest in importance after funding challenges. In results as such, it is difficult to attribute the real reason behind the main problem, is it bad management or lack of funding. It is like the chicken and the egg; which comes first. Nevertheless, it seems from the overall study results that the problem of management is the one that prevails over funding.

5.9.1 Potentials, Challenges, Future Perspective and Recommendation for Action

In sum, the study revealed that philanthropy in Egypt is rich and has promising potentials if properly guided towards development, yet there are also challenges that need to be addressed and confronted in order to enhance local philanthropy and direct resources and social assets towards the development of the community.

In this section we present in sum some of these potentials and challenges. The following few points are points of strengths:

5.9.1.1 Potentials of Philanthropy for Development

1. The study confirmed that the practice of philanthropy among Egyptians is very high (62.1%). Religious philanthropy is very strong; annually 85% of the people pay *Zakāt al Fiṭr* and 42% pay *Zakāt al Māl*. The total philanthropic contribution of Egyptians is estimated to be LE 5, 458,664, i.e. around US$ 1 Billion.
2. Volunteerism within the cadre of philanthropic organizations is relatively high as 66.3% of people working in NGOs are volunteers who do not receive any income in return of their services. However, this point is not as positive when we look at individual volunteerism apart from those working in the third sector. Only 6.4% from the public interviewed indicated that they volunteer their time and effort.
3. Foreign donor agencies' funding to NGOs turned up to represent the least source of income to local philanthropic organizations as they only make 1.9% of their income coming last on the NGOs chart of resources. This result has serious implications because Egypt is one of the highest aid recipient countries and accordingly one tends to think that NGOs rely on foreign and government funding. From this result onward, trust in the potentials of local NGOs that depend on local resources and sustain multiple projects providing services to a wide range of the population, is maintained. Accordingly, local mechanisms and resources are to be considered keys of success; local capital is immense and promises revolutionary developmental changes if considered an indispensable partner in development.
4. The study revealed the possibility of optimizing stimuli that enhance philanthropy for development and social change. Among the many significant stimuli is the cultural environment that commences by family, scholarly education, education curricula, the teacher as an idol, and extra-curricular activities. Another is the religious motivation that is the primary drive behind philanthropy, together with social compassion, which could be consolidated by theoretical knowledge and teaching that targets their optimal usage.
5. There are plenty of characteristics that reflect high potential, whether contextually in the rich heritage of philanthropy in Egypt or in religious texts or practically in the various indigenous models of local initiatives and institutionalized philanthropy. We attempted to highlight some of the models in the case studies listed in this publication, but there are many others that form a promising wave for change.

5.9.1.2 Challenges facing Philanthropy for Development

Although the potentials discovered, there are also serious impediments exposed. However, these are not problems as much as they are challenges. Acknowledging these challenging and bringing them to the surface is a starting point. Among these are the following points:

1. Most of the NGOs and religious institutions' resources are allocated to charitable activities and rarely is invested in developmental work.
2. In the context of this study, we raised several concepts to assess their comprehension among the people and therefore their impact. It is a serious impediment to realize that most of these concepts were not properly understood by a considerable part of the interviewee. Among these concepts are basic terms used by cultured individuals and the media channels, like philanthropy, development, social justice, civil society, transparency and also religious concepts like *Zakat*, *ʿUshūr* (tithes), *waqf*. This unawareness is attributed to two factors: mostly to the low educationlevel especially among the beneficiaries and the usage of foreign-driven terms that are remote from the cultural heritage of the people.
3. There were a number of challenges demonstrated by the giving habits and tendencies of the Egyptian public. Among these, is the preference to individual person-to-person giving versus institutional philanthropy; this leads to scattered ad-hoc philanthropy that is mostly charity based.
4. It was observed that the vast majority of the philanthropic organizations (68.8%) do not invest their resources and those 30% that do, mostly invest part of their revenues in Bank deposits. This challenges current investment opportunities of the third sector and invites models to demonstrate creative investment techniques to grow capital. This also challenges third sector laws governing investments and tax deduction laws that should encourage the private sector to invest resources in the third sector.
5. Funding is a challenge that hinders the realization of many activities and makes interventions that aim at development rather than meeting basic needs, an unaffordable luxury. Raising needs and diminishing resources is often accompanied together absorbing most resources and revenues. It is true that religiously motivated giving by Muslims and Christians sustains giving and institutionalize it in the philanthropic culture, but low overall economic condition influences resources. In addition, as mentioned earlier, religious giving is mostly channeled to charity and are not sustainable. In addition they do not contribute to peoples' ability to help themselves. Religious education on this issue is accordingly a major challenge, and channeling religious resources to development work is another.
6. Although some media programs highlight the work of some NGOs, media has much more to offer. Especially television and radio programs could allocate programs for philanthropic organizations and series that encourage young people and philanthropists to invest in building their communities by strategizing their efforts and philanthropy.

5.9.2 Future Perspective

The future perspectives mentioned here represent the points of view of the research respondents as indicated by them in the surveys and expressed in the intensive interviews. 75% of the public pointed out that philanthropy should be directed to development and not merely to charity that does not enhance peoples' potentials to grow. The following figure presents this result:

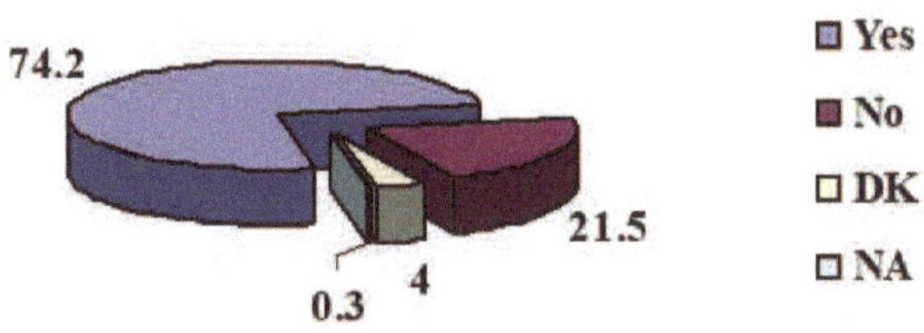

Figure 56: Philanthropy towards Investment not only Charity

In our intensive interviews with respondents on means to direct philanthropy towards development and social justice, the following visions, or future perspectives, came to reflect the opinions of all the segments involved: chairpersons of the NGOs' BoD, board members, *shaykhs*, priests, beneficiaries and donors.

5.9.2.1 Rebuilding Trust

Most respondents emphasized the importance of trust in any attempt to organize philanthropic efforts and channel giving towards development and social justice. Donors were mostly concerned with trust building between the public and the NGO sector. As one of the donors expressed, "To organize philanthropic resources, people of trust should be involved in the development field; people who do not need to get personal benefits. In addition, we must know where our money is going". Most board members agreed to the importance of trust and making people participate in what the NGOs are doing. In this respect, trust and transparency are two sides of one coin.

As also revealed by the study, the lack of trust is a major factor that contributes to weak institutionalized philanthropic structures. The prevailing charity-oriented giving is not only the result of lack of awareness, but it is also due to the lack of trust dominating the relationship between civil society, civic institutions, governmental social bodies and donors, whether individual philanthropists or businesspersons. This resulted in weak institutionalized philanthropy and a recently emerging corporate philanthropy that is striving to function in a fertile environment.

Transparency is one of the measures to build trust; firm measures to enforce it are a process that requires organized collective efforts. Although all Chairpersons of philanthropic institutions affirmed that they provide all possible means to be transparent, lack of trust in NGOs work is a reason that compels donors to resort to person-to-person charity. As one donor explained, "Trust is the most important thing. If I trust that my donations will reach whoever deserves it, I will not hesitate to donate to NGOs."

On the other hand, lack of trust in the central governmental institutions like the Azhar and the Ministry of Awqaf as sources of channeling donations is evident among respondents. Despite the high religiously-motivated civic philanthropy and the religious connotation of these governmental bodies, lack of transparency and trust characterizes this relationship. It is, therefore recommended to bring out these issues on the agenda of the governmental and non-governmental organizations involved, in order reach venues of reform.

Besides, and as revealed by the study's results, people of religion play a significant role in mobilizing people. One of the Chairpersons of the BoD explained, "People are willing to give, but who would take their hands and direct them to the right path? We have to make seminars led by religious people, either Muslims or Christians."

Another aspect of the problem of trust is reflected in the overall negative thinking prevailing. On the grass root level, there is a sensed hopelessness in real change. Among the common sentences elaborated by the respondents is what follows: "I can not do a real change"; "It is the responsibility of the government", and other negative phrases revealing a rather pessimist outlook towards the possibility of change.

People need to realize that collective efforts with *enlightened visions* for change would make a difference and would eventually compel all segments and members of the community, including the government, to work towards building a healthy environment where development and social justice prevail.

5.9.2.2 Awareness on Philanthropy for Development

The study affirmed that enhancing peoples' awareness is the key for any positive social change; without proper knowledge and awareness there is little chance for social mobility, development and social justice to prevail. When we addressed the cultural environment, and the impact of religion on peoples' awareness and action, it was evident that they have a strong connotation with the encouragement or discouragement of social justice philanthropy. Family upbringing, religion, educational curricula and extra-curricular activities, idols, and media are among the most influential factors that shape awareness. Philanthropy for development and social justice does not have a solid educational ground and therefore many of the related concepts are distorted. For example the saying of Prophet Mohamed that encourages the provision of tools or means to enable a poor person to start a job and support him/herself rather than giving charity money (*ḥadīth al iḥtiṭāb*). This hadith is not included in any of the scholarly curricula and is not known to many people. Similarly, conditions of paying *zakāt* that prioritize giving to enhance one's condition and enable him/her to reach subsistence level (*ḥadd al kifāya*), or to give *zakāt* in priority to needy people within the same geographical area of the donor, or to establish *waqf* as a form of *ṣadaqāt jāriyya* and other civil society development education are absent in most of the cultural channels. Lack of education results in lack of awareness and in return leads to distorted actions. People accordingly resort to forms of giving that in the name of religion are channeled in ways and to sources that do not necessarily relate to the real essence of religion. In light of this, and as one of the priests explained, "Institutionalized giving has to be achieved through awareness building." Another beneficiary elaborated, "Awareness is the most important thing, the *shaykh* in the mosque and the media are very important." Finally, one of the donors was quoted as follows: "People should understand the concept of philanthropy in the right way. They should also understand that when development is achieved, the returns will yield benefits to the donor himself."

From the above it is evident that education, religion, and media through their respective channels, have a significant role to play in enhancing awareness and mobilizing people to give for causes of development and social justice. These channels carry the responsibility of closing the gap between knowledge and action, theory and practice and enabling civil society to influence decision makers to achieve the desired change.

5.9.2.3 Enhancing Development Oriented Education

Most respondents confirmed that education is crucial in channeling philanthropy towards development and social justice and agreed that current curricula (whether in schools in all levels or in universities) do not encourage philanthropy. Service-learning is non existent in the majority of schools and universities and accordingly students do not get neither the theoretical nor the practical proper civic engagement that prepares them to be the future philanthropists and activists for social change. Hence, it was recommended by respondents to integrate philanthropy for development components and support theory with practical engagement that paves the way for on-the-ground action and the realization of creative philanthropic models led by young children and youth.

It was agreed by the majority of respondents that education is the most crucial, and that school curricula must involve what mobilizes philanthropy and volunteering, not only through theories and textbooks, but through injecting extra-curricular activities that leads to a change in children's' mindsets and actions, and through the implementation of pilot projects that enforces theory by demonstrating the "how to" in practice. The creation of good teachers that fill the empty place of the role model figure is also among the significant challenges if we seek change.

Religious education and figures are important; as one of the respondents highlighted: "People should understand that it is God's right to have us help each other, and transmitting this message is the responsibility of religious education and the curricula in schools and universities."

Among the most important sectors that should plant the seed of philanthropy in our society is the educational institutions through emphasizing on teachings that promote philanthropy for human and social development and for social justice. The results of this study revealed that education crucially affects the philanthropic behavior. Accordingly, it is quite important to provide a comprehensive curriculum that encourages philanthropy, both in theory and in practice. Educating children and youths on their social responsibility and at the same time empower them with the provision of knowledge on the best means to direct their resources (whether volunteer effort or material resources) is a crucial task of both schools and universities. Considering the faith-based giving nature, legitimizing the curricula by supportive religious teachings is crucial.

5.9.2.3.1 Religion and Development

As mentioned above, in a country where philanthropy is faith-based, transmitting the right religious teachings to the public is essential. Hence, using all the means to achieve this objective either through education or religious institutions should take a priority. NGOs and religious associations that believe in the import role of local philanthropy in development, should work with religious figures and religious institutions (whether mosques or churches) to bring the most accurate and positive messages through to children, youth and the public at large. The Ministry of Awqaf with its wealth of people of religion and resources is among the most prominent actors in creating awareness and promoting positive messages through their *shaykhs* in the various mosques. Same applies to an institution like the Bishopric for Services (*Usqfiyyat al khadamāt)* for the Christians.

5.9.2.3.2 Media and Development

Despite the importance of media and its effect on shaping behaviors, its current role in promoting philanthropy for development and social justice is marginal. Creating programs that mobilize philanthropy and the concepts of development and social justice is significant to set the tune for change. In addition, the use of literally translated terms from the West which are not common to the Egyptian public such as "civil or *madanī* " (for civil society) versus "*ahlī* " (a term more culturally imbedded to describe civil society), as well as other terms like transparency and others, must be carefully studied before introducing to the public by media and by governmental bodies. This is crucial to avoid ambiguity and misunderstandings among the public, as well as to show respect to the cultural and linguistic heritage that might be more influential in gaining credibility and acceptance among the citizens.

5.9.2.3.3 Channeling *Zakāt* Resources to Development

Many donors expressed their desire to direct *Zakāt* to development projects and to use it in ways that substantially solve social and economic problems by surpassing the level of meeting the basic needs of the poor. Recommendations to mobilize local resources and direct them towards development conditioned the change in educational programs (curricular and extra-curricular) to children and youth, enhancing religious awareness and mobilizing the efforts of *shaykhs* and Priests in this direction as well as a activating a responsible media that gears peoples' thinking and action through various programs. As one of the Chairpersons suggested, "*It is important to transform giving into production. Volunteer efforts and local resources should come together to establish productive projects through trusted organizations. The purpose of these projects is not to gain profit, but to employ youths and re-direct profit to establish other projects. This means that one project builds another project until we make a series of projects. This can be done through the donation and cooperation of businesspersons even with a part of their Zakāt* "

There are very few yet very successful examples that apply this philosophy as one of the *shaykhs* explained. He is among the prominent socially responsible activists who attempted to solve the problem of unemployment. He elaborated that, "*we attract newly graduate youths and assist them in starting their own small projects as much as the available money in the Zakāt committee permits. We give them small loans without interests to start their own projects.*" Another similar initiative is embraced in one NGO in Aswan Governorate where donations' money was accumulated to start projects that employ young people. As the Chairman of this NGOs indicated, "*we bought 3 ferryboats (to cross the Nile) and launched a project that offers means of transportation to people crossing from one side to the other. These boats are developmental projects that attract young people to work in, and simultaneously provide necessary service to a wide range of people. Currently, there are two young people working in the morning and two others working in the night shift in a regular job.*" From examples as such, one could deduct the feasibility of further models that facilitate channeling *Zakāt*, *ʿUshūr*, and *ṣadaqāt* resources into investments and income-generating projects to absorb labor. In case of *Zakāt* resources, beneficiaries or partners should own shares in the projects in order to respect the condition of ownership in the *Zakāt* money received.

The following figure presents the opinion of the respondents in directing giving to development rather than unorganized charitable activities:

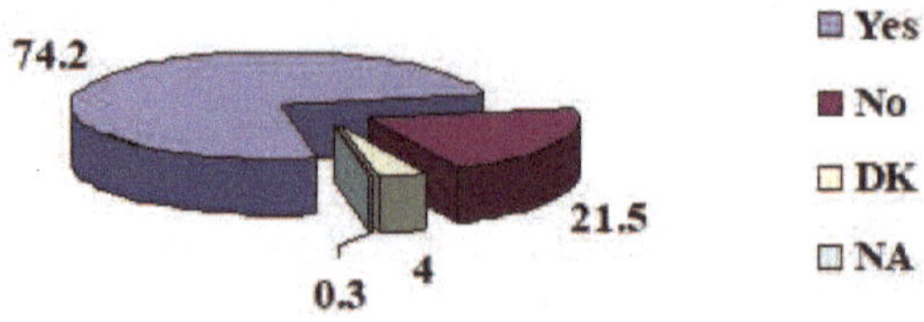

Figure 57: Would you care to direct Philanthropic Resources to Development rather than unorganized Charity?

5.9.2.4 Institutionalizing Philanthropy

Many respondents, especially donors, suggested that giving should be organized and coordinated through one big and trusted institution that has different branches throughout the country to organize and manage philanthropic resources. In an attempt to suggest models, one of the respondents proposed the following: "*We can establish an organization like that of the Friends of the Cancer Institute, and we can unite all organizations that work in the same field, then establish branches in all Governorates.*" A similar opinion was shared by another donor who suggested, "We can establish "*Bayt al māl*" (a traditional institution that used to exist in Islamic countries as the pot where *Zakāt* money is collected and redistributed). *Bayt al māl*, he continued, *could be divided into different branches*; *one for donations allocated to medical treatments, another for projects in rural areas and others*. Instead of making individual donations from one person to the other, our donated resources should be directed to this institution." Another donor affirmed the idea of institutionalizing giving through one organization by saying, "We can establish *Bayt al māl* for Muslims to enhance social justice in the country."

5.9.2.5 Creating Income-Generating Projects for Youth: A responsibility of the Private Sector

Many of the respondents emphasized on the social responsibility of the private sector. Suggestions for a more efficient role to be played by the socially responsible private sector and corporations in embracing projects that employs youth and enable people to have their own businesses, were common suggestions. Some respondents believed that private philanthropies of the private sector or philanthropists in general should fund the capital for projects that absorb youth. The creation of income-generating projects was an activity mostly attributed by respondents to the private sector that seemed in their eyes most able to carry out. Unemployment is a major challenge to peoples' lives and to development in the point of view of respondents all over, whether in urban or rural areas, and severely in villages in Upper Egypt. Hence, philanthropy to create jobs was the most sacred and the most valuable form of social responsibility in the eyes of respondents; especially seen as the responsibility of the private sector.

5.9.2.6 Centers for Studying and Promoting Philanthropy

An important partner and engine for change are university-based centers that encourage the study and promotion of philanthropy in Egypt, the Arab and Islamic World. Those centers would encourage researchers to conduct studies on philanthropy through exploring fields like *Zakāt*, *'Ushūr* (tithes), *ṣadaqāt*, *waqf*, social justice, *takāful*, etc and establish linkages between theoretical education and the practical on-the-ground developmental experience. Students' practical projects should be fueled by civic structures that in return would benefit from the students efforts, potentials and future expertise in the field.

It is envisioned that such centers would help promote philanthropic endeavors and assist in channeling giving and volunteering towards development starting with students taking the lead as socially responsible citizens. This exploratory study in hand explored the field of philanthropy in Egypt at large to pave the way for the establishment of such centers in the different universities in Egypt and the region.

5.9.2.7 Establishing Community Foundations

Local giving in Egypt rates high as seen from the estimates; and motives behind giving are faith-based but also responsibility-driven. People choose to give to respond to the miseries of others and to lessen the most marginalized in the society. In addition, tendency by the Egyptian public to give to people of kinship and of geographical proximity is the prevailing form of giving. Most recipients of donations (70%) are either related of kin or of geographical proximity to the donor. Thus, a model such as community foundations is a promising endeavor in Egypt. In addition, taken that NGOs do not enjoy sufficient financial sustainability and that private foundations are limited to foundations recently established by wealthy businesspersons or families, as the Sawiris Foundation, Talaat Mostafa Foundation and others, community endowed foundations need to emerge as important partners in development. This model was recently introduced by the researcher for the first time in Egypt with the establishment of the community foundation of Maadi, known as Mu'assaset Waqfeyet al Maadi el Ahleya. This *waqfiyya* with its board of trustees known as *Nuzār al Waqfiyya* is a leading initiative because it revives the *waqf* structure through the establishment of a community foundation serving the rich and the poor in one geographical area. It is envisioned that this initiative breaks the path for future community foundations of traditional yet modern nature to develop in various districts, governorates and eventually regionally with the collaborations of community leaders, socially responsible private sector, philanthropists and partners of all backgrounds.

5.9.2.8 Reviving the Waqf Structure

It was a shocking result to learn about the ignorance of 30% of the people about the *waqf* as a concept and the majority's misperception that *confused waqf* with government's properties. Considering the significant role that waqf institutions used to play as vivid civic endowed structures over the course of hundreds of centuries in Egypt, the deterioration of this civic form of institutionalized philanthropy signals an alarm to civil society in general and to development in specific. Accordingly, and as some of the voices in the field expressed, there is a pending need to revive this old structure, as a civic autonomous form of institutionalized philanthropy. Awareness on the waqf should be created and models as well as an encouraging environment should unfold to provoke change. Among the successful examples is the attempt of the Waqfeyat al Maadi Community Foundation, founded by Marwa el Daly, and that of El Sayed El Badawy NGO in Tanta to fundraise through selling shares of a "waqf pot" in order to finance some of the NGO's activities. Another initiative is the effort of Mohamed Shawqy Al Fangary who established the Fangary Waqf from a belief that *waqf* structures deteriorated because of successive governments' violations over these civic institutions and which used to enjoy autonomy and power. In response he established various pots of *waqf* money, allocating their profit to support students and Islamic studies.

Local initiatives as such are significant engines for change and development. They should accordingly be studied, empowered and highlighted to ensure their success and replication.

5.10 Practical Implementation: The Establishment of the Waqfeyat al Maadi Community Foundation (WMCF)

Waqfeyat al Maadi Community Foundation (WMCF) is the practical on-the-ground implementation resulting from the field study conducted by Marwa El Daly. It is an embodiment of the theoretical background information and the field work that reflects figures, trends, challenges, potentials, and aspirations monitored on the national level through the study. WMCF was the model derived by El Daly that represents sustainable and organized philanthropy leading to change and development, based on these outcomes. It is a nonpfrofit founded by Marwa el Daly and registered on the 13th of May 2008 under the Ministry of Social Solidarity as the first community foundation in Egypt. It has a Board of Trustees of seven persons and a group of full time, part-time employees, consultants and national and international interns. It is a community-led philanthropic change-agent that catalyzes change through community investments and Waqf to improve the standard of living for all community members. WMCF channels donations, zakat, sadaqat, tithes, and other forms of traditional giving to support community projects, individuals, and small community based organizations (CBOs) to empower the whole community and help in lessening the social and economic gaps between its members. Its existence as a model, the lobbying efforts of El Daly resulted in the inclusion of Clause 90 in the Egyptian Constitution, which stresses on the government's role to revive the waqf concept; this was the first time to have such clause included in the constitution of Egypt.

The major determinants that led to the establishment of WMCF are summarized as follows:

1. Philanthropic giving is considerable in Egypt but it is not strategically directed; it is ad-hoc, from person-to-person, lacking institutionalization and effectiveness.
2. Most if not all local NGOs in Egypt are charity oriented and rely on donations to offer traditional services to their constituencies. They do not target the root causes of the problems, nor apply any form of theories of change.
3. This study on philanthropy at hand, proved that people tend to satisfy the needs of their surrounding communities first; in addition, the legisalation of zakat implies that the needs of the surrounding community must first be met: "*al aqrabūn awlā bi al ma'rūf" is a verse from Quran indicating that those close to kin are worthy of your kindness. This* translates in peoples' minds that those close by kin or geography are more worthy to one's assistance. In a culture where faith-based giving is the driving force behind philanthropy as highlighted by this study, the community foundation seems to be a promising model for community mobilization and giving.
4. Most of the Civil Society Organizations (70%) as revealed by the study do not invest their resources and the vast majority of this sector is not financially sustainable. Hence, introducing the endowment system (waqf) and models of social ventures seeking financial sustainability for CSOs is a vital intervention to be undertaken by Waqfeyat al Maadi Community Foundation (WMCF).
5. 70 % of the people of Egypt do not know what *waqf* means and out of the 30% who claim to know the word waqf believe that it is the property of the government; and refer to the Ministry of Awqaf as the beholder of these properties. This is a great shame; not only because *waqf* was the backbone of a vivid civic sector for centuries and centuries but also because it is by all means a solid system of institutionalized philanthropy that finds its roots in the tradition of this nation and region at large. Hence, reviving this model and modernizing it, would give venue to civil society at large to strategically invest in development work. Waqf provides a solid base for social entrepreneurship and forms of social investment. It offers an alternative to the charity model that is regid when it comes to investment and growth.
6. Up to the point of the creation of Waqfeyat al Maadi Community Foundation, there was no model of community foundations in Egypt and there was no model as such combined with an attempt to revive the *waqf* mechanism. It was intended to establish WMCF in Maadi which is a well to do area surrounded by shanty towns and very disadvantaged population. The idea was to make this model work in a challenging environment that is also a representation of Egypt at large.
7. Marwa EL Daly formed an advisory board and invited prominent figures in Maadi area and those became interested in the importance of establishing a

community foundation that revives the *waqf* model and serves the people of Maadi and its surroundings based on the outcomes and recommendations of the study. Now the Board of Trustees of Waqfeyat al Maadi comprises topnotch business philanthropists, development practitioners, and academia from the Maadi community. They all set the mission and vision of the foundation and through regular monthly meetings, monitor its work and development.

5.10.1 The Foundation's Mission, Vision, and Role

Wafeyat Al Maadi Community Foundation aims at reviving and modernizing Al Waqf mechanism – old tool for organized social giving embedded in Egyptian history. The Foundation provides an innovative sustainable model of Community Foundations that employ modern applications of Al Waqf as a sustainable channel for mobilizing and channeling local resources towards sustainable local development of a given local community.

WMCF acts as a facilitator and catalyst for civil society organizations in adopting innovative and financially sustainable business models to function as waqf models financing development work.

The vision of WMCF is achieving a more just and equal society which allows all members of the community equitable access to services, resources, and opportunities enabling them to maximize their potential for further achievements and growth.

5.10.2 Line of Business and Programs

The Foundation's work is envisioned to serve five main axes:

1. Al Waqf Model Development
2. Provision of social services in Maadi and outskirts area as Operational and Grant-making Foundation.
3. Facilitation, coordination, and capacity building to other civil society organizations, and socially responsible businesses.
4. Conducting nationwide awareness raising campaigns about Al Waqf and its modern applications
5. Research and Development (Diwan el Waqfeya) supporting research and participatory research appraisals (PRAs) in the target areas.

5.10.2.1 A. Al Waqf Model Development

Corporate Social Responsibility (CSR) and social justice are concepts not novice to Egyptian culture as such. They have been part of our social fabric for centuries in many forms suitable to each era's needs. WMCF works on the development of various corporate social responsibility applications inspired by Al Waqf system, which is equivalent but not restricted to the concept "Endowment". The Foundation aims at empowering organizations to implement sustainable programmes through the marriage of business and development organizations. Innovative models are developed and applied as social ventures following a business model that permits their sustainability and growth. Examples of these ideas include and are not exclusive to the following:

- Social ventures that work as waqf and provide sustainable income as they are incubated in the foundation.
- The role of banks in reviving Al Waqf mechanism.
- The role of businesses in allocating a percentage of their profit to fund civic institutions and causes.
- The role of angel investors in building Al Waqf fund to support social enterprises.
- The role of businesses in growing endowment funds that respond to developmental benchmarks in a sustainable manner.
- Partnership in business between a Social Innovator/service provider and a development organization for ongoing cash flow
- Business models in projects implemented by the foundation, like establishing flat factories where people work from home as part of a supply chain.
- Launching incubators for social and business innovators within civil society organizations as a profit sharing initiative.

5.10.2.2 B. Provision of social services in the Maadi and outskirts area

Through the maintenance of certain *Waqfs* (endowments), the Foundation acts as an operating and grant making foundation to implement and support social service provision programs in underprivileged communities in the areas of, education, environment, water and sanitation, and job creation, primarily based on the outcomes of on-the-ground researches, Participatory Rapid Appraisals (PRAs) and other Needs Assessment tools for improving the standards of living in such communities and helping to close the gap between community members in this geographical area.

5.10.2.3 C. Facilitation, coordination, and capacity building to other civil society organizations

WMCF builds the capacity of Community-Based Organizations (CBOs) as well as social entrepreneurs and young-changemakers to decentralize its programs among other entities and their support groups. Developing strong partners is one of the foundation key interests.

5.10.2.4 D. Conducting nationwide awareness raising campaigns about Al Waqf and its modern applications

Based on the nationwide study on Philanthropy in Egypt conducted by the founder of WMCF, giving across the country is ad-hoc, short-term, person to person, and very much non-strategic. Through conducting awareness campaigns to the public, civil society, private sector, and development practitioners, WMCF provides "Best Practices" and models of donor-advised waqf and social enterprises that are sustainable and have long term, effective impact and results. Most of these practices rely on business models that make them financially sustainable and scaleable.

5.10.3 WMCF's Five Programs

5.10.3.1 The Livelihood Program (Bab Rizq)

This program helps in the formation of skilled workers providing them with opportunties to work. It is composed of five main projects which include:

- *#Help_them_work_from_home, a project where people are equipped and empowered to work from home to supply products branded and sold by WMCF as" Waqfeya Home Factory" products in different outlets.*
- *Seed fund for Small & Micro Enterprises:* WMCF conducts needs assessments and prioritizes the most disadvantaged families and most promising entrepreneurs in marginalized communities. They receive seed funding to start or expand their small business.
- *Grants for Community-Based Organizations (CBOs):* WMCF gives grants to CBOs to start their own income-generating projects and/or to fund entrepreneurs with seed funds.
- *Vocational Training:* WMCF provides young people with vocational training opportunities & soft skills to allow them to get jobs or start their own businesses.
- *Social Entrepreneurs Support Project:* WMCF supports Social Entrepreneurs through grants in applying creative projects.

5.10.3.2 The Youth Engagement Program (YEP)

The program targets youth and engages them as actors who contribute towards social change and development. This involvement helps in the reconstruction of their characters to become more dependent and self-fulfilled where they assess and design community projects, mobilize local resources (both human and financial), and gain skills and knowledge throughout the experience.

Through this program, the first five Youth Banks in Egypt and the Arab World were created linking them to 200 Youth Banks that exist worldwide; these Youth Banks are composed of trained young people following international agreed upon standards of fundraising, grant-making and program development to financially support projects of other young social entrepreneurs from 14 to 27 years.

5.10.3.3 Waqf & Philanthropy Consultancy Program

This program provides consultancies to philanthropists, including those who want to create *WAQF* funds in their names or for their loved ones, those who want to give their *zakat*, *tithes*, *sadaqat*, and time to empower others, and Corporate Social Responsibility (CSR) departments in companies.

5.10.3.4 Khan El Fenoun Art Program

Khan el Fenoun Program is a hub that raises awareness on the importance of art and culture in addition to providing space for people from different communities to meet through their talent exchange. The program started as a Property Waqf through the generous contributions from Prof. Dr. Fatma Abu Nawareg (Professor of Art Appreciation in Helwan University) reflecting her belief in the role of art in the advancement of the society.It became WMCF's first social enterprise whereby the income of art classes supports other art classes in disadvantaged communities and bridging the gap endeavors between community members. Moreover, WMCF collaborates with community members, clubs, youth centers and schools in organizing community events and street festivals to discover talents, bridge gaps, and build networks between people, social and business entrepreneurs, artists, etc.

5.10.3.5 The Environment Unit

This program aims to enhance environmental conditions through raising awareness among children and adults on how to protect their environment. The environment team consists of young agriculture engineers who regularly hold awareness campaigns providing green services such as roof plantations, landscaping and bio-agriculture projects. The main aim is to help combat pollution, provide healthy food and income to the families, in addition to spreading beauty especially in marginalized areas.

5.10.3.6 WMCF's Scope of Work

As indicated by the findings of this study, people, both Christians and Muslims, favor giving to relatives as their first choice and people of the same neighborhood as a second choice; "*al aqrabūn awlā bi al maʿrūf*" is the Arabic expression of this trend of favoring those to you by kin and geography. It is a faith-based driving force behind philanthropy that explains that Egyptians tend to assist those close to them, primarily by kin and secondary by geographical closeness. Moreover, the geographical aspect in giving *zakāt* is vital, as it is preferable to spend the *zakāt* money on those who deserve it in the same area you inhabit. Thus, community foundations which identify core geographic areas, in which they operate and provide grants and services, have great potential to develop, grow in number, and strategically ensure sustainable development in a country like Egypt.

Based on the above findings, Waqfeyat Al-Maadi Community Foundation has been established in 2007 as a pioneering model for grant-making and operating community foundations in Egypt. Its overall objective is to bridge the gap between the rich and poor in Al-Maadi suburb and its outskirts, while improving the quality of life for all people residing in the area. A major aim of the foundation is to promote youth and children's philanthropy so as to establish and empower a cadre of young people as community leaders capable of mobilizing philanthropic resources and managing youth and children thematic endowments. This is achieved through advancing programs of comprehensive and sustainable community development that build upon and enhance local philanthropic giving—from the Community Foundation itself, other foundations and civic associations, the private sector, youth groups, members of schools, universities, clubs in the area and individual philanthropists. This ensures sustainable sources of giving that are rooted within the communities of Maadi and its outskirts.

WMCF is an independent foundation that is governed by a Board of Trustees, known as *Nuzār al Waqfeya*, representing a cross section of Al-Maadi community. It covers the 7 provinces or zones of Al-Maadi suburb. These provinces include: Old Maadi, New Maadi, Zahra· El Maadi, Thakanat El Maadi, Arab El Maadi, Hadayek El Maadi and Torah. Based on the 2006 census data of the Central Agency for Population Mobilization and Statistics (CAPMAS), these zones had an estimated population of 200'000 of residents, inhabiting 14 km^2 during the time of the survey. Moreover, Waqfeyat al Maadi Community Foundation serves shanty towns located at the outskirts of Maadi, yet belong to other districts such as, El Basateen and Helwan. The estimated population of these suburbs is around 1.5 million residing in 30.5 km^2 and 1.2 million of residents inhabiting 69.4km^2, respectively.

The socioeconomic backgrounds of the residents of these areas reflect the rapid urbanization that took place in Maadi over the last few decades. Whereas the former zones are mostly resided by the upper- and upper-middle classes as well as expatriate communities, the latter zones as well as the areas in Basateen and Helwan are largely inhabited by the lower classes. As mentioned earlier, within these areas, there are many shanty towns where hundreds of thousands of people are crammed into informal settlements. Problems of density as well as a lack of organized infrastructure and basic services have long combined to make these areas a byword for urban deprivation. Moreover, problems of youth, such as gang activity, alcohol and drug abuse, unemployment and underemployment, teen pregnancy, violence and vandalism are not uncommon.

WMCF employs community-driven development approaches; its activities are prioritized based on community needs; it treats all residents and their institutions, with a focus on youth, as assets and partners in the search for solutions to developmental challenges; it supports and partners with other NGOs and youth groups operating in the same neighborhoods and/or fields; and it gives control over planning decisions and investment resources to community groups and local social entrepreneurs and philanthropists. In brief, WMCF operates on the principles of local empowerment, reviving authentic philanthropic business models, participatory governance, partnership, youth leadership, proactiveness, administrative autonomy, accountability and credibility, and enhanced local capacity.

5.10.3.7 WMCF's Overall and Specific Objectives

Over the course of hundreds of centuries in Egypt, *Waqf*[86] institutions have played the role of vivid civic endowed structures that aimed at community sustainable development and left behind great civic investments in establishing schools, hospitals, paving streets, enhancing research and development, and many other progressive civic acts reflecting refined social responsibility. Unfortunately this civic form of endowed structures was broken with governments' successive control of these endowments and completely deteriorated with the socialist regime of the 1950s by the firm control of the Ministry of Endowments over the *awqāf* and the abolishment of the family *waqf*. In brief this signaled an area where the government had been the sole social player and care provider. With Egypt following more liberal policies, civil society institutions began to re-emerge but in a different form prevailing in the NGO structures, a model imported from the West. However, in recent years the law governing NGOs allowed the establishment of endowed foundations and there are a number of private ones that have emerged recently. Yet, two things were still pending and missing: A traditional model for endowment building and a community foundation focusing on one geographical area. Emerging from this challenge, *Waqfeyat Al- Maadi* Community Foundation was a pioneering idea that manifested in the establishment of this body under the supervision of the Ministry of Social Solidarity in 2007, by Marwa El Daly (the Founder and Chairperson of WMCF).

WMCF aims at pro-active change through advocacy, arts and education. Moreover, the Foundation's specific objectives include:

- Providing innovative solutions and business models that revive the concept of *waqf* as a model similar to that of a social enterprise supporting a community cause yet being self-sustainable finanancially.

---

86 Waqf: (plural: awqaf)" is a major Islamic form of institutionalized philanthropy, which supported Egyptian civic life for centuries. The concept *Waqf* is derived from the Arabic word meaning "to-tie-up", and refers to tying-up profit to a social cause. For centuries, people in Egypt, as in many Muslim countries, tied-up properties by establishing a *waqf*, either directed to support charitable purposes, to support projects of public benefit *(waqf khayrī)*, or to the heirs and succesors (*waqf ahlī*) of the waqif (the personal who established the *waqf*), or mixed waqf (*waqf mushtarak*) which supported both charitable purposes as well as family members.

- Providing technical support to communities and other profit and non-profit making organizations to effectively set-up and mobilize endowments for sustainable development as well as to manage sustainable development programs that contribute to the benchmarks set for the development of the geographical area where they operate.
- Developing the concept of community foundation in Egypt that could be applied in various neighborhoods and eventually in the region.
- Strengthening local communities through philanthropy and civic engagement.
- Improving community-youth relationships through building awareness and understanding of youth concerns and strategies for dealing with them.
- Fostering and promoting the use of volunteers in serving their communities.
- Establishing and forging a network of partners from socially responsible businessmen, academics, community leaders, volunteers and development practitioners that would put strategies to promote concepts of philanthropy for sustainable development in Egypt.
- Involving youth in planning and implementation of activities.
- Establishing endowments and trust funds to support benchmarked sustainable development programs in Maadi and its outskirts to serve children, youth and adults of the area.
- Organizing activities and awareness programs that would promote philanthropy in Al-Maadi district as well as other neighborhoods, in collaboration with concerned parties.
- Collecting efforts to advocate for the promotion of an enabling legal environment that would promote philanthropy for development such as tax reduction for socially responsible investors.
- Establishing and forging local, regional and global networks to strengthen philanthropy for development.
- Linking corporate social responsibility departments of the private sector to non-governmental organizations operating in the same fields of intervention.
- Strengthening the private sector's role in local service delivery.

5.11 Summary

This chapter discussed four major issues:

First, it analyzed the theoretical component underlying philanthropy in Egypt and whether it is seen from a "right-based approach", i.e. the entitlement of the disadvantaged, or "their right" in a share in philanthropic resources as a religious obligation and not as a charitable volunteer act. It also discussed the connection between philanthropy as a religious duty and development as a social responsibility. Hence, we looked into the potentials of local philanthropy and the challenges of channeling it towards development. In this context the idea of the public good versus the individual interest was revisited and the influence of religious beliefs rooted in people's minds was discussed.

Second, and after presenting the theoretical component underlying philanthropy, the second major component dealt with in this chapter was philanthropic institutions in Egypt as represented by our sample, their establishment, geographical distribution, mission, activities and others. Religious organizations (Islamic and Christian) with philanthropic agendas were also included in the study analysis where their chairpersons of the Board of Directors, their donors and beneficiaries were intensively interviewed. Finally the economic conditions and sources of funding of these organizations were thoroughly discussed.

Third, we listed potentials for change and the future perspective as expressed by the respondents in relation to means of solving developmental problems and the possibilities of directing local giving and volunteering as well as local human capital towards the development of Egypt. These are recommendations and suggestions coming from the field, expressed by those involved, messages for them, us and to policy makers and agents of change; all partners in seeing a brighter future for them and their children.

Fourth, the chapters presented the model of Waqfeyat al Maadi Community Foundation (WMCF), the first community foundation in Egypt and one that was founded by the Dr. Marwa el Daly the author of this work. This was the on-the-ground product of years of research and field work to demonstrate the feasibility of revibing waqf as a local philanthropic model and developing social ventures with business models to sustain and scale up philanthropic operations and community empowerment.

References

Abdel Hamid, Abdellatif. Using SPSS Program through Windows: Statistical Package for the Social Sciences" (2001).

Abdel Salam Shehata. Dalil al-Dara'ib. Kitab Al-Ahram Al-Iqtisadi. No: 146, Marh 2000, page, 54

Ahmed Ismael Yehia. Al Zakat: 'ebada maleya wa idarah iqtisadeya. Cairo: Dar Al Ma'aref1986.

Al Fangary, Mohamed Shawky. Al Islam wal Tadamon al Ijtima'i. Cairo: Al Hay'a al Misriya al 'amma lel Ketab, 1990

Al-Qaradawy, Youssif. Fiqh Al-Zakat: A Comparative Study to the Rules and Philosophy of Zakat in Light of the Quran and Sunnah. Cairo: Wahba Library (24th edition), 2003.

Al Makhzangy, Alsayed Ahmed. Al Zakat wa Tanmeyat al Mujtama'. Saudi Arabia- Mekka: League of Islamic World; 2005

Al-Marsify, Said. Al-Mas'uliya al-ijtima'iya fi al-Islam. Al-Mansoura: Dar Al Yaqin, 2004.

Al-Nawawi, Rawdat al-talibun. Beirut, AH 1385, v. p. 314

Al Sharika Al-Tunisia lel Tawzi' (Publishers): Tunis: 1981.

Al Sheikh, Yaseen Ibrahim. Zakat: The Third Pillar of Islam. Lebanon: Al Maktab Al Islami in Beirut, 1998

Al-Sherbiny, Naguy. Kayfa tokaddir wa to'adi Zakat amoalak. Cairo: 1986.

An-Naim ,Abdullahi Ahmed and Asma Mohamed Abdel Halim. Rights-Based Approach to Philanthropy for Social Justice in Islamic Societies. This is a concept paper under publishing written by the two authors as a conceptual study for a research project on Islamic philanthropy in six countries, three of them with Muslim majority and three with Muslim minorities, among which is this study on Egypt that the research has lead.

Ashour, Anwar Ali: Quabs Min al-Fiqh al-Islami fi Alzakah, Al-I'tisam library, 1980. Pages5, 6.

Ateya, Mohamed Kamal. Halat tatbiqiya fi mohasabat al-Zakat wa 'ard lehalat tatbiqiya. (page 212), Monsha'at al-Ma'aref, Alexandria, 1988.

A workshop on the perception of philanthropy was prepared by Marwa El Daly as part of her MA Thesis on: Private Philanthropy in Egypt. The workshop organized by the Institute of Cultural Affairs and funded by the Ford Foundation in Cairo, demonstrated different perceptions of the term philanthropy, and the Arabic concept al 'ata' il ijtima'i was agreed upon to mean philanthropy and was first introduced as such by the researcher.

Babay, Ahmed. Sa'adat al-anam fi al-sa'i ila al-Zakat wal siyam, p. 23

Bishop Jacobos; Bishop of Zakazik and Menia el Qamh. Al'ata' wa kayfa yakoun. Egypt: Virgin Mary Church and Mar Johanna, 1998.

Burlingame, Dwight F. "Altruism and Philanthropy: Definitional Issues". Indiana University Center on Philanthropy, p 6–7.

Chapra, M. Umer. Islam and Economic Development: A Strategy for Development with Justice and Stability. Pakistan: The International institute of Islamic Thought and Islamic Research Institute, 1993

Deuteronomy (14:22–29 ; 15:7–11; 15:19–23; 12:6–7; 25:19).

El Daly Marwa. Private Philanthropy in Egypt: Institutionalized Private Philanthropy as a Mechanism for Sustainable Community Development. MA Thesis: The American University in Cairo, Dec. 2000.

El Daly, Marwa. Islamic Philanthropy: Institutionalized Giving in the Muslim Perspective. City University of New York; The Center for the Study on Philanthropy, 2001.

El Rashidy, Ahmed. Hoquq al insan: Dirasa moqarna fi al nazareya wal tatbiq. Al Qahira: Jami'at al Qahira: Kolleyat al Iqtisad wal 'olum al siyaseya, Page 35, 2003.

https://doi.org/10.1515/9783110697032-006

Elwan, Abdallah Naseh, Al takafol al ijtima'i fil Islam. Cairo, Dar Al Salam publishers, 6th edition, 2001.

Farishta G . de Zayas. The Law and Instiution of Zakat. Kuala lumpur: The Other Press; 2003

Ghanem, Ibrahim al Bayoumi. Al awqaf al Siasiya fi Misr.Cairo: Dar al Sherouk, 1998

Gregory Kozlowski, C. Muslim Endowments and Society in British India. NY: The Press Syndicate of the University of Cambridge. 1985.

Hujat Waqf Ahmed Pasha al Minshawi, page 47

Imams at-Tirmadhi and Abu Daudi.

Ibrahim, Medhat Hafiz. Dor al Zakat fi Khedmat al Mujtama'. Cairo: Dar Gharib lel Nashr wal Tiba'a.

Kamal Imam, Mohamad. Al Wasaya wal Awqaf fi al-Shari'a al-Islameya: Dirasa Fiqhiya wa Tashri'iya. Alexandria: Monsha'at Al-Ma'arif, 2002.

Mashhour, Neamat. Al-Zakat Mawared wa Masaref. www.islamonline.net/arabic/economics/2000/12/article2.shtml

Meksy Iskandar, Michael. Awal Mawsoua 'an al-ushour wa al-bokour, wa al-nuzur (75 sou'al wa gawab): Page 29, Cairo: Maktabet al Mahabba: 2000.

Nizam al Waqf wal mujtama' al madani fi wattan al 'rabi. Markaz dirasat al wihda al 'arabeya wal amana al 'ama lil awqaf fi dawlat al Kuwait. Beirut: 2003.

Qandil, Amani. Al mujtama' al madani fi masr fi matla' al alfeya al jadida. Al Qahira: Al Ahram, Markaz al dirasat al siyaseya wal istrategiya, 2000.

Qutb, Sayyid. Translated by John B. Hztfir. Social Justice In Islam. Cairo: Kaktabet Misr 2000

Quran, surat Ibrahim (14), 24–25.

Sabra, Adam. Poverty and Charity in Medieval Islam. Mamluk Egypt, 1250–1517; Cambridge Studies in Islamic Civilization; UK: Cambridge University Press, 2000

Saad Iddin, Ibrahim,. Al mujtama' al madani wal tahawul al dimoqrati fi misr. Al Qahira: Dar Qiba', 2000.

Said Al-Marsify. Al-Mas'uliya al-ijtima'iya fi al-Islam. Al-Mansoura: Dar Al Yaqin, 2004.

Samak, Nagwa Abdallah. Al Keta' Al Ahli wal Tanmeya Al Iktesadiya fy Misr. Center for the Study of Developing Countries, Cairo, 1999.

Selim El Awa, Mohamed. Azmat al Mo'assa al Dineya. page 42–43, Cairo: Dar El Sherouk, 2nd addition 2003.

Tarich Insha' al jami'a. Al Hilal Newspaper

The Diwan Al Ahbas was established during the reign of Hisham Bin Abdel Malak in the Omayad Period in Wgypt.

UNDP: Arab Human Development Report. July 2002

Yasseen Ibrahim Al-Sheikh. Zakat: The Third Pillar of Islam. Beirut: Al Maktab Al Islami (publishers), 2nd edition, 1998

Yehia Ismail, Ahmed. Al-Zakat: Ibadah maliya wa idarah iqtisadiya. Cairo: Dar El-Ma'aref, 1986.

Zohny Ihab Mohamed. Misr fi kitabat al ra'alah wal qanasil al firinsiyin fi al qarn al thamin 'ashar; Cairo: 1992

Appendices

https://doi.org/10.1515/9783110697032-007

Appendix 1: In Depth Interview with NGOs' Chairpersons and Members of the Board (Qualitative Study)

Intensive Interview with Board Members and Heads of Boards

I. Data about the NGO

Social Activities in the NGO

1. What are the activities the NGO offers (are they income generating projects or donations (charity)?
2. What are the goals of these activities and what is the general goal of the NGO?

II. Ideas and traditions related to the NGO's activities

Principals and traditions related to philanthropy

3. Do you know what philanthropy is? Are there any traditions or inherited ideas that encourage philanthropy? What are they?
4. Do you think philanthropy, as you explained, is reflected on the activities in the NGO?

– **Sources of Funding**

5. Who funds the NGO activities?
6. (If donor agencies) who are these agencies? What are the fields to which they prefer to donate?
7. Do you receive aid from any government agency, like, the Ministry of Social Affairs? How?
8. Do you receive aid from individuals?
9. What are the individuals' preferences of donations?
10. Are the rich the only segment that contributes to philanthropy?
11. What do people contribute more with; is it financial (money) or in-kind (clothes, food ... etc) or voluntary contribution?
12. To what extent do you depend on businessmen? Do they allocate fixed amount of money to be paid frequently to the Ngo?
13. What are the means you use to attract donations
14. Do you have any advocacy activity to incite people to make a change and to organize the philanthropy process?
15. Do people tend more to donate in their residence area or where their families were born? Give examples? (For example Diasporas) if there are Diasporas how could you reach them? What are their preferences of donations?
16. Do donors have a say in the kind of activities in the NGO?

17. Is it more difficult or easier to attract donations now than before? Why?
18. How far the resources of the NGO cover its activities and salaries for employees? (Give a percentage)
- **Relationship between NGO and Beneficiaries**
19. Who are the beneficiaries? How does the NGO distribute its resources?
20. Are there any problems in the resources distribution with the beneficiaries?
- **Social Justice**
21. What do you think this concept means?
22. Have you ever thought of this issue? If no, why not? If yes, what did your reach?
23. Do you see that social justice exists in our society? Why? If he says yes, how it has been achieved? If he says no, how could it be achieved?
24. If the rich gives money to the poor, could this decrease the gap between the two classes?
25. If people put their money and effort in establishing an organization or institution that aims at achieving social justice in Egypt, do you think people would like to support such organization? What could such organization do? Do we have in Egypt any organization of this kind?
- **Development**
26. How do you define development? What is the difference between charity and development?
27. Does the development concept prevail in the NGO activities?
28. Can we say that development achieves to some extent social justice?
- **Human Rights**
29. If we say human rights, what does this concept means to you? What are the most important of these rights?
30. Do the NGO activities concern about achieving human right and defending them as well? How?
- **The Effects of the NGO Activities on the Community**
31. If you think about the community around the Ngo, what is the effect of the NGO on the surrounding community regarding philanthropy, social justice, development and human rights?
- **Transparency**
32. In your opinion, what does transparency mean?
33. Do you face or have faced mistrust problem with donors?
34. Do you think transparency is achieved in the third sector (NGO or mosque or church)? How?
35. What are the procedures the NGO follows to show its transparency? Are they enough?

III. Main Principles in the Structure of the Organizations

– **Administrative and Structural Basis**

36. What did the persons or the group of persons who established the NGO do to collect the funds needed to found it?
37. Do you think many people in the community were willing to participate in founding the NGO?
38. Did you prefer another pattern to register the organization, like waqf or an investment project to serve the community? (The structure and explanation of its administration should be asked and if there is anything written about the NGO it is better to have it).
39. What is the situation of the founders from the NGO now?

– **Relation between the NGOs and Foundations with the Government and the Religious Institutions**

40. To what extent the procedures of founding the NGO were easy or complicated?
41. What are the facilitations or obstacles offered by the governmental agencies?
42. What is the degree of censorship exercised by the government either on the NGO activities or fund? What is the effect of this censorship on the NGO work?
43. Is there any kind of coordination concerning the activities between the Ngo and any other body; government agencies or organizations or other institutions?
44. Do you have any idea about the assistance fund box in the Ministry of Social affairs (MOSA)? Do you have any idea how this fund is distributed on the NGOs?

IV. The Surrounding Environment

– **Cultural and Social Environment**

45. What is the civil society?
46. Was there any kind of volunteerism in your school or university?
47. Did you practice any kind of these activities? Why? What was its effect on your personality?
48. During your education years, was there anything in the school curricula that encourages volunteerism or philanthropy?
49. Can you say public proverbs or Qur'an verses or prophet's sayings about philanthropy? What were their effects on you?

– **Philanthropy in Media and Arts**

50. What is the most influencing mean of media that affects people regarding philanthropy?
51. Did you use any of these means of media (television commercials, radio, newspapers or banks) to attract donations? How?

52. Have you been influenced by the television commercials, like the one about the cancer hospital or others, and donated to any of them? What about el Azhar?

– **The Cultural Legitimacy: How the Community Members Accept the Philanthropy Culture**

53. How can we encourage philanthropy and make the philanthropic process more organized?

– **The Religious Legitimacy: Religion as a Motive to Philanthropy**

54. What do you know about the conditions and percentages of the *Zakat* and tith?
55. Do you make an announcement that your NGO accepts *Zakat*?
56. Do you think people become more willing and compassionate to participate in philanthropic activities when it is under religious slogan? If yes, how did you make use of this compassion to attract people toward philanthropy?

– **The Legal Environment**

57. What did you expect to see in the new organizations' law? Are these expectations realized or not? How it affected the NGO?
58. Are the donors concerned about taking a receipt to use it in tax exemption?

– **The Economic Environment**

59. Most people say that the current economic status is very bad, how do you think this has affected the rate of giving, especially, the private sector? How?
60. Currently with this bad economic situation, did the number of the beneficiaries increase? If yes, how the NGO deals with this increase?
61. How could philanthropy contribute in solving economic problems like unemployment? Are there any examples? Is this related to religious teaching?

Appendix 2: Intensive Interview with Leaders of Religious Institutions Sheikhs/Priests (Qualitative Study)

I. Data of the Mosque/Church

1. Mosque/Church Name:
2. Address:
3. Governorate:
4. City: Village:
5. Person's name:
6. Profession:
7. How many working hours: Volunteering or paid?
8. Is there other job:
9. What is the kind of administration that supervises the mosque/church?
10. What is the administrative structure of the mosque/church?
11. Does this structure consist of employees or volunteers?
12. When the mosque was built and with whose effort?
13. Was there social contribution during the construction process?
14. What did you do to collect resources/fund for the construction?
15. Who is responsible for the social activities in the mosque/church?

– **Social Activities in the Mosque/Church:**

16. What is the kind of social activities in the mosque/church? (Are they seasonal associated with feasts, income generating activities or financial assistance?)
17. What is the goal of these activities?

II. Ideas and Concepts Related to the Mosque/Church Activities

– **Principals and Traditions Related to Philanthropy**

18. Do you know what philanthropy is? Are there any traditions or inherited ideas that encourage philanthropy? What are they?

– **Sources of Funding**

19. Who funds the mosque/church activities?
20. (If donor agencies) who are these agencies? What are the fields to which they prefer to donate?
21. Do you receive aid from any government agency, like, the Ministry of Social Affairs? How?
22. Do you receive aid from individuals?
23. What are the individuals' preferences of donations?
24. Are the rich the only segment that contributes to philanthropy?
25. What do people contribute more with; is it financial (money) or in-kind (clothes, food ... etc) or voluntary contribution?

26. To what extent do you depend on businessmen? Do they allocate fixed amount of money to be paid frequently to the mosque/church?
27. What are the means you use to attract donations
28. Do you have any advocacy activity to incite people to make a change and to organize the philanthropy process?
29. Do people tend more to donate in their residence area or where their families were born? Give examples? (For example Diasporas) if there are Diasporas how could you reach them? What are their preferences of donations?
30. Do donors have a say in the kind of activities in the mosque/church?
31. Is it more difficult or easier to attract donations now than before? Why?
32. How far the resources of the mosque/church cover its activities and salaries for employees? (Give a percentage)

– **Relationship between the Mosque/Church and Beneficiaries**

33. Who are the beneficiaries? How does the mosque/church distribute its resources?
34. Are there any problems in the resource distribution with the beneficiaries?

– **Social Justice**

35. What do you think this concept means?
36. Have you ever thought of the issue? If no, what not? If yes, what did you reach?
37. Can you say Qur'an verses or prophet's saying that encourage social justice?
38. Do people understand what social justice is in religion? Do they apply it in their life?
39. Do you see that social justice exists in our society? Why? If he say yes, how it has been achieved? If he says no, how could it be achieved?
40. If the rich gives money to the poor, could this decrease the gap between the two classes?
41. Do you have activities in the mosque/church that encourage and aim at achieving social justice and decreasing the gap between classes? How?
42. If someone went to pilgrimage or omra once, is it good to go another time or it is better to give the money to needy people?

– **Development**

43. How do you define development? What is the difference between charity and development?
44. Do you think religion encourage development? How? Explain with Qur'an verses or prophet's sayings.
45. Can we say that development achieves to some extent social justice?

– **Human Rights**

46. As a religious man, can you tell us what does this concept mean to you? Can you say Qur'an verses or prophet's saying?
47. What are the most important of these rights? What are of these rights you think don't exist?

48. Do the mosque/church activities concern about achieving human rights and defending them as well? How?

- **Effect of the Mosque/Church Activities on the Community**

49. What is the effect of the mosque/church on philanthropy?
50. If you think about the community around you, what do you think the effect of the mosque/church on the surrounding community regarding philanthropy, social justice, development, and human rights?

- **Transparency**

51. In your opinion, what do you think transparency is?
52. Is it preferred to be in privacy or in public?
53. Who is responsible for distributing the resources?
54. Does the donor know where his money goes?
55. What are the procedures you do to show the mosque/church's transparency? Are they enough?

III. Main Principles in the Structure of the Institutions

56. What are the facilitations or obstacles offered by the governmental agencies?
57. Is there any cooperation with other civic organizations? Is there any collaboration between the mosque/church with other organizations to estimate the number of beneficiaries in the district?

IV. The Surrounding Environment

- **Cultural and Social Environment**

58. What is the civil society?
59. Does the mosque/church use preaches as a means to encourage philanthropy? How?
60. Was there any of volunteerism in your school or university?
61. Did you participate in any kind of these activities? Why? What were their effects on your personality?
62. During your education years, was there anything in the school curricula that encourages volunteerism or philanthropy?

- **Philanthropy in Media and Arts**

63. What is the most influencing mean of media that affects people regarding philanthropy?
64. Did you use any of these means of media (television commercials, radio, newspapers or banks) to attract donations? How?
65. Have you been influenced by the television commercials, like the one about the cancer hospital or others, and donated to any of them? What about el Azhar?

- **The Cultural Legitimacy: How the Community Members Accept the Philanthropy Culture**

66. How can we encourage philanthropy and make the philanthropic process more organized?
- **The Religious Legitimacy: Religion as a Motive to Philanthropy**
67. How many people pay *Zakat*/tith
68. Do you make an announcement that your mosque accepts *Zakat*?
69. Do you think people become more willing and compassionate to participate in philanthropic activities when it is under religious slogan? If yes, how did you make use of this compassion to attract people toward philanthropy?
- **The legal Environment**
70. Are the donors concerned to take a receipt to use it in tax exemption?
- **The Economic Environment**
71. Most people say that the current economic status is very bad, how do you think this has affected the rate of giving, especially, the private sector? How?
72. Currently with this bad economic situation, did the number of the beneficiaries increase? If yes, how the NGO deals with this increase?
73. How could philanthropy contribute in solving economic problems like unemployment? Are there any examples? Is this related to religious teaching?

Appendix 3: In Depth Interview with Donors (Qualitative Study)

Data of the Donor

1. Name:
2. Address:
3. Governorate:
4. City: Village:
5. Person's name:
6. Profession:
7. Income average:
8. How many times do you come to the NGO:

I. Motive

9. What is the motive of your giving?
10. When you donate, do you feel that it is charity or that it is people's right that has to be delivered?
11. Do you exempt your donations from taxes?
12. When you contribute to the NGO, either with your money or effort, do you feel that your contribution gives you a better social status? Explain.

II. Concepts and Ideas Related to the Donor's Experience

13. What is philanthropy? Are there any traditions or inherited ideas encourage you on philanthropy?
14. Do you contribute with your money or your effort or both?
15. Do you donate to organizations or individuals? How and why? Explain.
16. What are the fields to which you prefer to donate?
17. What are the means that attract you to donate?
18. Where do you tend to donate your money, in the place you were born or to people in the same area where you live or where your family live or in the place where you work?
19. Do you mind donate to other countries?

– **Social Justice**

20. What do you think this concept means?
21. Have you ever thought of this issue? If no, why not? If yes, what did your reach?
22. Do you see that social justice exists in our society? Why? If he says yes, how it has been achieved? If he says no, how could it be achieved?
23. If the rich gives money to the poor, could this decrease the gap between the two classes?

24. If people put their money and effort in establishing an organization or institution that aims at achieving social justice in Egypt, do you think people would like to support such organization? What could such organization do? Do we have in Egypt any organization of this kind?
25. Do you feel your contribution has achieved small part in social justice? How?

– **Development**

26. How do you define development? What is the difference between charity and development?
27. When you donate or volunteer, do you put into consideration that this is aimed at charity or development? Explain.
28. Have you ever thought about making sadaqa jariya or a sustainable kind of giving?
29. Do you have any idea about the waqf?
30. Have you ever thought about donating money to the Ministry of Awqaf or to make waqf?
31. Did you invest your donation or volunteerism in teaching someone or give someone a capital to start a small project? If no, explain why you did not, if yes, what have you done? Did you think about doing that through any organization?
32. Can you say public proverbs or Qur'an verses or prophet's sayings that encourage philanthropy? How have they affected you?
33. Can we say that development achieves to some extent social justice?

– **Human Rights**

34. If we say human rights, what does this concept means to you?
35. What are the most important of these rights? What are of these rights you think don't exist?
36. Do you have a vision in your contribution to achieve social justice or human rights? If yes, how do you try to achieve that? If no, why?

– **Transparency**

37. In your opinion, what do you think transparency is? Do you think that transparency is important? How do you think it can be achieved? Do you face or have faced mistrust problem with organizations/do you completely trust the charitable NGOs you deal with?
38. What are the procedures that can make you trust these NGOs?

III. The Surrounding Environment

– **Cultural and Social Environment**

39. What is civil society?
40. What made you want to donate or volunteer? Is it the school, the family, the education, the economic standard that makes you feel the social responsibility or the religion?
41. Was there any kind of volunteerism in your school or university?

42. Did you participate in any kind of these activities? Why? What were their effects on your personality?
43. During your education years, was there anything in the school curricula that encourages volunteerism or philanthropy?
44. Can you say public proverbs or Qur'an verses or prophet's sayings about philanthropy?

– **Philanthropy in Media and Arts**

45. What are the most attractive means of media that encourages you to donate?
46. Have you been influenced by any of the TV commercials, like the one about the cancer hospital or other project and donated your money to any of them?
47. Can you donate to bank accounts?
48. What about the Azhar?

– **The Cultural Legitimacy: How the Community Members Accept the Philanthropic Culture**

49. How can we encourage philanthropy and make the philanthropic process more organized?

– **The Religious Legitimacy: Religion as a Motive to Philanthropy**

50. What do you know about the conditions and percentages of the *Zakat* and the tith?
51. Do you calculate you *Zakat* accurately? How much approximately do you pay?
52. Do you differentiate between where to put your *Zakat* and where to put your sadaqa?

– **The Economic Environment**

53. Most people say that the current economic status is very bad, did this have effect on your contribution? How?
54. How could philanthropy contribute in solving economic problems like unemployment? Are there any examples?

Appendix 4: In Depth Interview with NGOs' Aid Recipients (Beneficiaries) (Qualitative Study)

Data of the Beneficiaries

1. Name:
2. Address:
3. Governorate:
4. City: Village:
5. Person's name:
6. Profession:
7. Number of children:
8. Source of income:
9. Income average:
10. How many times do you come to the NGO:
11. Why have you resorted to the NGO or the individuals for help?
12. What are the organizations you deal with?
13. How did you know about them?
14. How did they decide to help you?

I. Ideas and Concepts Related to the Beneficiary's experience:

– **Principals and Traditions related to Philanthropy**

15. What do you think philanthropy is?
16. What is the kind of help you receive form the organization? Is it financial or in-kind or volunteering help?
17. What is your preference of help?

– **Social Justice**

18. What do you think this concept means?
19. Have you ever thought of this issue? If no, why not? If yes, what did your reach?
20. Do you see that social justice exists in our society? Why? If he says yes, how it has been achieved? If he says no, how could it be achieved?
21. If people put their money and effort in establishing an organization or institution that aims at achieving social justice in Egypt, do you think people would like to support such organization? What could such organization do? Do we have in Egypt any organization of this kind?
22. Do you think that this assistance could decrease the gap between your class and the rich one?
23. Do you feel this assistance from the NGO could achieve social justice in our society? If he says yes, how? If he says no, so what is the solution?

- **Development**

24. How do you define development? What is the difference between charity and development?
25. Do you feel the assistance you received was only charity or development?
26. What did you do with this assistance? How much it has affected your life?
27. If you take money, have you ever thought about establishing a small project with this money? If yes, what did you do? If no, why not?
28. Can we say that development achieves social justice to some extent?

- **Human Rights**

29. If we say human rights, what does this concept means to you?
30. What are the most important of these rights? What are of these rights you think don't exist?
31. Did the assistance you receive give you some of your rights as a human?

- **Transparency**

32. In your opinion, what do you think transparency is?
33. Do you take any help from individuals outside the NGO?
34. What is the difference between the assistance from the Ngo and that from individuals? Which one do you prefer? Why?
35. Is there any privacy in your relation with the NGO or individuals? Do you prefer this privacy or you don't care about it?

II. The Surrounding Environment

- **Cultural and Social Environment**

36. What is the civil society?
37. Was there any kind of volunteerism in your school or university?
38. Did you participate in any kind of these activities? Why? What were there effects on your personality?
39. During your education years, was there anything in the school curricula that encourages volunteerism or philanthropy?
40. Can you say public proverbs or Qur'an verses or prophet's sayings about philanthropy?

- **Philanthropy in Media and Arts**

41. Have you ever thought about going to any means of media to show them your problem? If yes, which one is it? If we assume that you will go to one, which one you will choose?
42. Have you thought of going to Al Azhar?
43. Have you thought of going to any organization made a television commercial?

- **The Cultural Legitimacy: How the Community Members Accept the Philanthropic Culture**

44. How can we encourage philanthropy and make its process more organized?

45. What are the things you prefer to have when you deal with the Ngo but do not happen?
46. When you see someone in need, do you help him? How?

– **The Religious Legitimacy: Religion as a Motive to Philanthropy**

47. What do you know about the conditions and percentages of the *Zakat* or the tith?
48. Do you pay *Zakat* or sadaqa?
49. Do you think people become more willing and compassionate to participate in philanthropic activities when it is under religious slogan? If yes, how did you make use of this compassion to attract people toward philanthropy?

– **The economic Environment**

50. Most people say that the current economic status is very bad, do you think this have an effect on individuals' giving? How?
51. How could philanthropy contribute in solving economic problems like unemployment? Are there any examples? Is this related to religious teaching?
52. Has the assistance enhanced your social status? Explain.

Appendix 5: The Philanthropic Institutions' Survey (Quantitative Study)

Philanthropy in Egypt: Philanthropic Institutions' Survey

V1: Country code

V2: Serial number

V3: Organization type
1. Governmental ( )
2. Non-government ( )
- Name of organization
- Address

V4: Governorate ……………………… Location ……………………

V5: Rural ( ) Urban ()

I. Data About Interviewee

V6 Respondent's name………………………………………

V7 Respondent's position ……………………………………

V8 Do you work in the organization full-time or part-time?
1. Full–time.
2. Part–time.
9. No answer.

V9 How many hours do you work per week ?

V10 Do you receive a salary for your work in the organization?
1. Yes (Go to V18)
2. No
9. No answer.

What are the reasons behind your volunteering time		Mentioned	Not Mentioned
V11	To feel satisfied for doing voluntary work	1	2
V12	To fulfill religious duties	1	2
V13	Important for development activities	1	2
V14	To gain personal experience	1	2
V15	To fulfill humanitarian needs	1	2
V16	To gain respect and esteem	1	2
V17	Others, please specify..		

V18 Do you hold other positions outside the organization ?
1. Yes.
2. No.
9. No answer.

V19 If "yes": What is your occupation? ....

II. Data on the Establishment of the Association, its Mission and Goals:

V20 Who came up with the idea to establish the association?
1. A group of community leaders.
2. A group of ordinary individuals.
3. Government officials.
4. A VIP person.
5. Others, please identify.......................................
8. Don't know.
9. No answer.

V21 How many founders were there for the association?

[ ]

8. Don't know.
9. No answer.

V21A Why more than one founders?
1. To collect sufficient support.
2. Because the Law demands that.
3. Create more financial support from collective participation.
4. Maintain collective participation of several individuals.
5. Others, please specify ....
8. Don't know.
9. No answer.

V21B Did all the founders contribute equally?
1. Yes, all individuals contributed equally.
2. No, there were individuals who contributed more them others.
3. Other, please specify..
8. I don't know.
9. No answer .

V21C Do those who have contributed more occupy different roles in the decision-making processes?
1. No, all individuals have equal-rights in the management.
2. Yes, those individuals who have contributed more money enjoy more rights in the management.
3. Other, please specify ....
8. I don't know.
9. No answer.

Where did your institution get the resources to own/rent the place at the time of establishment?		**Mentioned**	**Not Mentioned**
V22	Contributions from principals	1	2
V23	Donations from rich people in the area	1	2
V24	Hosted by other organization	1	2
V25	Through governmental facilities	1	2
V26	Providing a place for religious service	1	2
V27	Others, please specify..		

V28 What are the main goals/mission of the association?
-...
-...
-...
8. Don't know.
9. No answer.

V29 Does your organization promote certain ideas trying to advance certain principles that help formulate policies?
1. Yes.
2. No (Go to V49)
8. Don't know.
9. No answer.

If yes, list what you do?		Mentioned	Not Mentioned
Q30	Reservation of culture, arts, and historical heritage	1	2
Q31	Helping and protecting those who are in need.	1	2
Q32	Promoting religious plurality	1	2
Q33	Advocacy for improving health awareness	1	2
Q34	Advocacy for the protection of children and youth	1	2
Q35	Advocacy for animal protection	1	2
Q36	Advocacy for the advancement of sciences	1	2
Q37	Advocacy for the support of sports	1	2
Q38	Advocacy for enhancing environmental awareness among people	1	2
Q39	Advocacy for defending women's right	1	2
Q40	Advocacy to enhance human rights and social justice	1	2
Q41	Advocacy for bridging the gab between the rich and the poor	1	2
Q42	Other, please specify..		

What are the different mechanisms that are being utilized to advocate and actualize this change?		Mentioned	Not Mentioned
V43	Through panel discussions and lectures	1	2
V44	Through printing booklets and brochures	1	2
V45	lectures in Mosques Through	1	2
V46	Through TV advertisement	1	2
V47	Lobbying with Parliamentarians	1	2
V48	Other, please specify..		

V49 To what degree are you fulfilling your objectives? On a scale from 1 to 5, please reply with 4 or 5 if you have fulfilled your objectives (Mostly or Fully). If you have not fulfilled any objectives choose 1 or 2 if you have not fulfilled the objectives (Mostly or Fully).

Didn't fully fulfill its goals	Didn't fulfill most of its goals	Partly fulfilled its goals	Mostly fulfilled some of its goals	Fully fulfilled all of its goals
1	2	3	4	5

8 Don't know
9 No answer

What is the classification of the organization?		Mentioned	Not Mentioned
V50	Non-profit NGO	1	2
V51	A professional organization	1	2
V52	Religious organization	1	2
V53	A call for achieving social justice	1	2
V54	Providing support for the government	1	2

III. Information on the Association (Starting date, Employment, Activities, Resources, Problems, Points of Strength and Weakness)

V55 In which year did the association start performing activities?

....

8. Don't know.
9. No answer.

		Males	Females
V56	Number of trustees		
V57	Number of founders since the establishment of the association		
V58	Number of general assembly members		
V59	Number of administrative personnel		
V60	Number of salaried employees		
V61	Number of volunteers excluding administrative personnel		

Are the association resources from?		Mentioned	Not Mentioned	%
Q62	Economic activities	1	2	V62A...
Q63	Services activities	1	2	V63A...
Q64	Funds from foreign (Non-Arab) organizations	1	2	V64A...
Q65	Funds from Arab and Islamic donor organizations	1	2	V65A...
Q66	Funds from governmental donor organizations	1	2	V66A...
Q67	Donations from Egyptian businessmen	1	2	V67A...
Q68	Funds from local donor organizations	1	2	V68A...
Q69	Donates from community leaders	1	2	V69A....
Q70	Donations from Egyptian expatriates	1	2	V70A...
Q71	Endowments revenues (Waqf)	1	2	V71A...
Q72	Religious donations (*Zakat* El Fitr, Ashour, Sadaqa)	1	2	V72A....
Q73	Donations	1	2	V73A...

Are the association resources from?		Mentioned	Not Mentioned	%
Q74	Real-estate revenues	1	2	V74A...
Q75	Shares and bank interest	1	2	V75A...
Q76	Special endowment (Waqf) for the association	1	2	V76A....
Q77	Special permits to collect money (exhibitions and events)	1	2	V77A...
Q78	Membership Dues	1	2	V78A...

How does your institution allocate its resources?		Mentioned	Not Mentioned
V79	Disbursement according to the need of each activity	1	2
V80	Certain portions allocated to each activity in the budget	1	2
V81	Disbursement according to board of directors' decision	1	2
V82	The decision is left to a trusted person in the association	1	2

What are the activities that the institution does?

First: Economic, Social and Health Development:		Mentioned	Not Mentioned
V84	Managing economic enterprises	1	2
V85	Offering loans for small businesses	1	2
V86	Provision of care for senior citizen	1	2
V87	Provision of care for disadvantage group	1	2
V88	Provision of children and maternal care	1	2
V89	Family planning	1	2
V90	Girl's education	1	2
V91	Alleviation of illiteracy	1	2
V92	Others, please specify		

Second: Charity work		Mentioned	Not Mentioned
V93	Special weddings and funerals reception halls	1	2
V94	Services without charges	1	2
V95	Distribution of *Zakat* to the needy	1	2
V96	Distribution of Sadaqa to the needy	1	2
V97	Hosting of orphans	1	2
V98	Monthly payments and in-kind assistance for families and individuals	1	2
V99	Financial and in-kind assistance to families (Onetime)	1	2
V100	Financial assistance to families having no provider	1	2
V101	Others, please specify...		

V102 What is the number of the beneficiaries receiving assistance from the institution?

(....................)

8. Don't know.
9. No answer.

V103	What are the ways of reaching recipients?	Mentioned	Not Mentioned
V103a	Advertising campaigns calling for recipients	1	2
V103b	Most recipients are familiar with activities provided by institution	1	2
V103c	Referrals through networking with other institutions	1	2
V103d	Referrals through local community leaders	1	2
V103e	Referrals through MOSA and local government	1	2
V103f	Through the Media	1	2
V103g	Through the Mosques	1	2

V104 Are there instructions and conditions related to charitable disbursement adopted by the board?

1. Yes.
2. No. (Go to V105)
8. I don't know.
9. No answer.

V104A If the answer is "yes" What are these instructions or conditions ?

- ....
- ....
- ....

8. I don't know.
9. No answer.

V105 Does the institution seek recipient's opinion over the services that are being provided?

1. yes.
2. No (Go to V107)
8. I don't know.
9. No answer.

V106 How recipient's opinion is being thought?

....

V107 How much was the net revenue in the year 2002?

(.........................) net

8. I don't know .
9. No answer.

V108 Does the institution invest some of its revenues?

1. Yes.
2. No (Go To V114)
8. Don't know.
9. No answer.

How dose the institution invest its resources?		Mentioned	Not Mentioned
V109	Through investment certificate	1	2
V110	Through stock exchange	1	2
V111	Through fixed bank deposits	1	2
V112	Others, please specify		

V113 Why would this be done?

1. In order for the institution to cover the expenses for its activities .
2. To be able to pay salaries to staff.
3. In order to remain in operations.
8. Don't know.
9. No answer.

V114 Why wouldn't this be done?
1. Because this is religiously prohibited usury .
2. Because it is prohibited by Law.
3. The refusal of some members to avoid risks.
4. Because of insufficient resources.
5. Others, please identify……………………………………………………………
8. Don't know.
9. No answer.

V115 What are the activities that receive the highest proportion and get repeated in each budget?
1. ………………………………………….
2. ………………………………………….
8. Don't know.
9. No answer.

	Does the association's activities help in? Use scale from 1 to 5.	Didn't Help at All	Didn't Help	Help to Some Extent	Did Help	Help Greatly	NA
V116	Reducing the gap between the rich and the poor	1	2	3	4	5	9
V117	Enhancing love and mercy among people	1	2	3	4	5	9
V118	Helping families to face the demands of life	1	2	3	4	5	9
V119	Provision of services for people	1	2	3	4	5	9
V120	Making the poor feel secured	1	2	3	4	5	9
V121	Realize the principle of justice among people	1	2	3	4	5	9
V122	Contribution to social development	1	2	3	4	5	9
V123	Other, please specify …………………………………						9

When the association is in need for additional funding, what is the most likely channel it would follow?		Mentioned	Not Mentioned
V124	Getting a permit from the social affairs administration for fundraising	1	2
V125	Starting a new economic enterprise	1	2
V126	Contacting local donor organizations	1	2
V127	Contacting foreign donor organizations	1	2
V128	Contacting some community leaders or philanthropists	1	2
V129	Requesting financial support from the state	1	2
V130	Other, please specify		

What are the means that have been adopted to assure freedom of opinion within the board?		Mentioned	Not Mentioned
V131	The right to object to decisions	1	2
V132	Allowing discussion to know other opinion	1	2
V133	Decisions should not be approved unless the legal number of assembly is achieved	1	2
V134	Minutes of meeting should not be approved through passing	1	2

Several potential problems that an organization could face. please tell me how important this problem would be for the organization's operations by giving a score between 1 and 5.

		Not Important at all	Is not that Important	Important to Some Extent	Important	Very Important	NA
V135	Problems related to insufficient financial resources	1	2	3	4	5	9
V135A	Why this is the case?..............................						9
V136	Problems related to bureaucratic regulations	1	2	3	4	5	9
V136A	Why this is the case?..............................						9
V137	Problems related to state intervention	1	2	3	4	5	9
V137A	Why this is the case?..............................						9
V138	Problems related to lack of support from individuals in the community	1	2	3	4	5	9
V138A	Why this is the case?..............................						9
V139	Problems related to non-existence of accounting and control	1	2	3	4	5	9
V139A	Why this is the case?..............................						9
V140	Problems related to non-existence of specialized and good management	1	2	3	4	5	9
V140A	Why this is the case?..............................						9
V141	Problems related to insufficient of resourse and donations	1	2	3	4	5	9
V141A	Why this is the case?..............................						9
V142	Other ,please specify..............................						9
V142A	Why this is the case?..............................						9

In each association, there is always points of strength and points of weakness. in this association, what are points of strength and points of weakness

	(Points of strength)	Mentioned	Not Mentioned
V143	Board of director is strong and committed	1	2
V144	Transparency of decisions adopted by the board	1	2
V145	The existence of a good accounting system	1	2
V146	A general assembly that discusses decisions and negate them	1	2
V147	The non-existence of vested interest groups in the general assembly and the board	1	2
V148	The association enjoys a good reputation in local community	1	2
V149	The existence of honest staff members executing the activities	1	2
V150	The existence of assistance and support from the community	1	2
V151	Others ,please specify..................................		

	(Points of weakness)	Mentioned	Not Mentioned
V152	A constant conflict among board members	1	2
V153	An authoritarian chairman of the board	1	2
V154	The non-existence of a good accounting system to review documents	1	2
V155	Lack of transparency in the board's decisions	1	2
V156	A general assembly that does not negate decisions made by the board	1	2
V157	Doubtful impression expressed by the local community on the membership	1	2
V158	Lack of staff members to facilitate daily operations	1	2
V159	Favoritism to some members in the eyes of the community	1	2
V160	Others, please specify		

IV. The Relation of the Association with the Local Community

	Do the prevailing atmosphere within the community have any impact on the association?	Mentioned	Not Mentioned
V161	Legal and guidelines that influence the ways the association operates	1	2
V162	Impacts due to social conditions	1	2
V163	Impacts as a result of the current economic environment	1	2
V164	No influences affecting activities of the association	1	2

V165 Do you believe that the association is being influenced by certain individuals or governmental agencies in the community?

1. Yes Go to (V165A)
2. No Go to (V165B)
8. Don't know.
9. No answer.

V165A If yes (State why?) ……………………………………………………………………

V165B If no (State why?) ………………………………………………………

	V166	V167
In your opinion: Who has more impact on the association?	First Choice	Second Choice
Some leaders from the local community in general	1	1
Some individuals who donate to the institution	2	2
The government (Ministry of Social Affairs)	3	3
Funding agencies	4	4
Religious leaders	5	5
Others, please specify …………………………………		

	What is the relationship between the institution and the MOSA?	Mentioned	Not Mentioned
V168	Reducing all difficulties facing the association	1	2
V169	Providing opportunities for the staff to gain rewards	1	2
V170	Discovering errors during inspection campaigns	1	2
V171	Providing guidance during inspection and documents' review	1	2
V172	Encouraging the association to execute activities	1	2
V173	Putting obstacles in front of the association when implementing activities	1	2
V174	Putting obstacles for grants' approval	1	2

V175 Is there any cooperation between your association and religious organizations?
1. Yes.
2. No (Go to 176)
8. Don't know.
9. No answer.

V175A If yes, what is the form of this cooperation?
1. Joint-venture projects.
2. Receiving donations.
3. Sending donations.
4. Collaborative effort in civil activities.
8. Don't know.
9. No answer.

V176 Do members who donate have the right to know where the donations are going?
1. Yes.
2. No.
3. I never thought about that.
8. Don't know.
9. No answer.

V177 During the past year, has the organization/institution received any donation?
1. Yes.
2. No.
8. Don't know.
9. No answer.

What are the sources of donations?		Mentioned	Not Mentioned
V178	Cash donation from individuals	1	2
V179	In kind donation from individuals	1	2
V180	Cash donations from business community	1	2
V181	In kind donations from business community	1	2
V182	Donations from Egyptians living abroad	1	2
V183	Grants from foreign funding agencies	1	2
V184	Grants from local funding agencies	1	2
V185	Funding from the state	1	2
V186	Donations in the form of *Zakat*/Sadaqa/Ashour	1	2
V187	Donations in the form of volunteering time	1	2
V188	Others, please specify................................		

What are elements of the relationship between the institution and the government?		Mentioned	Not Mentioned
V189	The state should provide supervision of association's activities	1	2
V190	The state should provide the necessary information that the association might need	1	2
V191	The state should be involved in data collection	1	2
V192	Educational responsibilities	1	2
V193	Guidance responsibilities	1	2
V194	Encouragement responsibilities	1	2
V195	Participation in the decision-making process by providing information	1	2
V196	Others, please specify……………………………….		

What does the association do to get the trust of the local community?		Mentioned	Not Mentioned
V197	Provision of service needed in the community	1	2
V198	Fairness in the disbursements of assistance in case families are involved	1	2
V199	Services provided should be attainable by all categories of people	1	2
V200	Board members should be known for their good reputation	1	2
V201	Maintaining transparency	1	2
V202	Others, please specify………………………………………		

Do you think the new law would help in:		Mentioned	Not Mentioned
V203	Reducing the time required to acquire governmental approvals	1	2
V204	Giving associations more freedom to operate	1	2
V205	Enhancing philanthropy within the community	1	2
V206	Increasing benefits for some staff members	1	2
V207	Crippling the operations of some associations	1	2
V208	Decreasing some difficulties	1	2
V209	I don't know since the law has not shown its impact yet	1	2
V210	Others, please specify………………………………………		

Reasons for not donating to institutions		Mentioned	Not Mentioned
V211	Lack of transparency	1	2
V212	Lack of knowledge on the importance of role of association	1	2
V213	Lack of trust in the deployment of services to those who deserve them	1	2
V214	Others, please specify…………………………………………		

V215 Would it be possible to redirect philanthropic activity to investment rather than Sadaqa?

1. Yes.
2. No.
8. Don't know.
9. No answer.

V215A If yes: why?

……………………………………………………………………….

V215B If no: why?

………………………………………………………………………

What could affect the form of philanthropy in general		Mentioned	Not Mentioned
V216	The type of service provided	1	2
V217	Transparency of those responsible for charity work	1	2
V218	The concern over of including philanthropic activity under public accountability	1	2
V219	Advertising in local press	1	2
V220	Advertisement on TV	1	2

V221 In your opinion, what would be the new legal arrangement that might help in expanding the Waqf or organizational activities?

……………………………………………………………………………

……………………………………………………………………………

……………………………………………………………………………

8. Don't know.
9. No answer .

V222 Would you like to participate in a network that combine the organization/the institutions under of a mother organization?

1. Yes.
2. No.
8. Don't know.
9. No answer.

V223 What would you expect to achieve if you join this network?

....

....

Appendix 6: The Publics' Survey (Quantitative Study)

Publics and NGOs' Surveys – Quantitative Study – Philanthropy in Egypt

I. The Publics' Questionnaire

Q1 Country code: ....

Q2 Questionnaire number: ....
Date:
Interviewer name: ....

Q3 Name: ....

Q4 Address: ....

Q5 Governorate:
1. Cairo
2. Aswan
3. Menia
4. Menofia
5. Sharkia

Q6 Residence:
1. Rural
2. Urban

Q7 Respondent sex:
1. Male
2. Female

Q8 Respondent age: ....

Q9 Place of birth:
1. A village.
2. A small town.
3. A large city.
9. NA.

DEMOGRAPHIC DATA:

Q10 What is the level of your education?
1. Illiterate/never went to school.
2. Literate/left at primary school level.
3. Primary school certificate.
4. Preparatory school certificate.
5. Secondary school certificate.
6. University.
7. Post graduate level.
9. NA

Q 11 What is your employment status?
1. Employed.
2. Unemployed.
3. Retired.
4. Housewife.
5. Student.
6. Unemployed and not seeking employment.
9. NA

Q12 What is your job?
1. Professional (Doctor, Lawyers, Teachers,...)
2. Owner of private project.
3. Administrative occupations.
4. Salesman.
5. Services worker.
6. Social development workers.
7. Agriculture.
8. Skilled workers.
9. Others, please specify ....

Q13 Marital status:
1. Single (Go to Q15)
2. Married.
3. Widowed/divorced.
4. Engaged.
9. NA

Q14 Do you have any children? (Do not ask single respondents)
1.Yes.
2. No.
9. NA

Q15 Can you tell me how many persons are living in your household including yourself?

....

Total family members:

Q16 Male:....................

Q17 Female:.................

Q18 Total:...................

What does the family own?		Yes	No
Q19	TV	1	2
Q20	Private car	1	2
Q21	Taxi	1	2
Q22	Video	1	2
Q23	Mobile one or more	1	2
Q24	Computer	1	2
Q25	Air-condition	1	2
Q26	Satellite	1	2
Q27	Automatic-washer	1	2
Q28	Refrigerator	1	2
Q29	Dish-washer	1	2
Q30	Deep Freezer	1	2
Q31	Oven	1	2

	What is the average monthly family income/expenditures? (May ask for both or one option only)
Q32	Income:
Q33	Expenditures:

What are the resources of family income?		Mentioned	Not Mentioned
Q34	Stable and regular income	1	2
Q35	Real-estate	1	2
Q36	Agricultural lands/Buildings	1	2
Q37	Shop, workshop or factory	1	2
Q38	Others, please specify..		

II. Individual Orientations

The following are statements describing different attitudes towards certain issues. Could you tell me to what degree do you agree with each of these statements by giving a score between 1 and 5? please reply with 4 or 5 depending on how you agree with the statement (Mostly or Fully). if you don't agree, reply with 2 or 1 depending on how you disagree (Mostly or Fully).

		Strongly Disagree	Disagree	Neutral	Agree	Strongly Agree	NA
Q39	Restaurants and coffee houses should all be closed during the month of Ramadan	1	2	3	4	5	9
Q40	I am considering sending my child to a religious school	1	2	3	4	5	9
Q41	A religious person is more trustworthy than a non-pious person in commercial life	1	2	3	4	5	9
Q42	I do not approve of girls and boys being in mixed classes at high school age	1	2	3	4	5	9

Could you tell me to what degree do you agree with each of these statements by giving a score between 1 and 5?

		Strongly Disagree	Disagree	Neutral	Agree	Strongly Agree	NA
Q43	Being friend with another without considering his/her religion	1	2	3	4	5	9
Q44							
Q45	Giving somebody a hand without considering her/his religion	1	2	3	4	5	9
Q46							

Note: Q44 and Q46 will not be asked in Egypt

Could you tell me to what degree do you agree with each of these statements by giving a score between 1 and 5?

		Strongly Disagree	Disagree	Neutral	Agree	Strongly Agree	NA
Q47	Most people would provide help to their neighbors who suffer financially during an economic crisis	1	2	3	4	5	9
Q48	People pretend to care for others more than they really do	1	2	3	4	5	9
Q49	Most people inwardly dislike putting themselves out to help other people	1	2	3	4	5	9
Q50	People are usually out for their own personal interest.	1	2	3	4	5	9

Could you tell me to what degree do you agree with each of these statements by giving a score between 1 and 5?

		Strongly Disagree	Disagree	Neutral	Agree	Strongly Agree	NA
Q51	I would rather have my child cheat in an exam where most children do, than to have him/her fail in the exam	1	2	3	4	5	9
Q52	If you give the average person a job to do and leave him/her to do it, it is expected that most often the person will finish it efficiently	1	2	3	4	5	9
Q53	People usually tell the truth, even when they know they would be better off lying	1	2	3	4	5	9
Q54	Most people would cheat on their income tax, if they had a chance	1	2	3	4	5	9

Could you tell me to what degree do you agree with each of these statements by giving a score between 1 and 5?

		Strongly Disagree	Disa-gree	Neutral	Agree	Strongly Agree	NA
Q55	Everyone should have an equal chance to resources and equal access to express her/his opinions	1	2	3	4	5	9
Q56	It is the duty of every citizen to correct anti-minority remarks made in his/her presence	1	2	3	4	5	9
Q57	Poverty could be almost entirely eliminated if we made basic changes in our social and economic system	1	2	3	4	5	9
Q58	There would be no obstacles for women to get into prominent positions whether in the state or the private sectors	1	2	3	4	5	9

Could you tell me to what degree do you agree with each of these statements by giving a score between 1 and 5?

		Strongly Disagree	Disagree	Neutral	Agree	Strongly Agree	NA
Q59	One should always find ways to help others less fortunate than oneself	1	2	3	4	5	9
Q60	A person should always be concerned about the well-being of others	1	2	3	4	5	9
Q61	It is best not to get too involved in taking care of other people's needs	1	2	3	4	5	9
Q62	People tend to pay more attention to the well-being of others than they should	1	2	3	4	5	9

Could you tell me to what degree do you agree with each of these statements by giving a score between 1 and 5?

		Strongly Disagree	Disagree	Neutral	Agree	Strongly Agree	NA
Q63	One of the big problems in this country is that we don't give everyone an equal chance	1	2	3	4	5	9
Q64	More equality of incomes would avoid conflicts between people of different income levels	1	2	3	4	5	9
Q65	Incomes cannot be more equal since people's abilities and talents are unequal.	1	2	3	4	5	9
Q66	Incomes cannot be made equal since it is human nature to always want more than others have	1	2	3	4	5	9

Q67 What is your religion?
1. I am not a member of any religion.
2. Muslim.
3. Christian.
4. Jew.
5. Other (..)
9. NA

Q68 Would you say you are?
1. Very Religious
2. Somewhat Religious
3. Religious
4. Not Religious
5. Extent Person
8. Don't know
9. NA

Q69 Considering the last year, how often did you attend the place of worship apart from weddings or funerals?
1. More than once a week.
2. Once a week (Friday prayer or Sunday prayer)
3. Once a month.
4. In Ramadan and in the kandils.
5. In Bayrams, once or twice a year.

6. Less than once a year.
7. Never, almost never.
8. Don't know.
9. Not applicable.

Q70 How often do you interact with people at your Mosque?
1. Daily.
2. Weekly/nearly every week.
3. Once or twice a month.
4. Only a few times a year.
5. Not at all.
8. Don't know.
9. Not applicable.

Q71 Over the past three years did you get together with neighbors or friends to discuss how to resolve a local problem like getting a road paved, repair/construct a canal etc.?
1. Yes frequently.
2. Yes, from time to time.
3. No not really.
4. No not at all.
9. Not applicable.

III. Philanthropy as a Concept

From your point of view, what is philanthropy?		Mentioned	Not Mentioned
Q72	Financial or material assistance to the poor, the needy, and the homeless	1	2
Q73	Paying *Zakat*/Almsgiving, creating an Endowment or a sustainable Sadaqa	1	2
Q74	Interdependence (Mutual support/Takafol) from a religious perspective	1	2
Q75	Volunteerism and community service	1	2
Q76	Other, please specify.		

What is the motivation behind the philanthropy? (Three choice)	Q77 First Choice	Q78 Second Choice	Q79 Third Choice
-Traditions	1	1	1
-Religious duties	2	2	2
-Paying charities for the sake of Allah	3	3	3
-Reducing the number of the poor in society	4	4	4
-Support the state in poverty eradication	5	5	5
-For the public economic and social good	6	6	6

What does a philanthropist feel?		Mentioned	Not Mentioned
Q80	Happiness and self satisfaction	1	2
Q81	That s/he gave others some of their rights	1	2
Q82	That s/he help the needy to live	1	2
Q83	That s/he has performed a religious duty	1	2
Q84	That s/he has performed something s/he is used to	1	2
Q85	That s/he has brought happiness to others	1	2
Q86	Others, please specify.		

Q87 Can you mention any proverbs, instructions or popular sayings that encourage philanthropy?

....

From your point of view, what are forms of philanthropy in our country? please prioritize 3 choices or choose 3, then prioritize them	Q88 First Choice	Q89 Second Choice	Q90 Third Choice
Assisting some families or the needy to face the demands of life	1	1	1
Solving problems facing neighbors or friends	2	2	2
Volunteerism: without demanding compensation	3	3	3
Money to institutions for the poor	4	4	4
Contribution to build some places of worships, houses or hospitals	5	5	5
Undertake some charities on some occasions like Ramadan meals, or donations to charity boxes of Mosques or Churches	6	6	6

What makes people donate quickly and without thinking?		Mentioned	Not Mentioned
Q91	Donation for Mosques or Churches	1	2
Q92	Donation to build a hospital for chronic diseases	1	2
Q93	Donation to a charity organization to support its activities	1	2
Q94	Donation to a religious institution such as the Azhar or Madrasah	1	2
Q95	Donations to the governments at times of disasters or catastrophes	1	2
Q96	Donations for orphans or orphans' homes	1	2

I am going to read to you several conditions under which philanthropic giving can occur. please, evaluate each statement according to the degree to which each will help to help people get a better chance to compete in life: (On a scale from 1 to 5 for each option)

		Does not Effect Much	Does not Effect	Neutral	Does Effect	Does Effect Much	NA
Q97	If the state supervises the distribution of charitable revenues	1	2	3	4	5	9
Q98	If the donor him/herself distributes the revenues to the needy	1	2	3	4	5	9
Q99	If trust in charity institutions and organizations is achieved	1	2	3	4	5	9
Q100	When secrecy for the beneficiary is provided	1	2	3	4	5	9
Q101	When the collected donations and charity are done on the basis of the "right of the needy"	1	2	3	4	5	9
Q102	When one organization collects all the money and invests it in developmental projects	1	2	3	4	5	9

Q103 Do you believe that philanthropy can improve income equality among people to give them a better chance to compete in life?

1. Yes.
2. No.
8. Don't know.
9. Not applicable.

Who amongst the following is most responsible for helping the needy?		Mentioned	Not Mentioned
Q104	Every citizen	1	2
Q105	Wealthy individuals	1	2
Q106	The state	1	2
Q107	Religious individuals	1	2
Q108	Civil society organizations	1	2
Q 109	Mosques/Churches	1	2
Q110	Others, please specify..		

If you had a large sum of money, for whom would you spend this money? and for what purposes? please tell me your first three choices.	Q111 First Choice	Q112 Second Choice	Q113 Third Choice
Help people closer to me, friends or relatives	1	1	1
Provide service to as many people in the community as possible	2	2	2
Help some local organzations and institutions	3	3	3
Help Islamic or Christians associations abroad	4	4	4
Create a charitable project for the benefit of as many people as possible	5	5	5
Create an Endowment or a sustainable Sadaqa	6	6	6
Going to Hajj or Omra for more than once	7	7	7
Sponsor other persons who had never gone to Hajj or Omra	8	8	8

What is the optimum form of the association that would encourage you to donate?		Mentioned	Not Mentioned
Q114	An association with a freely elected board of directors	1	2
Q115	Where all board members have the right to discuss and object to decisions	1	2
Q116	Where there are rules to organize the distribution of services fairly on all association beneficiaries	1	2
Q117	When there is un-crippling supervision from the Ministry of Social Affairs	1	2
Q118	Where there is transparency in all operations of the institution	1	2
Q119	Where there is an accurate review of institutional accounts	1	2

Q120 Within this year, have you given any donations?
1. Yes.
2. No (Go to 168)
9. NA

If yes, in what form you give your donations?		Mentioned	Not Mentioned	If yes, please indicate how much
Q121	Cash	1	2	Q121A ______ L.E
Q122	In kind	1	2	Q122A ______ L.E(annum)
Q123	Voluntary effort	1	2	Q123A ______ hours (day/week/month)

(It Depends on Each Country's Currency)

Q124 How do you channel your donations?
1. Through institutions. Go to Q 125–Q 158
2. Directly to individuals. Go to Q 159–Q167
3. Both individuals and institutions. Go to Q 125–Q167
9. NA

To which of the following organization you give your donations?		Mentioned	Not Mentioned
Q125	Sports clubs	1	2
Q126	Youth associations	1	2
Q127	Environmentalist associations	1	2
Q128	Human rights' associations	1	2
Q129	Charity associations	1	2
Q130	Religious associations	1	2
Q131	Labor unions	1	2
Q132	A community development association for a neighborhood or a village	1	2
Q133	Alumni club	1	2
Q134	Chambers of commerce, unions, or other professional associations	1	2
Q135	A student-aid association	1	2
Q136	Migrants' associations	1	2
Q137	Agricultural cooperatives	1	2
Q138	Arts and folklore associations	1	2
Q139	Congregational associations	1	2

To which of the following organization you give your donations?		Mentioned	Not Mentioned
Q140	Health development associations or hospitals	1	2
Q141	A political party	1	2
Q142	Women associations	1	2
Q143	Ministry of Social Affairs	1	2
Q144	Others, please specify		

Please specify value per year:		Mentioned	Not Mentioned	If yes, please indicate how much
Q14 5	Cash	1	2	Q145A ______ L.E
Q14 6	In kind	1	2	Q146A ______ L.E(annum)
Q14 7	Voluntary	1	2	Q147A ______ hours (day/week/month)

(It Depends on Each Country's Currency)

Could you tell me to what degree you find the philanthropic associations as being effective in our social life by using a scale from 1 to 5 where 5 is the most effective?

		Does not Effect Much	Does not Effect	Neutral	Does Effect	Does Effect Much	NA
Q148	Helping the poor to live with dignity	1	2	3	4	5	9
Q149	Lead to equality among people	1	2	3	4	5	9
Q150	Achieve social justice	1	2	3	4	5	9
Q151	Reduce poverty rate within the community	1	2	3	4	5	9
Q152	Achieve security for people	1	2	3	4	5	9

Q153 Have you ever been obliged to donate to an institution to which you don't feel particularly close?
1. Yes.
2. No (go to Q154)
9. NA
Q153A If yes, specify..

Q154. Do you believe that donations given to religious institutions or associations ever reach those who deserve them?

1. Yes.
2. No.
3. To a certain degree.
8. Don't know.
9. NA

Q155 Do you believe that donations given to non-religious institutions ever reach those who deserve them?
1. Yes.
2. No.
3. To a certain degree.
8. Don't know.
9. NA

Q156 Do you usually know where does your donations go?
1. Yes.
2. No.
3. To a certain extent.
8. Don't know.
9. NA

Q157 Do you have the opportunity to object as to the way your donations are distributed?
1. Yes.
2. No.
3. To a certain extent.
9. NA

Q158 Do you have the opportunity to object to the implemented activities?
1. Yes.
2. No.
3. To a certain extent.
9. NA

If you have a sum of money to donate, to who would go your preference? Please tell me your first and second choices.	**Q159 First Choice**	**Q160 Second Choice**
Someone born in the same region as mine	1	1
Someone with the same political views as mine	2	2
Someone who is living in the same neighborhood	3	3
Someone who speaks the same language and culture	4	4
Someone who has the same religious beliefs as yours	5	5
Someone who is a relative	6	6

What is the type of charity that you practice?		Mentioned	Not Mentioned
Q161	Offering some food or money	1	2
Q162	Provide clothes to some of the poor	1	2
Q163	Pay a monthly payment to some poor	1	2
Q164	Pay school fees for poor students	1	2
Q165	Buy medicines or treat sick people	1	2
Q166	Orphans' support (or Kafala)	1	2
Q167	Others, please specify …………………………………………………………		

Q168 Are you a beneficiary receiving any monetary or in-kind assistance?
1. Yes.
2. No (Go to 189)
9. NA

How were you reached?		Mentioned	Not Mentioned
Q169	Through personal contact	1	2
Q170	Through religious persons	1	2
Q171	Through a philanthropic institution	1	2
Q172	Through relatives	1	2
Q173	Through neighbors	1	2
Q174	Through friends	1	2
Q175	Through an application to developmental institution	1	2
Q176	Through the Mosque/Church	1	2
Q177	Through the Mosque/Church	1	2
Q178	Through colleagues at work	1	2

What are the types of service or assistance that you received/or still receive?		Mentioned	Not Mentioned
Q179	Regular monthly or temporary salary from an institution	1	2
Q180	Regular monthly salary or assistance from an individual	1	2
Q181	Material assistance from relatives or neighbors	1	2
Q182	Services provided by some institutions for the poor and the elderly	1	2
Q183	Orphans or children with special need regular support (Kafala)	1	2
Q184	Pay tuition fees for students	1	2
Q185	A capital from an individual to initiate a project	1	2
Q186	A capital from an institution to initiate a project	1	2
Q187	Other, please specify		

Q188 Do you consider the service or assistance that you have receive is of any importance to your life?
1. Yes.
2. No (Go to 189)
3. To some extent.
9. NA

If yes, what has been the importance?		Mentioned	Not Mentioned
Q188A	It helps to sustain a better life	1	2
Q188B	It has convinced me that the world is fine and there is still hope in life	1	2
Q188C	It has proved to my family that care and love do exist between people	1	2
Q188D	It has strengthened my religious faith	1	2
Q188E	It has saved me and my family from deviance	1	2
Q188F	It has helped me to keep my children at school	1	2
Q188G	It has made me start a project from which i am making my living with my family	1	2
Q188H	Others, please specify		

IV. Religious Philanthropy

Q189 Do you pay *Zakat* or Ashour?
1. No.
2. Yes (Go to Q196)
9. NA

	In case you don't pay *Zakat*, could you mention why?	Mentioned	Not Mentioned
Q190	I do not know that I have an obligation to pay *Zakat*	1	2
Q191	I do not have any control over what i own for which i should pay *Zakat*	1	2
Q192	I pay taxes to the government instead of *Zakat*	1	2
Q193	I don't trust those in charge of *Zakat* collection	1	2
Q194	I do not trust those in charge of the distribution of *Zakat* or Ashour	1	2
Q195	Others, please specify..		

Q196 Do you calculate your *Zakat* or Ashour every year?
1. Yes.
2. No.
9. NA

Q197 Do you give a constant amount of *Zakat* every year?
1.Yes.
2. No.
9. NA.

Q198 Do you go to religious people to calculate your *Zakat* or Ashour?
1. Yes.
2. No.
3. I never thought about it.
9. NA

There are different forms of *Zakat*, select from this list those forms you pay *Zakat* on:		Mentioned	Not Mentioned	If yes, please indicate the average per annum
Q199	Agricultural products	1	2	Q199A annum .... L.E
Q200	Livestock	1	2	Q200A annum ....L.E
Q201	Animal product, honey or milk for instances	1	2	Q201A annum ....L.E
Q202	Gold and silver	1	2	Q202A annum .... L.E
Q203	Trading and industries	1	2	Q203A annum .... L.E
Q204	Savings and deposits	1	2	Q204A annum .... L.E
Q205	Extracted treasures (Rikaz)	1	2	Q205A annum .... L.E
Q206	Prizes	1	2	Q206A annum .... L.E
Q207	Salary	1	2	Q207A annum .... L.E

Q208 Do you pay your *Zakat* El-Mal every year?
1. No.
2. Yes (Go to Q213)
9. NA

In case you didn't pay your *Zakat* El-Mal, could you tell the reason why?		Mentioned	Not Mentioned
Q209	I cannot afford to pay *Zakat*	1	2
Q210	I don't know how to calculate it	1	2
Q211	I found no needy people in my neighborhood	1	2
Q212	Other, please specify......................................		

In what form do you usually give your *Zakat* El-Mal?		Mentioned	Not Mentioned	If yes, please indicate how much
Q213	In cash	1	2	Q213A __________ L.E
Q214	Basic food	1	2	Q214A .... liter/kg equal to L.E .....
Q215	Buy clothes/tools...etc for the needy	1	2	Q215A .... = L.E ....

Q216 Do you pay *Zakat* El-Fitr?
1. No.
2. Yes (Go to Q222)
9. NA

In case you don't pay your *Zakat* El-Fitr, could you tell the reason why?		Mentioned	Not Mentioned
Q217	I do not own enough to pay *Zakat*	1	2
Q218	I don't know how to calculate it	1	2
Q219	I don't trust the persons in charge of *Zakat* collection	1	2
Q220	I did not find any needy people in my neighborhood	1	2
Q221	Others, please specify.		

In what form do you usually give your *Zakat* El-Fitr?		Mentioned	Not Mentioned	If yes, please indicate how much
Q222	Cash	1	2	Q222A _________ L.E
Q223	Basic food	1	2	Q223A .... liter/kg equal to L.E .....
Q224	Other basic food, clothes, tools	1	2	Q224A .... = L.E ....

(It Depends on Each Country's Currency)

Q225 Do you give Sadaqa?
1. No.
2. Yes (Go to 230)
9. NA

In case that you didn't pay Sadaqa, could you tell me why?		Mentioned	Not Mentioned
Q226	I do not own enough to give Sadaqa	1	2
Q227	I don't know how to pay Sadaqa	1	2
Q228	I found no needy people in my neighborhood	1	2
Q229	Others, please specify		

Q230 Please specify how regular do you pay your Sadaqa?
1. Once a month.
2. Once in three months.
3. Once in six months.
4. Once a year.
5. Once in two year.
6. More than once in two years.
7. Not regular.
8. DK
9. NA

How do you usually pay Sadaqa?		Mentioned	Not Mentioned	If yes, please indicate how much
Q231	In cash	1	2	Q231A ________ L.E
Q232	Basic food	1	2	Q232A ... liter/kg equal to L.E .....
Q233	Buy clothes/tools...etc for the needy	1	2	Q233A .... = L.E ....
Q234	Volunteering effort	1	2	Q234A How many hours per day/week/month..........

Q235 Do you pay Zakat/Ashour/Sadaqa through institutions or individuals?
1. Through institutions Go to Q 236–Q 252
2. Personal Go to Q 253–Q266
3. Both Go to Q236 - Q266
9. NA

Why did you choose institution to distribute your *Zakat*/Sadaqa?		Yes	No
Q236	Institutions are more capable	1	2
Q237	Because i trust those responsible for distribution	1	2
Q238	Because they do the distribution according to religious law or Shar'ia	1	2
Q239	Because they direct the money towards developmental projects	1	2
Q240	Because i am busy	1	2
Q241	Others, please specify		

In your opinion, do you agree to distribute *Zakat*/Sadaqa for the following purposes?		Yes	No	No idea
Q242	On victims of natural catastrophes	1	2	9
Q243	On the construction of public utilities	1	2	9
Q244	On the empowering the poor	1	2	9
Q245	On health sector	1	2	9
Q246	On the printing of books	1	2	9
Q247	On research activities	1	2	9
Q248	On atrs,heritage, and culture	1	2	9
Q249	On basic education	1	2	9
Q250	On environmental conservation	1	2	9
Q251	On the establishment of an Endowment (Waqf)	1	2	9
Q252	On the promotion of social justice	1	2	9

Why do you personally distribute your *Zakat*/Sadaqa to individuals/causes directly?		Yes	No
Q253	Since the amounts of *Zakat*/Sadaqa are so small and itermediary agent is not required	1	2
Q254	I usually give these amounts to my relatives	1	2
Q255	I do not trust institutions	1	2
Q256	I usually give these amounts on special occasions	1	2
Q257	I do have a trusted individual who does the distribution of *Zakat*	1	2
Q258	I don't know anything about the institutions and the role they play	1	2
Q259	Others, please specify		

Do you think, the following categories of people have the right to receive *Zakat*?		Yes	No	No idea
Q260	The poor and the destitute	1	2	3
Q261	Those who collect and manage the distribution of the *Zakat* funds	1	2	3
Q262	Those who are in the service for the sake of Allah. (Fisabilillah)	1	2	3
Q263	The non-Muslim	1	2	3
Q264	The refugees	1	2	3
Q265	Persons who are at risk of deviance (e.g. prostitutes who are being pressured by procuress)	1	2	3
Q266	Those who have been suffering from chronic diseases	1	2	3

Q267 Do you usually put your *Zakat*/Sadaqa/Almsgiving in the boxes provided at the Mosques?

1. Yes.
2. No.
9. NA

Q268 Do you usually donate your Zakat/Sadaqa and Almsgiving through the TV commercial sponsored by Al-Azhar?

1. Yes.
2. No.
9. NA

Q269 Do you usually give the Sadaqa and Almsgiving to institution that are using the TV commercial calling for donation?

1.Yes.
2. No.
9. NA

Q270 Have you ever given your Zakat/Sadaqa to other countries or governorates?
1. Yes.
2. No.
9. NA

Q271 Do you mind giving your religious obligations such as Zakat or Sadaqa to people irrespective of their gender?
1. Yes.
2. No.
3. Others, please specify ....
4. NA

What is your primary motive for paying *Zakat*/Sadaqa? (Three answers maximum)	**Q272 First Choice**	**Q273 Second Choice**	**Q274 Third Choice**
To help the poor.	1	1	1
To purify my soul and wealth.	2	2	2
To develop Muslim communities' economy	3	3	3
To promote religious values	4	4	4
To maintain social relationship	5	5	5
To reflect my self satisfaction with my life	6	6	6
It is the right for the needy	7	7	7
Others, please specify			

Q275 Should be necessary to announce the audit report of local NGO'S that collect Zakat/Ashour from the publics?
1. Yes.
2. No.
9. NA

Q276 Do you think it is important to financially audit the institutions that handle Zakat and Ashour annually?
1. Very important.
2. Fairly important.
3. Not very important.
4. Not at all important.
9. NA

Q277 Do you agree that the giver of Zakat or Sadaqa should obtain deductible taxation?
1. Completely agree

2. Fairly agree
3. Not agree
4. Not at all agree
9. NA

Q278 What is the meaning of El-Sadaqa El-Jariaya?

....

8. Don't know
9. NA

Q278A What is the meaning of Zakat or Ashour?

....

8. Don't know
9. NA

From your point of view, is it obligatory for every Muslim to pay the following categories of *Zakat*?		Yes	No	No idea
Q279	*Zakat* on agricultural crops	1	2	9
Q280	*Zakat* on livestock	1	2	9
Q281	*Zakat* on gold and silver	1	2	9
Q282	*Zakat* on trading and industries	1	2	9
Q283	*Zakat* on agricultural products apart from staple foods	1	2	9
Q284	*Zakat* on animal products, e.g.: milk & honey	1	2	9
Q285	*Zakat* on money saving and deposits (*Zakat* El-Mal)	1	2	9
Q286	*Zakat* on extracted treasures (Rikaz)	1	2	9
Q287	*Zakat* on prizes	1	2	9
Q288	*Zakat* El-Fitr	1	2	9

Q289 What do you know about Waqf ?

....

Q290 What are the Waqf institutions that you know in Egypt ?

....

Q291 what is the difference between Charitable organization and Waqf ?

....

Q292 To what extent would the activities provided by the Ministry Endowment solve the social problems ? please place your opinion on the scale from 1 to 5 where 1 indicates "no help at all" and 5 indicates "help a great deal"
1. No help at all

2. Don't help
3. Help to some extent
4. Help
5. Help a Lot
8. Don't know
9. NA

Q293 Have you ever established a Waqf?
1. No.
2. Yes. (Go to Q296)
9. NA

Q294. For those who never established a Waqf. why didn't you ever establish one?
1. I do not understand what is Waqf.
2. I don't understand Waqf law.
3. I can not afford establishing a waqf.
4. I do not trust Waqf administration.
5. I should expend my wealth in a huge portion.
6. It is not an obligation.
7. other……………………………………………………
9. NA

Q295. Regardless of any obstacle, would you belive that establishing a Waqf services serve your charitable goals?
1. Yes.
2. No.
8. Don't know.
9. NA

In what form is your Waqf? You can answer more than one option		Mentioned	Not Mentioned	If yes, please indicate the average
Q296	Agricultural products	1	2	Q296A ……. m2 equal to L.E …
Q297	Livestock	1	2	Q297A ……. equal to L.E ……
Q298	Animal products	1	2	Q298A ………………… L.E
Q299	Gold and silver	1	2	Q299A ………equal to L.E ……
Q300	Trade, industry	1	2	Q300A ………equal to L.E ……
Q301	Realestate, lands	1	2	Q301 A number/area ……………
Q302	Others, please specify……………………………………………………………………			

Q303 Who are the beneficiaries from your Waqf?
1. Individual.
2. Institution.

3. Both.
4. Other,...................................
8. DK
9. NA

Q304 Is the Waqf that you have established considered collective or individual?
Collective.
Single.
9. NA

What is your primary motive for establishing/contributing to a Waqf ?		Mentioned	Not Mentioned
Q305	The religious rewarding of Waqf will continue even after the donor dies	1	2
Q306	To spread Islamic teaching	1	2
Q307	Social responsibility	1	2
Q308	To enhance my social status	1	2
Q309	To reflect on my self-satisfaction	1	2
Q310	Other, please specify................................		

Q311 If you have much money, would you go to Omra or second Hajj if you know that the money is needed
For the community?
1. Yes.
2. No.
3. I never thought about that.
8. I don't know.
9. NA

Q312 Some people tend to give in secret (So that no one would know neither the giver nor the receiver).
Do you think it is necessary to maintain this secrecy in charity?
1. Yes.
2. No.
3. Both.
8. I don't know.
9. NA

Q312A Why ?

Appendix 7: Qur'an ic Verses and Prophet's Saying (*Ahadith*) On Philanthropy

- **The Cow**

  177. It is not righteousness that ye turn your faces to the East and the West; but righteous is he who beleiveth in Allah and the last day and the angles and the scripture and the prophets; and giveth wealth, for love of him, to kinsfolk and to orphans and the needy and the wayfarer and to those who ask, and to set slaves free; and observeth proper worship and payeth the poor-due. And those who keep their treaty when they make one, and the patient in tribulation and adversity and time of stress. Such are they who are sincere. Such are the God-fearing.

  195. Spend your wealth for the cause of Allah, and be not cast by your own hands to ruin; and do good. Lo! Allah loveth the beneficent.

  245. Who is it that will lend unto Allah a goodly loan, so that he may give it increase manifold? Allah straiteneth and enlargeth. Unto him ye will return.

  261. The likness of those who spend their wealth in Allah's way is as the likness of a grain which growth seven ears, in every ear a hundred grains. Allah giveth increase manifold to whom he will. Allah is All-Embracing, All-knowing.

  271. If you publish your almsgiving, it is well, but if you hide it and give it to the poor, it will be better for you, and will atone for some of your ill-deeds. Allah is Informed of what you do.

  273. (Alms are) for the poor who are straitened for the cause of Allah, who cannot travel in the land (for trade). The unthinking man accounteth them wealthy because of their restraint. Thou shalt know them by their market: they do not beg of men with importunity. And whatsoever good thing ye spend, lo! Allah knoweth it.

- **Women**

  36. And serve Allah. Ascribe no thing as partner unto him. (Show) kindness unto parents, and into near kindred, and orphans, and the needy, and unto the neighbour who is of kin (unto you) and the neighbour who is not of kin, and the fellow-traveller and the wayfarer and (the slaves) whom your right hands possess. Lo! Allah loveth not such as are proud and boastful.

  86. when ye are greeted with a greeting, greet ye with a better than it or return it. Lo! Allah taketh count of all things.

- **The Table Spread**

  2. O ye who believe! Profane not Allah's monuments nor the Sacred Month nor the offerings nor the garlands, nor those repairing to the Sacred House, seeking the grace and pleasure of their Lord. But when ye have left the sacred territory, then go hunting (if ye will). And let not your hatred of a folk who(once) stopped your going to the Inviolable Place of Worship seduce you to transgress; but keep your duty to Allah. Lo! Allah is serve in punishment.

8. O ye believe! Be steadfast witness for Allah in equity, and let not hatred of any people seduce you that you deal not justly. Deal justly, that is nearer to your duty. Observe your duty to Allah. Lo! Allah is informed of what ye do.

– **The Ascending Stairways**

24. And in whose wealth there is a right acknowledged.

25. For the beggar and the destitute.

– **Repentance**

103. Take alms of their wealth, wherewith thou mayst purify them and mayst make them grow, and pray for them. Lo! Thy prayer is an assuagement for them. Allah is Hearer, knower.

– **The Family of Imran**

140. If ye have received a blow, the (disbelieving) people have received a blow the like thereof. These are (only) the vicissitudes which we cause to follow one another for man-kind, to the end that Allah may know those who believe and may choose witness from among you; and Allah loveth not wrong-doers.

– **Iron**

11. Who is he that will lend unto Allah a goodly loan, that he may double it for him and his may be a rich reward?

18. Lo! Those who give alms, both men and women, and lend unto Allah a goodly loan, it will be doubled for them, and theirs will be a rich reward.

– **Divorce**

2. Then, when they have reached their term, take them back in kindness or part from them in kindness, and call to witness two just men among you, and keep your testimony upright for Allah. Whose believeth in Allah and the last Day is exhorted to act thus. And whosoever keepeth his duty to Allah, Allah will appoint a way out for him.

– **The Morning Hours**

9. Therefor the orphan oppress not.

10. therefor the beggar drive not away.

– **Exile**

7. That which Allah giveth as spoil unto his messenger from the people of the townships, it is for Allah and his messenger and for the near of kin and the orphans and the needy and the wayfarer, that it become not a commodity between the rich among you. And whatsoever the messenger giveth you, take it. And whatsoever he forbidden, abstain (from it). And keep your duty to Allah. Lo! Allah is stern in reprisal.

9. Those who entered the city and the faith before them love those who flee unto them for refuge, and find in their breasts no need for that which hath been given them, but prefer (the fugitives) above themselves though poverty become their lot. And whose is saved from his own avarice such are they who are successful.

- **Sad**
  39. (Saying): This is our gift, so bestow thou, or with-hold, without reckoning.

- **Time or Man**
  8. And feed with food the needy wretch, the orphan and the prisoner, for love of him.

- **The Most High**
  14. He is successful who growth.

  15. And remembereth the name of his Lord, so prayeth.

  16. But ye prefer the life of the world.

  17. Although the Hereafter is better and more lasting.

- **The Troops**
  9. Is he who payeth adoration in the watches of the night, prostrate and standing, bewaring of the Hereafter and hoping for the mercy of his Lord, (to be accounted equal with a disbeliever)? Say (unto them, O Muhammad): Are those who know equal with those who know not? But only men of understanding will pay heed.

- **The Angels**
  28. And of men and beasts and cattle, in like manner, divers hues? The erudite among his bondmen fear Allah alone. Lo! Allah is Mighty, Forgiving.

Prophet Mohamed's (pbuh) Sayings (Ahadith) on Philanthropy

It was related that Anas Ibn Malik said that the Prophet (Prayers & Peace be upon him) said: "if any Muslim plants any plant and then it is consumed by a human being or animal, he will receive a reward as if he had given the same amount in charity."

It was related that Abu Huraira said that The Prophet (Prayers & peace be upon him) said: "a person who practices charity so secretly that his left hand does not know what his right hand has given". (i.e. nobody knows how much he has given in charity).

It was related that Abu Huraira said that The Prophet (Prayers & peace be upon him) said: "Tow angles come down from heaven every day and one of them says: 'O

God! Reward every person who spends in your Cause,' and the other one says: 'O God! Obliterate the misers'."

It was related that Hudhaifah said that The prophet (prayers & peace be upon him) said: "Once while the angels were seizing the soul of a man who had died before your time, they asked him: 'Have you done anything good? He said" 'I used to order my employees to respite the person who has difficulty in repaying his debts and to forget the debt of the rich" He said: "So God forgave him his sins."

It was related that Jabir Ibn Abd Allah said that the Messenger of God said: "May God have mercy on the one who is lenient in his buying, selling and when he demands his money back."

It was related that Hakim Ibn Hizam said that The prophet (prayers& peace be upon him) said: "The hand that gives is better than the hand that takes. So give first to your dependants. The best charity is that which is given by the rich, and whoever refrains from asking others for money, God will give him, and God will Spare him from needing to ask."

It was related that Abu Musa said that the prophet (prayers& peace be upon him) said: "All Muslims must give charity." The people asked: "O Messenger of God! If someone has nothing to give what should he do?" He replied: "He should work with his hands and earn something to give in charity." The people asked: "And if they cannot do that?" He replied: "he should help the needy who ask." Then the people asked: "And if he cannot do that?" He replied: "Then he should do good deeds and avoid sin and this will suffice as charity."

It was related that Abu Huraira said: "A man came to The Prophet (Prayers & peace be upon him) and asked: 'O Messenger of God! Which charity will earn the better reward?' He replied: ' The charity you perform when you are healthy, niggardly and fear poverty and wish to become wealthy. Do not put it off until death approaches and then say: ' Give something to so and so and something to so and so.' It will be too late'.

It was related that Abu Huraira said that the Messenger of God said: "A man said he would give charity. He took his charity and went to find someone to give it to, but he put it in the hand of a thief, then the people said: "He has given charity to a thief.' Then he said: "And praise be to you O God! I will give another charity.' And he went out with his charity and put it in the hand of an adulteress. Then the people said: 'He has given charity tonight to an adulteress. 'So he said:' All praise be to you

O God! For my giving charity to an adulteress. I will give another charity.' So he went out with his charity and put it in the hand of a rich man.' So he said: 'All praise be to you O God! For my giving charity to a thief, an adulteress and a rich man.' Someone came to him and said: 'The charity you gave to the thief may prevent him from stealing, as to the adulteress it may prevent her from committing adultery, and as for the rich man it may be an example he will take notice of so he would spend from what God has granted him'."

It was related that 'Adi Ibn Hatim said: "While I was sitting with the Messenger of God, two people approached him, one of them complained of poverty and the other complained about the prevalence of theft. The Messenger of God said: 'As for theft and waylaying, a time is approaching when caravans will go to Makkah unguarded. And as for poverty, the Hour will not come until a person will seek to give in charity and will not find anyone to accept it And each one of you will stand before God and there will be neither a curtain nor an interpreter between him and God, and God will ask him: 'Did not I give you wealth? He will answer: 'Yes.' Then God will ask: 'Did I not send a Messenger to you? And again he will answer 'Yes'. Then he will look to his right and he will see nothing but the Fire, and then he will look to his left and will see nothing but the Fire, and then he will look to his left and will see nothing but the fire. And so you should all save yourselves from the fire by giving even half of a date in charity. And if you do not have even half a date, then be charitable by saying a kind word to someone''."

It was related that AlNu'man Ibn Bashir said that the Messenger of God said: "You see the believers showing mercy to each other, and showing love to each other and being kind to each other as if they were one body, so that if any part of the body suffers malaise, then whole body shares in the malaise and fever."

It was related that Abu Musa said that the Prophet (Prayers & Peace be upon him) said: "A believer as a building whose various parts support each other. "The Prophet (Prayers & peace be upon him) then clasped his hands with his fingers intertwined, as the Prophet (Prayers & peace be upon him) was seated there, a man came and asked for something. The Prophet (Prayers & peace be upon him) turned to face us and said: ' Help him and invite him, and you will be rewarded, and God fulfills what He pleases through the tongue of His Prophet."

Muslim

Book 035, Number 6518:

Abu Huraira reported Allah's Messenger (may peace be upon him) as saying: He who alleviates the suffering of a brother out of the sufferings of the world, Allah would alleviate his suffering from the sufferings of the Day of Resurrection, and he who finds relief for one who is hard pressed, Allah would make things easy for him in the Hereafter, and he who conceals (the faults) of a Muslim, Allah would conceal his faults in the world and in the Hereafter. Allah is at the back of a servant so long as the servant is at the back of his brother, and he who treads the path in search of knowledge, Allah would make that path easy, leading to Paradise for him and those persons who assemble in the house among the houses of Allah (mosques) and recite the Book of Allah and they learn and teach the Qur'an (among themselves) there would descend upon them the tranquillity and mercy would cover them and the angels would surround them and Allah makes a mention of them in the presence of those near Him, and he who is slow-paced in doing good deeds, his (high) descent does not make him go ahead.

It was related that Aisha said that the Prophet (Prayers & peace be upon him) said: “Gabriel Persisted in commending to me the good treatment of neighbours, to the point that I though he was going to order me to make them inheritors.”

It was related that Amr Ibn Al Harith, the brother of the wife of the Messenger of God, Juwairiya bint Al Harith, said: “when the Messenger of God died he left no Dirham or Dinar, eno slave or slave woman nor anything but his white mule, his armor and a piece of land which he had assigned to charity.”

Narrated Az-Zubair bin Al'Awwam:

The Prophet (p.b.u.h) said, “It is better for anyone of you to take a rope (and cut) and bring a bundle of wood (from the forest) over his back and sell it and Allah will save his face (from the Hell-Fire) because of that, rather than to ask the people who may give him or not.”

Al Bukhari

Volume 7, Book 63, Number 224:

Narrated Sahl:

Allah's Apostle said, “I and the one who looks after an orphan will be like this in Paradise,” showing his middle and index fingers and separating them.

Appendix 8: Biblical References for al-Ushour (Christians Tithes)

- **Num 18:24**
  But the tithes of the children of Israel, which they offer [as] an heave offering unto the LORD, I have given to the Levites to inherit: therefore I have said unto them, Among the children of Israel they shall have no inheritance.

- **Num 18:28**
  Thus ye also shall offer an heave offering unto the LORD of all your tithes, which ye receive of the children of Israel; and ye shall give thereof the LORD'S heave offering to Aaron the priest.

- **Deu 12:6**
  And thither ye shall bring your burnt offerings, and your sacrifices, and your tithes, and heave offerings of your hand, and your vows, and your freewill offerings, and the firstlings of your herds and of your flocks:

- **Deu 12:11**
  Then there shall be a place which the LORD your God shall choose to cause his name to dwell there; thither shall ye bring all that I command you; your burnt offerings, and your sacrifices, your tithes, and the heave offering of your hand, and all your choice vows which ye vow unto the LORD:

- **Deu 26:12**
  When thou hast made an end of tithing all the tithes of thine increase the third year, [which is] the year of tithing, and hast given [it] unto the Levite, the stranger, the fatherless, and the widow, that they may eat within thy gates, and be filled;

- **The Book of Sirach 35:11**
  In every gift shew a cheerful countenance, and sanctify thy tithes with joy.

- **Amo 4:4**
  Come to Bethel, and transgress; at Gilgal multiply transgression; and bring your sacrifices every morning, [and] your tithes after three years:

- **Mal 3:8**
  Will a man rob God? Yet ye have robbed me. But ye say, Wherein have we robbed thee? In tithes and offerings.

- **Mal 3:10**
  Bring ye all the tithes into the storehouse, that there may be meat in mine house, and prove me now herewith, saith the LORD of hosts, if I will not open you the

windows of heaven, and pour you out a blessing, that [there shall] not [be room] enough [to receive it].

- **The First Book of Maccabees 3:49**
  And they brought the priestly ornaments, and the firstfruits and tithes, and stirred up the Nazarites that had fulfilled their days:

- **The First Book of Maccabees 10:31**
  And let Jerusalem be holy and free, with the borders thereof: and let the tenths, and tributes be for itself.

- **The First Book of Maccabees 11:35**
  And as for other things that belonged to us of the tithes, and of the tributes, from this time we discharge them of them: the saltpans also, and the crowns that were presented to us.

Biblical Refrences for Tithes and First Fruits

- **Gen 25:31**
  And Jacob said, Sell me this day thy birthright.

- **Gen 25:32**
  And Esau said, Behold, I [am] at the point to die: and what profit shall this birthright do to me?

- **Gen 25:33**
  And Jacob said, Swear to me this day; and he sware unto him: and he sold his birthright unto Jacob.

- **Gen 25:34**
  Then Jacob gave Esau bread and pottage of lentiles; and he did eat and drink, and rose up, and went his way: thus Esau despised [his] birthright.

- **Gen 27:36**
  And he said, Is not he rightly named Jacob? for he hath supplanted me these two times: he took away my birthright; and, behold, now he hath taken away my blessing. And he said, Hast thou not reserved a blessing for me?

- **Gen 43:33**
  And they sat before him, the firstborn according to his birthright, and the youngest according to his youth: and the men marvelled one at another.

- **Deu 21:17**
  But he shall acknowledge the son of the hated [for] the firstborn, by giving him a double portion of all that he hath: for he [is] the beginning of his strength; the right of the firstborn [is] his.

- **1Ch 5:1**
  Now the sons of Reuben the firstborn of Israel, (for he [was] the firstborn; but, forasmuch as he defiled his father's bed, his birthright was given unto the sons of Joseph the son of Israel: and the genealogy is not to be reckoned after the birthright.

- **1Ch 5:2**
  For Judah prevailed above his brethren, and of him [came] the chief ruler; but the birthright [was] Joseph's:)

- **Luk 2:36**
  And there was one Anna, a prophetess, the daughter of Phanuel, of the tribe of Aser: she was of a great age, and had lived with an husband seven years from her virginity;

- **Hub 12:16**
  Lest there [be] any fornicator, or profane person, as Esau, who for one morsel of meat sold his birthright.

Biblical Refrences for Charitable Deeds

- **The Book of Tobit 12:8**
  Prayer is good with fasting and alms more than to lay up treasures of gold:

- **The Book of Tobit 12:9**
  For alms delivereth from death, and the same is that which purgeth away sins, and maketh to find mercy and life everlasting.

- **The Book of Tobit 4:11**
  For alms deliver from all sin, and from death, and will not suffer the soul to go into darkness.

- **The Book of Tobit 4:12**
  Alms shall be a great confidence before the most high God, to all them that give it.

- **The Book of Sirach 3:33**
  Water quencheth a flaming fire, and alms resisteth sins:

- **The Book of Sirach 7:10**
  Neglect not to pray, and to give alms.

- **The Book of Sirach 17:18**
  The alms of a man is as a signet with him, and shall preserve the grace of a man as the apple of the eye:

- **The Book of Sirach 29:11**
  But yet towards the poor be thou more hearty, and delay not to shew him mercy.
- **The Book of Sirach 29:15**
  Shut up alms in the heart of the poor, and it shall obtain help for thee against all evil.
- **Mat 6:2**
  Therefore when thou doest [thine] alms, do not sound a trumpet before thee, as the hypocrites do in the synagogues and in the streets, that they may have glory of men. Verily I say unto you, They have their reward.
- **Mat 6:3**
  But when thou doest alms, let not thy left hand know what thy right hand doeth:
- **Luk 11:41**
  But rather give alms of such things as ye have; and, behold, all things are clean unto you.
- **Luk 12:33**
  Sell that ye have, and give alms; provide yourselves bags which wax not old, a treasure in the heavens that faileth not, where no thief approacheth, neither moth corrupteth.
- **Act 3:2**
  And a certain man lame from his mother's womb was carried, whom they laid daily at the gate of the temple which is called Beautiful, to ask alms of them that entered into the temple;
- **Act 3:3**
  Who seeing Peter and John about to go into the temple asked an alms.
- **Act 3:10**
  And they knew that it was he which sat for alms at the Beautiful gate of the temple: and they were filled with wonder and amazement at that which had happened unto him.

Biblical Refrences for Vows

- **Lev 22:18**
  Speak unto Aaron, and to his sons, and unto all the children of Israel, and say unto them, Whatsoever [he be] of the house of Israel, or of the strangers in Israel, that will offer his oblation for all his vows, and for all his freewill offerings, which they will offer unto the LORD for a burnt offering;

- **Lev 23:38**
  Beside the sabbaths of the LORD, and beside your gifts, and beside all your vows, and beside all your freewill offerings, which ye give unto the LORD.

- **Num 29:39**
  These [things] ye shall do unto the LORD in your set feasts, beside your vows, and your freewill offerings, for your burnt offerings, and for your meat offerings, and for your drink offerings, and for your peace offerings.

- **Num 30:4**
  And her father hear her vow, and her bond wherewith she hath bound her soul, and her father shall hold his peace at her: then all her vows shall stand, and every bond wherewith she hath bound her soul shall stand.

- **Num 30:5**
  But if her father disallow her in the day that he heareth; not any of her vows, or of her bonds wherewith she hath bound her soul, shall stand: and the LORD shall forgive her, because her father disallowed her.

- **Num 30:6**
  And if she had at all an husband, when she vowed, or uttered ought out of her lips, wherewith she bound her soul;

- **Num 30:7**
  And her husband heard [it,] and held his peace at her in the day that he heard [it]: then her vows shall stand, and her bonds wherewith she bound her soul shall stand.

- **Num 30:11**
  And her husband heard [it], and held his peace at her, [and] disallowed her not: then all her vows shall stand, and every bond wherewith she bound her soul shall stand.

- **Num 30:12**
  But if her husband hath utterly made them void on the day he heard [them; then] whatsoever proceeded out of her lips concerning her vows, or concerning the bond of her soul, shall not stand: her husband hath made them void; and the LORD shall forgive her.

- **Num 30:14**
  But if her husband altogether hold his peace at her from day to day; then he establisheth all her vows, or all her bonds, which [are] upon her: he confirmeth them, because he held his peace at her in the day that he heard [them].

- **Deu 12:6**
  And thither ye shall bring your burnt offerings, and your sacrifices, and your tithes, and heave offerings of your hand, and your vows, and your freewill offerings, and the firstlings of your herds and of your flocks:
- **Deu 12:11**
  Then there shall be a place which the LORD your God shall choose to cause his name to dwell there; thither shall ye bring all that I command you; your burnt offerings, and your sacrifices, your tithes, and the heave offering of your hand, and all your choice vows which ye vow unto the LORD:
- **Deu 12:17**
  Thou mayest not eat within thy gates the tithe of thy corn, or of thy wine, or of thy oil, or the firstlings of thy herds or of thy flock, nor any of thy vows which thou vowest, nor thy freewill offerings, or heave offering of thine hand:
- **Deu 12:26**
  Only thy holy things which thou hast, and thy vows, thou shalt take, and go unto the place which the LORD shall choose:
- **The Book of Judith 16:22**
  And it came to pass after these things, that all the people, after the victory, came to Jerusalem to adore the Lord: and as soon as they were purified, they all offered holocausts, and vows, and their promises.
- **Job 22:27**
  Thou shalt make thy prayer unto him, and he shall hear thee, and thou shalt pay thy vows.
- **Psa 22:25**
  My praise [shall be] of thee in the great congregation: I will pay my vows before them that fear him.
- **Psa 50:14**
  Offer unto God thanksgiving; and pay thy vows unto the most High:
- **Psa 56:12**
  Thy vows [are] upon me, O God: I will render praises unto thee.
- **Psa 61:5**
  For thou, O God, hast heard my vows: thou hast given [me] the heritage of those that fear thy name.
- **Psa 61:8**
  So will I sing praise unto thy name for ever, that I may daily perform my vows.

- **Psa 66:13**
  I will go into thy house with burnt offerings: I will pay thee my vows,
- **Psa 116:14**
  I will pay my vows unto the LORD now in the presence of all his people.
- **Psa 116:18**
  I will pay my vows unto the LORD now in the presence of all his people,
- **Pro 7:14**
  [I have] peace offerings with me; this day have I payed my vows.
- **Pro 31: 2**
  What, my son? and what, the son of my womb? and what, the son of my vows?
- **Jer 44:25**
  Thus saith the LORD of hosts, the God of Israel, saying; Ye and your wives have both spoken with your mouths, and fulfilled with your hand, saying, We will surely perform our vows that we have vowed, to burn incense to the queen of heaven, and to pour out drink offerings unto her: ye will surely accomplish your vows, and surely perform your vows.
- **Jon 1:16**
  Then the men feared the LORD exceedingly, and offered a sacrifice unto the LORD, and made vows.
- **Nah 1:15**
  Behold upon the mountains the feet of him that bringeth good tidings, that publisheth peace! O Judah, keep thy solemn feasts, perform thy vows: for the wicked shall no more pass through thee; he is utterly cut off.

Maecenata Schriften

Previous publications:

Volume 20
Iris Rozwora
Die gemeinnützige Aktiengesellschaft als Akteurin der Zivilgesellschaft –
Eine empirische Untersuchung, 2021
ISBN 978-3-11-073749-3, e-ISBN (PDF) 978-3-11-073262-7,
e-ISBN (EPUB) 978-3-11-073272-6

Volume 19
Antonia Karaisl von Karais
The House is in a State –
Christian Wolff's Oeconomica in the context of public welfare, 2021
ISBN 978-3-11-071392-3, e-ISBN (PDF) 978-3-11-071409-8,
e-ISBN (EPUB) 978-3-11-071419-7

Volume 18
Rupert Graf Strachwitz, Eckhard Priller, Benjamin Triebe(Ed.)
Handbuch Zivilgesellschaft, 2020
ISBN 978-3-11-055129-7, e-ISBN (PDF) 978-3-11-055347-5,
e-ISBN (EPUB) 978-3-11-055140-2

https://www.degruyter.com/view/serial/MAEC-B